PAUL KOVI'S
Transylvanian Cuisine

PAUL KOVI'S
Transylvanian Cuisine

by Paul Kovi

Edited by Kim Honig

Translated from Hungarian by Clara Gyorgyey

Crown Publishers, Inc., New York

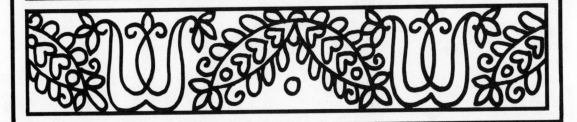

Published by Crown Publishers, Inc., One Park Avenue,
New York, New York 10016 and simultaneously in
Canada by General Publishing Company Limited
Manufactured in the United States of America
CROWN is a trademark of Crown Publishers, Inc.
This book was previously published in different form in
Hungarian under the title *Erdélyi Lakoma*.

Library of Congress Cataloging in Publication Data
Kovi, Paul.
    Paul Kovi's Transylvanian cuisine.
    Bibliography: p.
    Includes index.
    1. Cookery, Hungarian.   2. Cookery, Romanian.
3. Transylvania (Romania)—Social life and customs.
I. Honig, Kim.   II. Title.   III. Title: Transylvanian
cuisine.
TX723.5.H8K69 1985   641.59439   84-21339
ISBN 0-517-55698-7

Design by Dana Sloan
Woodcuts by Joseph Domjan

10 9 8 7 6 5 4 3 2 1
First Edition

I dedicate this book
to my beloved mother

Throughout my travels in Transylvania
this thought accompanied me:
God, if you are
look at me also
if I am

CONTENTS

IN REVERENCE OF FOODS

INTRODUCTION

A partial contemporary map of Europe today, which incorporates an overlay of Hungary at the turn of the century, since the stories, recipes, and historical essays herein generally involve the last three hundred years in the life of Transylvania, finishing just at the beginning of World War I or a little bit after.

INTRODUCTION

The rich traditions of one's native land can be truly appreciated only by those who had left it a long time ago. The elusive, haunting memories of events —particularly of food flavors and aromas—the overpowering emotions surrounding our childhood and early youth, unexpectedly burst forth like a long-dormant volcano, especially when we are traversing *mezzo giorno,* the middle years of our lives.

It was my old alma mater, the University of Kolozsvár, that inspired this spiritual quest to return to Transylvania. As the years passed, a feeling of indebtedness did begin to develop in me. I recently felt pursued by a secret obligation, a voice reminding me of an unsettled score. This book will honor those people whose traditions, religious convictions, and culinary skills created the marvelous experiences about which I now reminisce. In some small way, it will enable me to express my gratitude to that country whose people contributed so significantly to my values and my being.

While living in Kolozsvár as a college student, I absorbed the sacred quality of that historical place. Over the centuries, this lovely capital of Transylvania bore several names: Kolozsvár in Hungarian, Klausenberg in the Saxon tongue, Cluj in Rumanian, and today Napoca, so named by the Roman legions long ago.

Kolozsvár and the entire region known as Transylvania was unique in southeastern Europe. Surrounded by devastating religious wars in other countries and centuries of persecutions, it was here that, for the first time, religious freedom was declared and flourished. Subsequently, a mélange of five ethnic groups—Hungarians, Rumanians, Saxon Germans, Armenians, and Jews—lived for many decades in peace and mutual respect. This tranquil and romantic country had often been called "an East European

Switzerland," despite the later popular myth about it being a macabre haven for vampires. Translyvania as a historical reality is gradually disappearing—a fata morgana, or fading dream, beset by ideological and nationalistic fanaticism. For me, this was yet another reason to embark upon the adventure of writing this book.

But the most important motive still remains my deep love for Transylvania. I felt compelled to find a way of paying back at least some of the intellectual and emotional riches I had received there. My work in the restaurant field—more than work, a real vocation—had inspired me to study and collect Transylvanian gastronomic treasures and family traditions hidden in old books and manuscripts in different parts of the world. I have searched for more than two decades. Finally, five years ago I decided it was time to write a book about the exciting and varied cuisine of this region, before its colorful tradition became swallowed up by the onslaught of gray uniformity we are experiencing throughout the world. This volume, thus, is my humble gift of gratitude for my real education in Kolozsvár, my beloved second home.

I'd like to linger briefly at some of the milestones on this long journey of researching and collecting memorabilia. I was profoundly influenced by George Lang's excellent cookbook, *The Cuisine of Hungary,* published in New York City in 1967. George is a good friend of mine, and I not only admire this work but consider it better than most other books devoted to the mysteries of food. His unique opus is more than a mere collection of recipes; it is a chronicle of Hungarian gastronomy and a fascinating delineation of the factors that influenced the development of Hungarian cuisine. Lang clearly indicates the effect various kitchens of the world have had on Hungarian cooking, while at the same time pointing out the originality of the Magyar culinary art. In addition to the valuable recipes, it includes excellent samplings of history, poetry, folk songs, and folklore related to the "Feast of Food," which describes the essence of Hungarian cuisine. In it, the close relationship between the joys of food, as symbols of human love and community, and the spiritual values of Hungarian culture are expounded. George Lang's work has been one of the major inspirations for me in researching and writing this volume.

---

*A NOTE ABOUT TRANSYLVANIA (*ERDÉLY)

Transylvania was part of Hungary for about a thousand years, but for most of this century it was ruled by Rumania. Today Transylvania is located in northern Rumania. Its population about the turn of the century consisted of approximately 4 million Hungarians, 4 million Rumanians, 500,000 to 600,000 Saxon-Germans, 50,000 to 75,000 Jews, 20,000 to 25,000 Armenians, and other ethnic minorities. The Hungarians themselves were divided into two groupings: the Székelys, or Seklers (including the Sabbatarians), and Hungarians proper. This map (left) indicates the location of the various ethnic groups.
NOTE: The above figures are approximate, and I am sure every ethnic group will find it incorrect from its own viewpoint and special calculations.

Some years ago in New York City, I had the good fortune of meeting the notable gastronomer Egon Ronay, author of the bestselling English restaurant and hotel guide. (Mr. Ronay is of Hungarian origin, and one of his father's famous restaurants in Budapest was the only one with Transylvanian cooking. Each day the chef would contribute exquisite homeland specialties to the menu.) In a recent interview, Ronay elaborated on his theories, based on years of study and experience. He stated that in the history of food, there are essentially three outstanding cuisines: the French, which is the foundation of the Western European and American cuisines; the Chinese, with its unbelievable variety, richness of flavor and color, and three thousand years of tradition; and the Transylvanian. His listeners seemed surprised, since most of them had never heard of Transylvania except as the home of Dracula.

In the course of my arduous research, I chanced upon innumerable unexpected riches, and also made fascinating discoveries. Here are, for instance, the first two pages of a truly remarkable book about a "new cooking," published by János Keszei in 1680,

Two pages from a cookbook published by János Keszei in 1680. The page on the left is a dedication to Anna Bornemisza; the page on the right is the title, Egy Ujj Fözésrül Való Konyv, *"a book about the new type of cooking."*

dedicated to Anna Bornemisza, who was then the wife of the Prince of Transylvania. The second page contains the title of the book, *Egy Ujj Főzésrül Való Konyv,* "a book about the new type of cooking." (It was the nouvelle cuisine of that age!) Interestingly, Keszei refers to a book by Marcus Rumpolt (1604), which constituted the base for his works.

The greatest finding of my search surfaced in the Chicago home of my dear colleague Dr. Louis Szathmary, a Transylvanian and a fine restaurateur. His library contains what is generally regarded as the greatest privately owned gastronomical collection in the world. Works about Transylvanian cuisine alone comprise more than 350 volumes. My friend not only put his treasure at my disposal but enriched me with ideas, invaluable advice, and guidance. One great treasure I found in his library was the incomparable cookbook of Marcus Rumpolt.

Perusing scores of his old tomes, I found out that Marcus Rumpolt had been considered the greatest master in German culinary history. As cook of the High Magistrate at Mainz, he published an epoch-making book in 1581 that included numerous extraordinary recipes. Here are three illustrations from this work.

Some years ago in Italy, I visited San Lazzaro Island near Venice, the site of an old Armenian Mechitarist monastery. There, to my utter surprise, I found a unique collection of books dating back to the eighteenth and nineteenth centuries, describing customs and foods of the Transylvanian Armenians. These incunabula, written in both Hungarian and Armenian, also contain a large number of recipes, some of which are included in this book.

While reading through books, manuscripts, and various menus for festive dinners, I began to feel the presence of the "Chinese connection" and recognized definite similarities between the Transylvanian and Chinese gastronomies. For example, ginger, one of the most important Chinese spices, was equally popular in Transylvania. To my knowledge, it is only these two cuisines that combine cabbage, pork, and freshwater lobster or crayfish. In both places this combination was served in egg-pastry rolls. Similarly, the almost identical dish of pan-fried crayfish with vegetables and spicy sausages must be more than a coincidence.

Subsequently I came across Baron Radvánsky's monumental work and recipe collection compiled from sixteenth-century sources; it was published in 1883. The Baron discusses the use of Oriental spices, condiments, and herbs commonly used in the Translyvanian kitchen at that time. The question automatically arises: how did these spices find their way to remote Transylvania? In my opinion, the short, very hot paprika-pepper, popular both in China and Transylvania, is of Chinese and not of Mexican origin, unlike most other peppers of Europe. My theory is based on the assumption that during medieval times and well into the sixteenth century, the continental China-Europe trade route must have had its end station in Transylvania. Other information supported my hypothesis. Having read the stories about the art of serving food in Andreas

Dedicated to the most Serene High-born Princess and Lady, Lady Anne, née Queen of Denmark, Duchess of Saxony, Countess in Thuringia, Margravine of Meissen, Baroness of Magdeburg, and My Most Gracious Lady.

Your Serene Highness Elector G.F. has won renown and deserved praise for venturing at all times to encourage the intelligent members of the human race and to support with great earnestness those who have inherited great gifts from the gods so that they may be of benefit to all of mankind.

A NEW COOKBOOK

This is a thorough and full description of how someone may learn to cook and prepare correctly and excellently all manner of foods, whether boiled, fried, braised, or roasted, according to the fashion of the Germans, Hungarians, Hispanics, Italians, and the French: chops, stews and braises, various pastries and pies, gelatins, etc., to be made not only from four-legged native and wild animals, but also from a goodly variety of birds and game, greens, and dried fish, also you may learn to prepare all kinds of vegetables, fruits, sauces, mustards, sweets, and electuary syrups.

Herein it can also be learned how you may properly make ready magnificent great banquets, together with all appropriate hospitalities.

For the benefit of all people, the high-born and the lowly, female and male; published now for the first time, the likes have never before been put forth.

Also including a thorough account of how wine may be preserved from all injury; how the sickly may be made well; how herbal potions, wine, beer, vinegar, and other drinks may be brewed so that all people may drink them naturally and without harm.

Milos's writings, I found an additional unmistakable Chinese influence: in Transylvania the festive hunter's dinners were served in many courses of three dishes each—still a common custom today in China.

Yet another interesting discovery was learning that black coffee was already popular in Transylvania at the beginning of the seventeenth century, long before it became widespread in Vienna. Coffee was used not only as an after-dinner drink, but also to thicken sauces. I found several early seventeenth-century receipts documenting the sale of coffee to Translyvanian noblemen by Greek merchants. Additionally, I discovered several exotic sauce recipes prepared with coffee from that era.

The more I studied the culinary habits of the various ethnic groups in Translyvania—Hungarian, Saxon, Armenian, Rumanian, and Jewish—the more I realized their interrelationships. While each represented a singular flavor in Transylvanian cuisine, they each enriched one another as their tastes overlapped.

As my material grew I came to realize that to write an authentic book about Transylvanian cuisine, a recipe collection alone was not enough. Consequently, I decided to go back to my adopted second homeland to trace its culinary history. With the assistance of

> Denn weil ich ein geborner Vnger/ vnd aber der grausam Wütrich vnnd Erbfeindt Christliches Namens/der Türck/nach dem er meine Voreltern von Landt vnd Leuten vertrieben/das vnsere/ so in klein Walachey gelegen/ biß auff den heutigen Tag innen hat/ auch vns nach Leib vnd Leben trachtet/ Als hab ich mich von Jugendt auff vnter frembden müssen erhalten/ darauff geflissen vnd bedacht seyn/ wie ich heut oder morgen meinen vnterhalt vnnd außkommen haben möchte. Hab derwegen von einem Landt in dz ander/meiner notturfft/ vnd der Herren/so ich gedienet/ Geschäffte halben/ verreisen müssen/ also/ daß ich einer Sprach nach notturfft nicht hab obligen können.

I am a Hungarian by birth, but that cruel tyrant and archenemy of all with Christian names, the Turk, after having expelled my ancestors from family, home, and country, rules until this very day over our land, situated in Wallachia, and threatens us all body and soul; therefore I have lived among strangers from my earliest youth on, endeavoring and striving most devotedly to find ways how I might support myself today or tomorrow. Accordingly I have sought to meet my needs in one country after another, serving many masters and traveling as affairs warranted; so that I have not been able to master a language with attentiveness.

several dedicated teachers, authors, museum curators, and others, an enormously rich amount of additional material was gathered. During my pilgrimage I met outstanding writers who were willing to join my adventure and contribute articles to this work; their talents lend poetry and color to this volume. In the end, from the vast number of historical and current recipes my friends and I had collected, I was able to sort out the most significant ones, which are now included in this publication.

I feel obliged to express my gratitude to a great many people. First of all, my heartfelt thanks go to my business partner, the co-owner of The Four Seasons Restaurant in New York City, Tom Margittai. He never ceased to encourage and assist me in my work; he stood by me steadfast at those times when I felt frustrated and ready to abandon this complex and often thankless task. I am very grateful to my nephew, Miklós Havay, who accompanied me on my travels in Transylvania, and to my old professor from Kolozsvár, István Papp—I cannot forget his spiritual help and practical encouragement.

My infinite thanks are also due to the group of distinguished writers from Transylvania who so generously contributed to this volume: Andor Bajor, Tibor Bálint, Gyula Dávid, József Éltető-Wellman, Romulus Goga, Ildikó Marosi, István Szőcs, and Zaciu Mircea; and to the two food experts there who assisted us: Anikó Fehér and Gabriella Gál. I can hardly express my gratitude enough to the brilliant authors András Sütő and Gyula Szabó for their warm memories conveyed in the two short stories included in this work. I am also specifically thankful to Erzsébet Ádám, the well-known Transylvanian actress, and Győző Hajdú, for their kind assistance in finding in the various parts of Transylvania the right paths for collecting the material used for this book, and George Skorka for helping me go through the recipes.

Last but not least, I must acknowledge my most sincere appreciation to those friends and co-workers who have tirelessly helped me in preparing, typing, and proofreading the manuscript—especially my faithful and most competent translator from Yale, Clara Györgyey, and Kim Honig, who edited this book so ably.

Paul Kovi
New York City

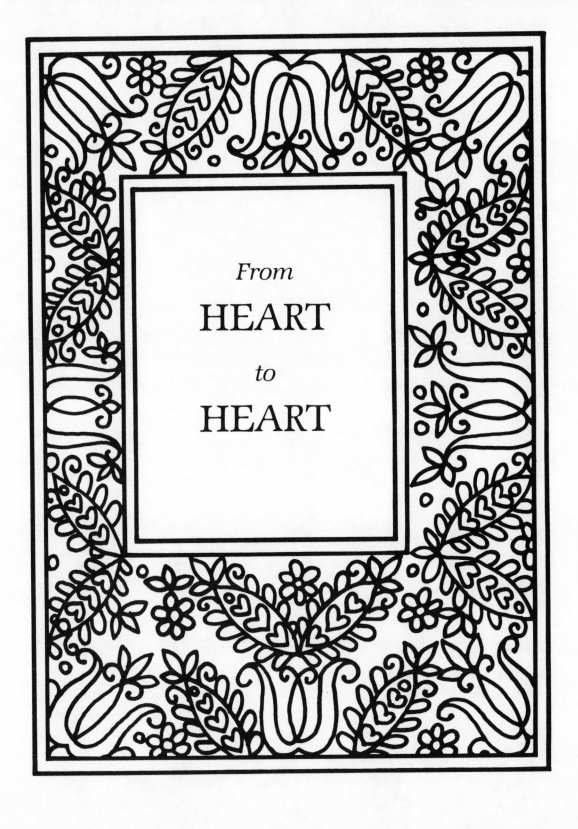

From

HEART

to

HEART

A LINK BETWEEN THE EARTH AND SKY:

A Chronicle of Hungarian Flavors in Transylvania

by István Szőcs

I dreamt about you, Transylvania
when I was an adolescent, Transylvania
mountains and princes
greeted me from afar.
You were my book, Transylvania
you became the house of my youth
*   and my study.*
For three long years, Transylvania
I lived on your soil, Transylvania
I ate your cornette loaf
*   and scones from Torda.*
I knew your colors, Transylvania
your fairly colored autumn, Transylvania
the diamond-edge of your
glass peaks cutting the sky . . .

—MIHÁLY BABITS
(Dean of Hungarian poets in
the first half of the century)

Is it a sacrilege for a poet who longs for the land of his dreams to recall the cornette loaf and scones from Torda, together with books and princes? No, for Torda connotes religious freedom and the cornettes are not simply milk loaves but edible symbols of the pennants flown in heroic battles. Is this poem really a kind of fatal forecast or prophecy about the future of the planet, when mediocrity will deluge the world, and commercial tourism and the catering industry will set bleak standards of taste?

3

Today, restaurants are built everywhere, even on the edge of volcanoes and beside undersea research stations, or near famous landmarks. The Acropolis appears to be merely an attractive backdrop and tempting advertisement for a food stand. Here, at the very foot of the marble pillars, lemonade and grilled sausages are sold! A new observatory is hardly completed when the snack bar, to be situated directly under the giant telescope, has already posted its ads.

The food industry is moving in everywhere: in the Malayan House of the Dead, in the depths of the sunken Spanish galleon, and in Dickens's former stagecoach. Today most people remember the name of large cultural regions only from the bill of fare, and nations, provinces, and historical cities become familiar only in connection with the names of salads, soups, or appetizers on the menu.

Could this be the sole purpose of our book? Namely, that the name Transylvania— once the land of Ilona, the great beauty of a local fairy tale, and the former Dacia Montana, as the Romans called this region; the land of infinite forests and mineral-water streams; the land of three nations, and seven hundred and seventy-seven castles; the land of the freedom of religion; the birthplace of eminent globe-trotters and scientists; the land of folk music and wooden belfries, of ballads and mountain foundries— should be remembered only for its cornette loaf and Torda roast, squeezed between the Russian salad and French Cognac on a menu?

We hope not. There is, we feel, something different on these pages, something that may help our contemporaries to appreciate the uniqueness and high standards of this almost vanished land and era.

Today the world feels alien, because humanity has become uniform; we eat in the same manner, and dress in the same way, and, ironically, we are bored with this conformity. I once met an urban engineer who was constantly traveling on behalf of his firm. He was as familiar with at least thirty countries as with his own. Eventually he had no idea where he belonged. I asked him what he had learned in his thirty years of wandering. He said the reading lamp in one hotel is on the left side of the bed, and on the right side in another, but the waiters, the breakfasts, lunches, nightclubs, offices, workshops, drawing tables, and chests seemed identical everywhere.

Our ideals are different. And, without trying to be self-righteous, we merely intend to document a culture before it disappears into obscurity. We want to present ourselves, and the experiences and customs of our ancestors, in the way the earth, the wind, the water, the climate, and the work shaped, polished, and ennobled them during the past millennia.

It is to that end that we focus on the culinary customs and cuisine of the Hungarian Transylvanians and the Seklers, and on our gardens, forests, and pastures. These are epicurean, not hedonistic, pleasures that we pursue. The flavors and aromas, every drop of our food and drink, are links between the earth and sky: the earth, from which acids, minerals, and elements emanate; the sky, from which the sun, wind, snow, and rain come. These distilled components are the quintessence of our ancestors' gastronomic art.

Both the soil of Transylvania and her peoples are unique and complex. While some traits common to all the population emerged, a closer look at the physiognomy of the regions, ethnic groups, or parts of regions shows an overall picture of extreme variety. For example, at the beginning of the century, just within a Rumanian mountain village in Hunyad County (and even in Saxon villages), different dialects were spoken in the upper, middle, and lower sections of the same village.

Hungarians, Rumanians, Saxons, Armenians, and Jews coexisted here for centuries, enriching one another, yet each of these cultures retained its own distinctive characteristics. The ethnographer will be astonished while wandering in this small area from valley to valley, from plateau to plateau. He will find men blowing mountain horns and wooden structures like in Tibet, towers and belfries such as those seen in the Caucasus, carved gateways reminiscent of China, ancient Roman triumphal arches, gravestones shaped like headboards as seen in the Basque region, and embroidery recalling Siberian and Macedonian influences.

Despite these borrowed influences, one senses the true Transylvanian spirit so indigenous to this region and to its cuisine. Translyvanian people have tasted the meals of their neighbors near and far, evaluated and respected them, even learned how to prepare them, but have always retained their own dishes. This holds true, for example, among the Hungarians in Transylvania, whose methods of preparation for one delicacy can vary from town to town: a different marinade is used for the bacon at Szatmár than at Marosvásárhely. It is difficult to decide which is better, but it is not important; nobody wants to unite the two into one representative Transylvanian bacon. One is pleased that so simple a food can taste equally good when prepared in so many different ways.

The secret of preparing a good dish or a good meal goes beyond the recipe; a certain intuitiveness and dedication are necessary. It is an art and must be done with dignity and moderation, not by tasting food ceaselessly, or sprinkling spices by the handful, or flooding the kitchen with fat, honey, or butter.

Transylvanians are not gourmets who eat for amusement. Their culinary habits are dominated by practicality, simplicity, and common sense. The working peasant awakens at five o'clock in the morning on a hot summer's day and eats a piece of bread and a large bunch of grapes, because the brown bread and golden grapes contain sufficient sugar and calories for the long hours ahead of him.

The Transylvanian cuisine still alive today belongs to those who, during the week, work hard and live soberly and economically, but act quite differently on the holy days. Then they are extravagant and make great sacrifices not only for the stomach but for friends and guests alike, by preserving the traditions in a bold, almost reckless way. They celebrate in a manner that is remembered years and even decades later.

❧ ❧ ❧

Transylvania—this plateau on the eastern goblet of the Carpathian Basin, an area of characteristically mixed population—is embraced by the pure Rumanian ethnic block from the south and from the east; it snuggles up to the main territories of the Hungarians from the west and northwest; in the north it has a short common border with the Ukraine, which once belonged to Poland. If we suspend a string on the map between Vienna and Istanbul, and push the midpoint somewhat to the northeast, we find Transylvania. Its center is equidistant from Vienna and Istanbul. Even if this circumstance strongly influenced its politics for centuries, it would be incorrect to believe that its culture, including its culinary art, strived for some balance between the Austrians and the Ottomans. Though it has something in common with both, its essence and character are entirely different. This area did come under the attacks and influence of the Turks for several hundred years, and some of its parts belonged for 150 years directly to the same empire as Baghdad, Damascus, Anatolia, and Egypt, but, surprisingly, its internal culture and customs have remained independent and intact. It is a frequently mentioned example that although the poppy seed was always a favorite condiment both in Transylvania and Hungary, and consequently poppy growing was widespread, opium smoking (popular among the Turks) remained completely unrooted here. Smoking in Transylvania spread only when it caught on in Europe, despite the fact that in their language the word *dohány* (tobacco) is of Turkish origin and was transmitted by the Turks.

On the other hand, Transylvanians did learn coffee drinking from the ardently coffee-loving Turks. In accordance with the general Oriental etiquette, discussions involving politics, economics, taxes, ransoms, or booty during meals were forbidden among the Turks. After dessert, the "black soup," coffee, was served, along with the *defter*—the list of taxes to be collected! Small wonder that our ancestors had no pleasant memories about *such* feasts.

Throughout Transylvania, corn is called "Turkish wheat," indicating the trade route of the cereal. Similarly, the Hungarian name for corn, *tengeri,* means a plant from overseas. It is true that the Rumanian gastronomic terms include several words of seemingly Turkish origin. It is, however, more accurate to speak about the transmission of these words through the Turkish language from the original Persian, Greek, or Arab. Sometimes one can even discover the ancient Byzantine-Balkan or Roman language roots in some words.

One should always keep in mind that Transylvanian Hungarian cusine, in addition to being Translvanian, is a variation of the Hungarian gastronomic art. Similarly, the Transylvanian Rumanian cuisine is an organic part of the entire Rumanian gastronomic art. And therefore, differences between Hungarian and Rumanian cuisines do exist within Transylvania. It is easy to illustrate this difference by comparing the cooking of the poor, rather than the gentry or the food of the restaurants.

In the basic Hungarian cuisine, a *roux* is the most important thickener of soups and sauces; onions and flour (but usually just the latter) are browned in fat, thinned with a liquid, then added to the soup. Another thickener is made from just flour, sour cream, and eggs. The Seklers of Transylvania and Rumanians are not fond of a *roux,* hence many of their soups are of a different type. They also use a lot of vegetables and meat cooked in a great deal of water, without any prior browning. The central source of calories in Hungarian cuisine is pork fat, while the Rumanians use oil, chiefly from sunflower or pumpkin seeds. The Hungarians, at least in the past, used cooking oil only for Lenten dishes. They still use primarily vinegar to sour their dishes, while the Rumanians like sour bran. The Hungarians frequently add roasted or fried food to a dish, while the Rumanians use semiraw saladlike garnishings. Cornmeal—the simplest repast of the Transylvanian poor—is a good example to further illustrate these differences. Rumanians prepare cornmeal with milk or curd, or with oil and salted or smoked fish, while the Hungarians fry a little onion for a garnish or fry the cornmeal itself.

Now, compared to the Hungarian cuisine, what makes the Transylvanian Hungarian (and Sekler) cuisine special? Several things, such as the use of herbs and spices (wild thyme, ginger, and saffron) in larger quantities and more imaginative ways, with more fidelity to tradition; the particular cult of scones, leavened and other kinds of baked pastries (at the expense of pastas); the frequency of fruit soups and fruit sauces; and, finally, an obvious influence of the other Transylvanian ethnic cuisines and Far Eastern, especially Chinese, cooking. Particularly conspicuous is the prodigious use of certain local vegetables such as eggplant and corn, since they are not used in traditional Hungarian cooking. Finally, the method of mass food preparation left a smaller imprint on the Transylvanian Hungarian cuisine than on the cooking of the great plain of Hungary, and mostly in Budapest.

We often see films, dramas, and operettas taking place in Eastern European or Mediterranean countries, where after the Western travelers taste the local specialties, they grab their throats and scream and moan, as if the poor devils have swallowed live fire. Such scenes insinuate that Westerners are soft and underdeveloped weaklings in comparison to the tough and resilient Orientals or Southern Europeans. Well, these inauthentic tales would never apply to the Transylvanian cuisine, because here the word *spicy* does not mean hot and burning but something completely different—although it is true that in Old Transylvania, as in the aristocratic Hungarian kitchens, the chefs of the rich competed in the use of various, more expensive Oriental or colonial spices. In general, the Transylvanian cuisine *is* fond of pepper and sweet paprika, but only in moderation, while the Rumanians, on the other hand, use a great deal of hot spices and paprika. Those who are curious to know what spicy Transylvanian food is really like should taste the lamb soup with tarragon. Another dish, "slushy" cabbage in the Transylvanian manner, for instance, features dill and savory but not paprika. The caraway seed flavors not only their liqueur, but even the simplest soup, and especially the roast chops. Similarly, aniseed is not only an additive in spirits but is also used in different scones and buns. And many additional herbs may be added to marinades for ham, bacon, or game: coriander, marjoram, juniper berries, and wild thyme, to mention only a few. These spices do not burn the mouth; if they did, people would not taste any flavor. When a dish still tastes a little too hot, Transylvanians eat a bit of horseradish, which has a sharpness that does not bite into the mouth or throat. Rather, it cleans the facial and frontal cavities with its fieriness. It is also believed to purify both the lungs and the brain.

Strangers to our food are astonished at the variety of fruit soups—cherry, gooseberry, red currant, apricot, apple, or plum—which can be sweet, slightly sour, or flavored with smoked meat. The skill and art needed to prepare any good sour fruit soup is realized by most people upon first tasting it. Since Transylvania is a fruit-growing country, there are a thousand methods of preserving and drying fruit there; dried fruit is used for soups, sauces, and teas. In addition to herb teas, cranberry, myrtle-berry (from both black and red berries) and rose hip teas are common. Fruit vinegars, primarily made from wild apples and pears, are used more often than wine vinegar. In the past, at least three types of vinegar had to be offered on a table: wine, apple, sour cherry, rose, or other vinegars, one of which was customarily seasoned with tarragon or thyme. Today, most of the apple vinegar used is commercially produced by state distilleries. Several varieties of mustard also had to be served: common mustard and the so-called Hungarian mustard cooked with grape juice, minced quince, and mustard flour. Even today, no decent pork feast is complete without a choice of mustards.

Transylvanian cuisine uses a large amount of preserved smoked meat in its dishes, and there are unique varied preparations of beans, vegetables, and other produce. The spring soup, called *fuszulyka* soup, contains green beans, lettuce, and fresh hops, while the *zakotas* soup contains pork, lettuce, tarragon, parsley, onion, savory, sour cream, and eggs. There are other similar soups with names just as mysterious. The always resourceful poor prepared various "purées" from what was available: for example, a type of jelly cooked from blanched porridge flour, eaten with milk or plum juice. There was hardly a plant, herb, tree, or flower that did not have a special role in Transylvanian cuisine. It was as if the Transylvanians followed the ancient Sumerian proverb: "Do not tear out anything: it may once bear fruit."

While quoting the past, it should be noted that the milk loaf, doughnuts, buns, and the famous scones of Torda are remnants of ancient sacrificial treats brought to Transylvania, probably by the Khazar Jews. Sacrificial scones—actually a honey bread—made of wheat, rye, and honey, and baked in the ancient river region of Persia and in Egypt, recall Abraham's pilgrimage to Melchizedek. There he sacrificed bread, as did the Jews to the father-in-law of Moses six centuries after, and to Christ, two thousand years later.

The most ancient terms of the Hungarian cuisine can be traced to the first written relics of civilization. We find the Hungarian word *sül* (bake) in early Sumerian and Egyptian texts, where other etymons of basic words were also discovered. *Sül* is still used in connection with scrambled eggs or meat fried in bread crumbs.

In the old Transylvanian villages, meals and everything connected with meals followed a strict order and were surrounded by keen rapture. Whenever food was transported, such as from the home to a picnic in a field, or to a working place, or from the shop to the home, it had to be carried under a cover, such as a *serviette* or cloth. To carry uncovered food was as unacceptable as eating from an unlaid table: when a woman took food to the field, she laid it down on a tablecloth, or a teacloth. This custom was particularly adhered to among the Transylvanian Hungarians.

All this was by no means empty formality. Meals were social events—an opportunity for the family to safeguard human values as well as educate the young and honor the old. After most of the ancient beliefs, superstitions, blessings, prayers, and sacrificial rites fell into extinction, piety and order emerged, as the essence of their "new" lifestyle. Nothing could be more alien to the Transylvanian than eating a fast-food hamburger, wrapped in paper, while on the go. Catered sandwiches have only recently started to replace the old-style sumptuous lunches, dinners, or high teas. (It is interesting to note that it was the aristocracy that first gave up traditions, while the peasants and the shepherds went on preserving them.)

Bread baking has always been accompanied by extensive ceremonies, from the preparation of the dough to the removal from the oven and the cutting of the bread. Even the most "headstrong" Protestants drew a cross on the bread with the edge of the knife before cutting it. It was a major sin to step on dropped bread crumbs; after the bread was eaten, the tablecloth was shaken over the fire. Various formations, usually garlandlike scones representative of ancient sacrificial rites, were made from the dough before baking.

Naturally, some religions often questioned the validity of the customs and rules of other religions, but, by the same token, they always followed their own traditions. For example, the Orthodox Rumanians observed Lent and food prohibitions much more than the Hungarians. It was a widespread custom that Friday lunch should include bean soup or bean purée, either with smoked meat (as prepared by the Protestants) or without; whereas poultry or stuffed cabbage was served (whenever possible) on Sundays. On Thursday, the customary day of bread baking and laundering, "slushy" cabbage was served, followed by pancakes, doughnuts, and jam turnovers. Fasting on Good Friday was strictly adhered to by the Protestants; the main dish to break the fast in the evening was bean purée in oil with fried onions or buttered pasta made without eggs, followed by prunes. In some regions on the Saturday before Christmas large beans were cooked in salted water, without any fat.

The Christmas, New Year, and Easter holy days are still celebrated by the Seklers with a nut and poppy seed loaf. In the past, nuts cooked in honey or roasted in the shell were eaten in abundance, for quite surprising reasons. Many religions believe that nuts have a mythological significance. The nut tree (both its foliage and fruit) is highly respected as the symbol of purity and durability. Consumption of nuts on holy days was also practical, because it complimented the heavy fatty meal of stuffed cabbage and roast meats with its own oil content. In addition, nuts provide an excellent foundation for wine: they absorb it well, make the taste more perceivable, and also clean the gums. Finally, nuts were often thought to work as an aphrodisiac—a boon when carnival time was approaching!

While at Christmas and on other holy days all these religious groups served poultry as the main dish, no poultry would be served or eaten on New Year's Day, because the belief prevailed that animals of the poultry farm pecked backward and would cause a "backlog" in the new year. Instead, pork was recommended, since pigs rooted with their noses forward.

The carnival feast still takes place on the "tail of the carnival," namely, from the last Sunday before Lent until midnight on Shrove Tuesday, which in many places in Transylvania is called "Hump Back Day." On this day a large amount of doughnuts, pastry horns, and pancakes with rose-hip jam is consumed. The pastry horn is a true Transylvanian specialty, not authentically produced in other parts of the world. The genuine pastry horn is of finger-thick, feather-light leavened dough; made with egg yolks, it is rolled around a wooden cylinder, brushed with melted butter and sugar, sprinkled with chopped nuts, and baked to perfection over charcoal embers. The "good roast of Torda" (roast lamb), or the "vendor's roast" (roast pork) of Marosvásárhely, is really tasty only when prepared over hot charcoal, and the lamb (or pork) *flekken*—medallions cut from the leg of baby lamb—is authentic only when the outside is reddish brown and crisp and the inside milky-white and soft.

But today we are losing the old customs and traditions that were always so essential to Transylvanian life. Unfortunately, people today, especially those living in urban areas, no longer have the opportunity to choose the wood to carve the dish, the water of the salty wells, or the stone for pressing the cabbage, and most of them have no idea what buttermilk or curd is. In some places it is difficult even to buy charcoal, not to mention the many herbs and spices grown in our moderate climate. Nevertheless, one still can find resourceful people who grow tarragon or savory in pots on their balconies or windowsills, to recall the flavors of the old homeland. Despite the changing times, respect for food and its thorough preparation should not be sacrificed, and the multifaceted and traditional cuisine of Transylvania ought to be preserved.

AS IF IT WERE
MY MOTHER'S COOKING:

From the Kitchen of
Rumanians in Transylvania

by Zaciu Mircea

Rumanian cuisine can fire the imagination of the foreigner and, particularly if he is a gourmand, can whet his appetite and satisfy his most refined tastes. This cuisine is a felicitous blend of ancient culinary arts that used the many and varied products of a fertile land. Our ancestors not only enjoyed the aroma of fruits, the taste of meat, the fragrance of fresh bread, but enriched them with flavors from the Far East and from Western Europe. In the eighteenth century, the Prince of Moldavia, Dimitrie Cantemir, noted how much pleasure his compatriots found in the various dishes and in the different kinds of drink of the Rumanian Transylvanians.

Almost a hundred years later, two writers, Mihail Kogălniceanu and Costache Negruzzi, assembled an anthology, *200 Selected Dishes.* It's sufficient to list only a few of the dishes to show how the indigenous ones mingle with recipes borrowed from the cuisine of other countries: crayfish soup, French soup, thread sausage, roast wild duck, roast lamb, saddle of deer, carrot stew, rice garnished with goose liver, ham with various kinds of dressing, meringue puffs, almond and pistachio pudding, doughnuts, soufflés, Spanish bread, and so on. Their names, or base materials, reveal that these came from the south—from the regions of the Mediterranean, Greece, and Asia Minor—or from German pastry shops or French cuisine. To Americans accustomed to the intermingling of races and peoples, this comes as no surprise. In Transylvania, where Rumanians, Hungarians, and Saxons have lived together for centuries, this interrelationship is also natural. The taciturn, learned Transylvanians prefer everything to be native and natural. Throughout the centuries they have become accustomed to the crisp air of the mountains and plateaus, streams teeming with fish, thick forests abounding with game, and grazing herds of cattle and flocks of sheep. They share at least one trait with the robust first colonists of the United States—the partaking of food is a kind of religious ritual. For Transylvanians, eating is a serious, beautiful, and simple act. It is restricted to the basic materials that nature offers in abundance: honey, fruits of the vineyards, lamb and tender piglet, and the fishes of the mountain streams. The produce of the patriarchal farms have a leading role in the recipes of Transylvania: cottage or sheep cheese made with dill; mushroom dishes prepared by shepherds; spawn of carp; grits; French toast with corn flour; corn porridge served in various ways; apple soup; green bean soup; chicken with vegetables; wether (castrated male sheep) roasted on a spit with sweet or sour cabbage; cabbage stuffed with pork; and so on. Their herbs also come from the fragrant kitchen garden: wild thyme and dill, basil, marjoram, lovage, tarragon, parsley, and horseradish. Fruits like quince, plum, apples, unripe grapes, and cranberry add a pleasantly sour or sweet taste to meats.

Anyone who wants to know what and how the Transylvanians ate can leaf through the existing literature; I think a few Rumanian references are the most interesting in this respect. In his mock epic, Ion Budai-Deleanu (1760–1820) talks often about liver sausage and praises their wines; however, he condemns the cooks who add too much salt to the food. Ioan Slavici (1848–1925) describes food in his folktales. Florita, the heroine, saves herself by appeasing the hunger of a band of robbers (with bottomless stomachs) by feeding them soup, roast pig, and chicken. In a little village tale, *At the Cross of the Village,* the plot revolves around a busy housewife who is oblivious to the outside world because "the oven is hot, and the strudel dough has to be rolled out." In the works of Ion Agîrbiceanu (1882–1963), almost every banquet takes place in the open air, on the thick grass or in the shade of the forests. "Cold roast lamb, duck, and pig interspersed with great, golden pieces of *brioche*" are placed on the "white tablecloth" laid out on the grass. Should a visitor drop by, the mistress of the house is never caught unprepared. She at once wrings the neck of a fattened turkey or goose. Then the men enjoy themselves alone in the woods, partaking in the ritual of preparing the roast.

One ritual that took place around Christmas was the slaughtering of a pig. Such scenes can be found in the stories by Agîrbiceanu, and also Liviu Rebreanu (1885–1944). In *Son,* Rebreanu's chief work, the village is in an uproar from the desperate squealing of the farmer's pigs, which will soon be turned into ham and sausage. After the slaughter, the farmer's appetite is aroused by the sight of the bloody meat; so to appease him, his wife gladly whips it up into a thick, peppery stew and prepares a cauldron of steaming corn porridge as an accompaniment. The tail and ears of the pig scorched on the straw fire are always reserved for the children. The ceremony of this porcine slaughter is also observed in *I Set Off from the Village,* by Ion Vlasiu (b. 1907).

The ceremony of eating is linked especially to feasts at christenings and burials. Here, Pavel Dan (1907–37) describes the burial feasts: "The cauldrons simmering with chicken soup steamed up to the beams, and filled the entire house with delicious aromas." In the works of Liviu Rebreanu, whenever a suitor turns up, the marriageable young women make "gigantic" preparations: they kill a chicken, procure some beef, and bake three kinds of cakes and *brioche.* They boil the milk the day before so that "by tomorrow its cream will be thicker." Milk is a basic, virtually symbolic food. Fresh, unboiled milk has a special taste and a refreshing effect. "It is as if wonderful powers lay in its warm breath," writes Ion Alexandru (b. 1941). It is as if everything connected to the immaculately white milk were directly linked with cosmic forces. Lucian Blaga (1885–1961) can never forget his childhood experience when at the sheep pen in the Sebeş Mountains he was offered "cheese, cottage cheese, and sour ewe's milk which melted in my mouth like a miraculous and cool balm."

The concept of "rite" evokes the idea of ritual and even sacrifice. For example, women who cooked for their working husbands mixed their very being into the daily meal. Ion Alexandru describes it poetically:

> *Around this time the women make dinner*
> *They cook it with their lungs and salt it with their sweat*
> *They put the fresh whey of ewe's milk into potato soup,*
> *And with smoked side of bacon, they enrich it.*

The most common sacrificial and ceremonial food is bread. Just breaking it is symbolic:

> *Round loaf opens its white breast—to the knife*
> *To the delight of the awakening children*
>   —Ion Brad

In another poem by Ion Brad (b. 1929), communication with the staple foods produced from the earth takes on a symbolic dimension and becomes the sacrifice in the "transubstantiation":

> *They grow round before our eyes, from fire and earth we got them.*
> *Is it eternity or is it mortality that is in them?*
> *White, round half-moons before us, new bread.*
> *The longing, beautiful starry eyes of the little ones urge us,*
> *Cut a slice of it for your hungry little servants.*
> *Give them melon, red on the inside, and golden honey.*
> *Look at them eat greedily, watch them with pleasure*
> *Give them dew-drenched apricots, let them delight in them.*
> *Look, the grape drops a tear when torn from its cluster*
> *When the darkness of the earth is magically changed into sunlight!*
> *Apples on apple trees, like a starry night,*
> *Take them and eat them, for they are the body of my land.*

Such an attitude clearly reveals the Transylvanian peasant's devotion to eating. He chose his menu carefully, and with moderation, and would not tolerate any kind of excess. He wanted bread and wine, milk and honey, bacon and onions, basic foods that ensured his bodily health. Gourmet dishes described in complicated recipes didn't interest him. And it was only during the holidays that food was given more importance than merely satisfying hunger. For this reason, eating was much more of a kind of communion with nature than a luxuriating in the senses. This facet gives it its solemnity, or, one might say, its "religious" character.

With the gradual transformation of Transylvania into a stratified society at the turn of the century, and the fact that the inhabitants of villages who used to live the ancient ways of life came into contact with new ways, the cuisine eventually became richer and assumed more significance in their lives. In his autobiographical confessions written in the 1920s, *The Chronicle and Song of the Ages of Life,* Lucian Blaga observes this phenomenon as soon as he descends from the Sebes Mountains, leaving the world of sheepfolds and villages whose inhabitants have lived a way of life unchanged from time immemorial. During a visit to Cugir, which had just been transformed from a "village at the foot of a hill" to a small industrial city (thanks to the large steel works in the area), the poet notes the "desire to get rich" that attracts a motley crew of "wild west" types. Ion Agîrbiceanu recounts the same thing in his novel *Archangels* (1914), in which the "gold fever" changes even the thinking of the erstwhile farmers and foresters as, from one day to the next, they find themselves the owners of land containing gold. This change is demonstrated even in their feasts, which become lavish, endless celebrations. The traditional inns begin to resemble American saloons. Not only do Balzacian-type figures settle in the cities, but restaurants, pastry shops, and beer houses patterned after German ones spring up like mushrooms. Blaga observes the "hospitable houses with open doors" where ceaseless sounds of cooking emanate from the kitchen and where "they were killing turkeys, plucking geese, cracking nuts, and pulverizing sugar in a mortar. They were making ice cream in quantities that indicated the threat of flood."

People's appetites and taste buds had begun to occupy their everyday thoughts. In the great Germanic cities of southeastern Transylvania, whose population came from the region of Luxembourg or from Flemish areas, the simple Rumanian cuisine was enriched with Hungarian and Saxon elements. In this sense, the memoirs of the great Rumanian linguist, Sextil Puşcariu (1877–1948), entitled *Old Brasso,* serve as a fascinating document. He writes that a veritable gastronomical orgy could be savored in this city. And that the residents of Brasso in the late nineteenth century were fond of *brioche;* blood pudding with black raisins; cracklings; crackling scones (biscuits) sprinkled with pepper; doughnuts called *Krapfen,* modeled after the Viennese *Faschingskrapfen;* cold pork in aspic with garlic, lavishly sprinkled with paprika; stuffed cabbage originating from the Sekler county of Hétfalu; chicken roasted on a spit or with bread crumbs; sour *ciorbă* soup of Eastern origin; red and black caviar; crabs; olives, and turbot, pike, and catfish. Brasso was located at the crossroads of the great trade routes, from the north, south, and west. In addition to the various kinds of pastries from Vienna, merchants brought *halvah* (ground sesame seed candy) and Turkish corn porridge *(rahat)* to Brasso via Bucharest. The halvah and *rahat* were served with Turkish coffee in tiny coffee cups. "Every house had its own coffee grinder!" recounts Sextil Puşcariu, and its own *dulcsasza* service. "When a stranger came to Brasso, he often wondered how *dulcsasza,* very sweet fruit preserves (especially delicious made from blackberries), were eaten. It was licked from teaspoons, as was raspberry sherbet." However, there were also local, traditional desserts, of layered *crêpes* with sour cream and cottage cheese; large dishes of dilled eggs; *kürtős,* the Hungarian equivalent of a pastry horn; Viennese pastries; strudel with cottage cheese or apples; *Kochs,* flavored puddings made from eggs and gelatin (but with rice or grits when these ingredients were unavailable); cream buns and Linzertorte. The children savored the plum dumplings, which were sprinkled with bread crumbs and cinnamon mixed with sugar. Puşcariu also lists the requisite order of the dishes for dinner. After the soups came cooked meats with a sauce made from onions, raisins, horseradish, dill, or tomatoes; followed by the roasts: beef, calf, wether, lamb, poultry or pork (in the given order); then stewed meat with paprika and sour cream or a kind of goulash; game; and finally dessert and coffee.

As time passed, this culinary paradise declined. This is rendered by another Transylvanian writer, Nicolae Breban (b. 1936), in one of his novels, *The Annunciation*. He parodies the old gastronomic tradition through the dinner ritual of a petit bourgeois family. They serve chicken giblets, necks, and backs, homemade sausages, and blood and liver sausage with onions cooked in vinegar, which are pronounced "special and delicious." These are followed by poultry and *pilaf,* meat with rice (which was left over from the noon meal), and finally fruits such as ripe and sour apples and dried grapes. The meal was crowned by a dessert, which was the specialty of the house: a peculiar concoction of nuts and honey with a thin cocoa cream sprinkled with wine. The characters, the foods, the ways of serving, the conversation at the table (usually limited to clichés and platitudes) become objects of caustic satire in Breban's hands. The dinner, scraped together from leftovers, gathers shipwrecked people around the table, who only pretend to have good appetites and good humor. In effect, Breban portrays them as mere puppets in the maelstrom of history.

Thus, Transylvanian writers have immortalized these rustic eating ceremonies in their works. From the embers of Transylvania's heated ovens comes the same sacred bread that was kneaded by the very hands of those who sowed and harvested the wheat: our ancestors. As the words go in an old folk song:

A rosy-red loaf, fresh from the oven
insolently disturbs the universal order,
and cares about nothing.

DINNER IN THE CHURCH FORTRESS:

The Gastronomic History of Saxon-Germans

by József Éltető-Wellman

In the lap of the Carpathian Mountains live a reserved and distant people—the Saxons of Transylvania. Their houses, which from the outside look like small fortresses, reveal little about their owners, for the high, austere stone walls hide their courtyards from curious eyes. Their churches are military structures equipped for long-lasting defense. Passersby can discover little about their lives, for the streets and squares are not an essential part of the Saxon way of life. They are used only for commuting and for the subtle exchange of goods. The Saxons were always reluctant to accept the fact that the streets and squares in their towns were public and any uninvited persons could enter them.

Despite their 800-year-old history in this region, they are still described as *prudens et circumspectus*. It seems though, that the fast-moving pace and profound changes of our time will achieve what centuries of political turbulence could not; that is, break up the Saxons' closed community. Since 1224, even the Hungarians were forbidden to settle in Saxon cities without the permission of the Saxon council. For centuries their religion, language, law, and customs surrounded them like a great protective shroud. Yet, already in medieval times, observant outsiders saw the Saxons as a two-sided people: to strangers they exhibited a deliberate, cold, tightfisted puritanical image, while among themselves they were as warm, cheerful, and colorful as the folk art they made.

Saxons enjoy imbibing wine, and in Transylvania they are recognized as masters of both the vineyard and the wine cellar. Indeed, the Saxon is red-cheeked and jovial, inclined to put on weight, and of an amorous disposition. The perpetual contradictions concerning these people have long been a source of confusion among their non-Saxon neighbors. "A cold fish," jeers the Székely Sabbatarian next door, while doing everything he can to learn his adversary's secret of wine making. "They're a miserly people who torment themselves," opines another neighbor, while actually emulating the Saxons' comfortable home and lifestyle. There used to be a popular saying that "the Saxon is an egotistical, naughty, and selfish individual." This hardly explains their unselfish sacrifice in providing their community with the most beautiful schools, churches, hospitals, and public institutions.

Historically, Transylvania has been fraught with outside threats and internal feuds, frequently culminating in the different nationalities setting fire to each other's cities and villages. While on the surface there was turmoil between the various inhabitants of Transylvania, the overall picture is one of groups who were inherently good to one another. How else could this region be referred to as the "Blessed Land" by the Catholics? But the perpetual tension, caused by the struggle for survival and the strenuous attempt to preserve each of their identities, hardened the militant factions of these ethnic groups. And perhaps the Saxons struggled the most. The fact that the spiritual presence of the Saxon has permeated this land, from the time of Saxon writers Johannes Honterus in the fifteenth century to Herman Oberth in the twentieth century, is the best proof that Hungarians and Rumanians not only tolerated but learned a thing or two from these resilient people. It was more than curiosity that prompted the neighbors to glance behind the high Saxon walls. The secret of their survival, the flourishing of their culture, and how they preserved their character with dignity taught others a valuable and practical lesson. The unique aspects of life in Transylvania were polished by complex interactions, held in balance by the forces of nature and the will of men. Many helped shape this land and, in turn, were shaped by it. Their spirit became the spirit of Transylvania.

Perhaps one of the most important and most expressive components of this spirit is cooking. A closer examination of the cuisine reveals insight into their way of life. One's first impression of Saxon cooking is that it was not inspired by an "ethereal muse" but by necessity. And, after studying the Saxons, this is neither paradoxical nor surprising, for their chief characteristic is the ability to distinguish between the essential and the merely incidental.

On our visit to a Saxon household, out of precaution, I have not started with the kitchen, but gone first to the storehouse. This essential part of the Saxon village community was located in the church-fortress. Its thick walls and installations were built with far-reaching care to provide defense and security for the entire village, for long periods, if necessary. The corner bastions and ramparts provided a hiding place for the larders that were assigned to each family. At all times, there was a complete supply of grain and bacon locked up there—along with an array of beautiful painted hope chests for the girls, with their trousseau and dowry in the drawers. This cautious community tradition was well thought out: in case of enemy attack, there was no need to rush about to stock up on provisions; everyone simply filed into the church-fortress, where everything necessary for survival was stored. (Only nature in its bounty can provide a secure cache as simple and effective as this.) Yet the peacetime side of this custom is even more interesting. Naturally, no one could use this great communal, and yet individual, storehouse according to his whim; it was available only within the bounds of strict expediency. Normally the storerooms were open only two days of the week, when everyone could publicly "draw a few days' worth of rations" from his own goods in the presence of an official specifically chosen to administer this task. "Feast and famine" were thus unimaginable, at least concerning the two traditional basic elements of the Saxon's cuisine: bread and bacon. A wise community knew that its strength and security lay in its individual members. Thus, no one could squander his family's food supply or his daughter's dowry (the financial base of a future family), if he didn't want to be ostracized forever by the community. So, for centuries, these reserved Saxons withstood the plundering enemy and created a community where paupers and beggars were unknown.

This tradition still lives on in our time; only the number of hope chests has diminished. (Actually, a young woman's trade or diploma is her easily defensible dowry today.) The strictness of the "rationing" has also been eased. Additionally, those who go to work in the city buy bread in the shops there; and bacon is losing its importance as a staple.

The prudence and foresight of the Saxon community did not stop at the storehouses. The greater community of the village was divided into smaller, closed communities—the neighborhoods. Associations were established to help each town, and their rules were followed in all Saxon cities and villages. The strictness of the town councils was understandable: left to their own devices, people would use every opportunity to break out of the simplicity and practicality of everyday life with sumptuous feasting or other excesses! The Saxon citizen could indulge in such practices only at home, because up to the eighteenth century, inns and public feasts were considered disreputable. In reading some documents that censure the citizens of Szeben, for instance, I learned that they did indeed seize the opportunity provided by family celebrations, meetings of the guilds and neighborhoods, and other similar occasions for great feasting. The neighborhoods were stocked for these occasions with a supply of communal pots, pans, and tableware. Excess or not, profligacy or not, these events were organized in a true Saxon fashion. It was planned in minute detail who was going to bring what to the revelry, and to what extent the cost would be covered by the community till. For example, when someone bought a house in a new neighborhood, the buyer furnished the food and the neighbors supplied the drinks for the housewarming. On "neighborhood day," for there were such celebrations, the community paid for the supper. (It is interesting to note that women were not allowed to participate in these neighborhood festivities.)

Such "secret" feasts proliferated to such an extent that in 1565 the magistrates of Nagyszeben thought it advisable to intervene and decreed that henceforth only one food course would be permitted at such occasions except on the "neighborhood day of Ash Wednesday," when two courses were allowed. In 1651, further measures were taken to reduce the number of feasts to only two annually. This rule was often violated, and the town council was forced to further tighten its restrictions between 1702 and 1752. Indeed, by the end of the eighteenth century it began to use Draconian severity in dealing with the revelers. This was tilting at windmills. Inns and taverns maintained permanent kitchens and excellent winecellars, and since some of the innkeepers were elected members of the town council, their position made it easier for them to break the rules. For instance, it was punishable by a fine of thirty gold pieces to hold a huge feast for the birth of a child, marriage of a daughter, or death of a villager. Hence, it was a better idea to invite friends to the inn, where one could eat and drink as much as one pleased and at the same time contribute to the enrichment of a compatriot innkeeper (and indirectly to the growth of the town). Celebrations in this fashion were permitted. Of course, there were always stubborn, wealthy citizens who simply paid the fine and caroused to their hearts' content.

On the other hand, the Saxon knew when to be tightfisted and when to be openhanded. They did not begrudge food for their help, for it was known that "what the plowman eats is repaid many times over by the work he does." The centuries-long prohibitions and exhortations for temperance had yet another result. When, in 1817, famine raged throughout virtually all of Europe, the government of Nagyszeben set up a soup kitchen (that's where the fines of thirty gold pieces went!) that fed the city's poor for more than three months. For once the stingy magistrates did not count the pennies.

After these brief glimpses at the Saxon lifestyle to complete this picture their cooking should be looked at closely. Old Saxon cuisine is very simple and lacks gastronomical refinement. The Saxon peasant and citizen did not invest their imagination in a masterly harmony of flavors, but rather he produced the most practical foods in the most economical way. The basic dishes of the Saxon kitchen eloquently demonstrate their motto: "We don't live to eat, but eat to live." They maintained that "we have to eat so that we can bear our hard work and yet we must not consume everything that we produce so we can thrive, grow strong, and survive. To survive, circumspection and supplies are needed. We must cook what is available, and prepare tasty dishes from all of it. We must make virtue out of necessity, and not take on future necessity for the sake of virtue nor renounce virtue at the command of necessity." This wisdom has stood the test of time, and it must be taken into consideration while examining old Saxon cuisine. Furthermore, those who for centuries ate this food labored twelve to sixteen hours a day in hot wheat fields and in vineyards. They also built houses, fortresses, palaces, and churches, worked in metals, and printed books.

The staples of the ancient Saxon cuisine were bread, meat, and bacon; and their oldest and most common dish was *Kächen*. Early medieval records indicate the word *Kächen* was used to mean "food." (Linguists trace it back to the Latin *coquina* or *cocine* [kitchen], derived from the old High German *kuchina*.) *Kächen* is a meat and vegetable dish—really a cross between a soup and a stew. It is a filling, economical one-pot meal, rich in calories and nutrition. Its enormous varieties reflect the abundance of the larder and the foods available in the season. But its basic ingredient was pork, chiefly the bony parts that have been salted, or smoked bacon or bacon rind. It is sometimes thickened with sour cream, eggs, or a *roux. Kächen* is still a traditional food of the farmers.

Another typical one-pot meal with a lot of sauce is *Brock* (loosely translated as "bread soup"), which has occupied a central position in Saxon cuisine. This, too, has innumerable variations, but a common ingredient is bacon. Basically, however, cooking *Brock* provides the optimal use for bread that has begun to grow stale. Similarly, such practicality brought into being the most famous Saxon specialty, *Hangklich,* customarily made out of leftover bread dough or scrapings. Its name supposedly comes from *"eine Hand gleich"* and refers to its literal meaning: a handful of dough. With its numerous versions it has since grown in rank, prestige, fame, and popularity to become an important dish on its own: a kind of Saxon pizza. Its virtue is forged from necessity.

Other main dishes of traditional Saxon cuisine are more familiar. It would be difficult to discern in a good many everyday Saxon foods what is original and what is the result of complex interactions. But it is likely, although it cannot be proved with complete certainty, that the chief masters of various cabbage preparations (especially of sauerkraut) in this region were the Saxon chefs. Linguistic data indicate that the characteristic Saxon word *Kampest* (cabbage) refers back to the old High German *cabuz,* a derivative of the medieval Latin *captium,* which means that cabbage had already been known in ancient Saxon homes. There is also a commonly known historical fact that Prince Gábor Bethlen wrote a letter to Kolomann Gotzmeister in 1623 expressing the hope of tasting some good Saxon cabbage in the course of his visit to Szeben. Poets were equally enthusiastic about this inimitable dish, and many wrote odes to praise its delectable pleasures. Here is one by Sigerius:

> *O, du gesegnetes Sauerkraut,*
> *Im Paradies bist du gebaut!*
> *Swlig, der dir die Bratwurst angetraut!*
>
> *O Sauerkraut, created in Paradise, you are blessed!*
> *Whosoever placed sausage with you*
> *Should be blessed too!*

Many people still consider sauerkraut to be of Hungarian origin. It is difficult to establish the truth in this matter, but it is known that at the old guild festivals and "neighborhood days," even in the twentieth century, the main course served was invariably a first-rate stuffed cabbage. It is clearly under Hungarian influence, however, that in the villages the Saxon soup called *der Lawend* gradually became thinner and distinct from the old *Kächen*.

Other kinship with Magyar treats is frequent in the realm of pastries: *Klotsch*, or honey bread, is *kalács* in Hungarian; and *Retesch*, their famous strudel, is *béles* or *rétes*. *Palukes* made its path from Turkey to the kitchen of the Transylvanian Saxons, with the Rumanians and Hungarians acting as the intermediaries. *Palukes* is just a form of ordinary cornbread *(puliszka)*, a staple the Saxons have consumed in several variations.

By and large, Saxon cooking has gradually conformed to other Transylvanian cuisines, except for traditional holidays. At Saxon weddings, for example, *Reiskächen* (a meat dish) is still a mandatory treat.

In this book, we intend to preserve the flavors of the ethnic cuisines that are slowly disappearing. This will, we hope, offer opportunities to the imaginative devotees of the gastronomical arts so that they may create new culinary symphonies based on time-tested harmonies of tastes, thereby enriching their repertoire.

NOTE: In the course of writing this piece, I interviewed Master Zeck (the present chef of the Römischer Kaiser, the famous and historic restaurant of Szeben). When M. Zeck was asked about the secrets of Transylvanian Saxon cuisine—present and future—he quoted *prudens et circumspectus* and took refuge in deep silence. No revelation, no betrayal of any secrets! As compensation, however, he prepared a "culinary poem" as dinner, based strictly on the oldest traditions of Saxon cuisine while respecting the demands of modern gastronomy. The meal was simply heavenly, but its recipes unfortunately cannot be given away.

ON THE ARMENIAN TRAIL

by Paul Kovi

In midsummer the road from Budapest to Nagyvárad reveals the bleak, gray, and dust-covered landscape of the Alföld, the great plains of Hungary.

The trip through the town of Nagyvárad is short in distance but time-consuming, because of the winding, twisting little streets. At one time Nagyvárad was known as the "little Hungarian Paris," but now it is a sad and sleepy provincial town. We drove through it in a half hour. The once distant dark blue mountains took on an orgiastic emerald green hue. We passed meadows of blue grass, and the gurgling Kőrös River. This is the Királyhágó, or Royal Mountain Pass. As we gradually reached the plateau of this region, the quiet villages of the county of Kalotaszeg came into view. There stood characteristic peasant houses with ornate gates, and embroidered homespun table-cloths and shirts hanging out to dry; these reflected a thousand years of culture and design.

Suddenly we were amid the hustle and bustle of Kolozsvár. Every corner of the city evoked a distant memory in me; I spent my student years here. On the left, the rushing Szamos River, and beyond, the rows of buildings of my Alma Mater, enclosed by the antiquated Székely *kapu* (a handcrafted gate unequaled for beauty and craftsmanship anywhere in the world). Inside was the large courtyard where we took the thorough-breds out for a run each morning and where we played football at sundown. On our drive around the main square I saw that everything looked the same as thirty-five years ago—the trees, the church, and the statue of King Matthias. We stayed in the "new" Napoca Hotel, which already showed signs of age. In the hotel everyone answered my questions cordially but carefully—I spoke Hungarian, which is not too welcome here nowadays; Rumanian is the required language. I asked the telephone central to locate István Papp, my old assistant professor from the academy. (He is now a famous professor and the author of several textbooks.) A sweet voice from the telephone central said, "Of course I know him, he is a friend of my husband's." So I set out to find his house on the little street next to the academy. The professor greeted me cordially, but, I regret, with a certain reserve—perhaps even a little coldness.

The following day we traveled to Marosvásárhely, and then down to Háromszék, the land of the Seklers and the heart of Hungarian Transylvania. We returned to Kolozsvár on Saturday at noon to go shopping. I bought a little ewe cheese for my mother, a Székely doll for my young niece, and some old Hungarian books. Should I go back to say good-bye to Professor Papp? I felt the need to resolve my uneasiness about him. Then I recalled that when I was a student at the Transylvanian University of Kolozsvár (in the early 1940s, during the war), István Papp, who was then a young assistant professor, spent most of those years in the army. Therefore, he did not know me well and could not remember my name; hence his coldness. Papp and I began conversing in his garden, and upon hearing my old "Palócz" (North Hungarian) accent through the open kitchen window, István's wife came out, recognized me (after thirty-five years!), and kissed me on both cheeks. From then on the conversation took on another tone. The atmosphere warmed up with the help of a little brandy. István's wife told me about her cousin, Domonkos Korbuly, an Armenian-Hungarian research scientist from Transylvania, now living in Budapest. I promised to visit him as soon as I arrived in Budapest and deliver a fine bottle of wine.

His apartment in Budapest was flanked by new high-rises on both sides of the street. A horrendous barking greeted me from behind his door. Then someone calmed down the dog and opened the door. It was Domonkos Korbuly, a serious man with great warmth in his smile. He promised to help me as soon as he unpacked the crates, explaining that he had just moved into this new apartment. We talked for a while, and finally he suggested that, as I was going to Italy in the next few weeks, I look up his nephew, Miklós Lukács Fogoján, who is an Armenian Mechitarist Father of Transylvanian descent. He could certainly provide access to information about the Armenians of Transylvania. We toasted, emptying our wineglasses, and I left.

My next stop was Venice—the Isola San Lazzaro. I took two bottles of wine with me for my meeting with Fogoján.

What intimacy, depth, peace, and condensed history were contained within the walls of the monastery. And what a marvelous library awaited me! It embraced about three thousand years of Armenian history, including those few centuries of the Armenians in Transylvania. Before my eyes were revealed an exquisitely beautiful gastronomical past and culture of these incredible people. Finishing our wine, I departed with a promise from the good Father to help me in my research.

EASTERN ROSE HONEY
AND ARMENIAN CUISINE

by Paul Kovi and István Szőcs

I was concerned about the fact that the Transylvanian Armenians' history, recipes, and contribution to the life of Transylvania were disappearing because the Armenian population there has dwindled to merely a few hundred. But thanks to the efforts of Professor Korbuly, Father Fogoján, and the late Marci Tarisznyás I have collected a great wealth of information about one of Transylvania's lost treasures, the rich Armenian heritage. The following essay, which I coauthored with István Szőcs, is the result of this research.

The name Armenian evokes romantic images: cloud-covered peaks of the Caucasus and Ararat, caravans replete with expensive ointments, magnificent Oriental rugs, exotic spices, and heavenly tasting, aromatic sweets. If you have ever seen an original box of halvah, smelled its aroma, and tasted its contents, you know what I'm talking about.

Unfortunately, the Armenian name is fraught with gloomy, ill-omened, and tragic overtones. In their many-thousand-year-old history, the cruelest blow of all fell on the Armenian people at the beginning of this century. Their land, already dismembered, was then occupied by the Turks. About two million civilians—half of the Armenian population—were massacred. This lachrymose story is told in Franz Werfel's novel *The Forty Days of Musa Dagh.* Sadly enough, he was only a voice crying in the wilderness, for Werfel's warning merely aroused shock and horror in the readers but did not serve justice, as there was no retribution or reparation. Thus, the atrocities of Musa Dagh set the precedent for more horrifying genocides of our century.

But the dreadful sufferings of the Armenians never broke their spirit or took away their love of life, their *savoir-vivre,* or their cult of pleasure (of which their ancient culinary art is an important element). Their cuisine is not a separate continent of the Eastern gastronomical world; rather, it is an independent and original subcontinent.

The Armenian culture has roots in the ancient cultures of Persia and India. India's sugar and strong spices, the honey of Iran's rose gardens, the fruits of Asia Minor's mountains, and the varied products of sheep's milk have all played a part in Armenian cuisine. Most of the Turkish sweets came from Constantinople (Istanbul) and are of Armenian origin. Of course, not only the Armenians' desserts but also their vegetable and meat dishes have influenced the culinary art of many nations. The Armenians, in turn, adopted the recipes from other regions that they sampled during their travels, and incorporated them into their gastronomical treasure trove.

In the seventeenth century, a great number of Armenians, rendered homeless either by the floods or by religious persecutions, took refuge in Transylvania. The Armenians settled in the counties of Gyergyó, Csik, Torda, Beszterce, and mostly in the towns of Szamosujvár, Gerle, and Ebesfalva (which later changed its name to Erzsébetváros/ Dumbräveni). They were not only reliable merchants but outstanding artisans and intellectuals. And although they participated in the affairs of the local inhabitants, the Armenians maintained their own traditions and original culture. They preserved their cuisine, and even today faithfully keep it alive. While Armenian families have not spoken their native language for generations, and have lost many of their old customs, they have nurtured their ancient cuisine.

Transylvanians—irrespective of their nationality—have always been fond of Armenian cooking. In fact, the varied use of spices and honey in the cuisine of the Hungarian nobility shows Armenian influences, possibly through a Caucasian connection. This rich and manifold interrelationship is obvious, for instance, in the sweet liver *pâté* of Marosvásárhely, which is cooked with ground meat, rice, and raisins. It is highly reminiscent of Armenian *pilaf* with meat. Sometimes the Hungarians also made their *pilaf* sweet and added raisins. The Hungarian butchers of Marosvásárhely also learned a great deal from the Armenian masters. Regrettably, some of these dishes are being forgotten, and unless one has tasted these delicacies, it is hard to imagine how well the seemingly discordant flavors go together. Their old songs and poems praise the most popular dishes, as in the following song, from an Armenian musical popular between 1890 and 1894:

> Dalauzi *and*
> Pethadzkhenis
> *heavenly food*
> *we all cherish.*
> *Even the Bishop*
> *after one bite,*
> *licks his thin fingers*
> *clean with delight.*

For Dessert take
dákták hálvá,
and our sumptuous
rich páchláva
or ángáds-ábur,
like a lady,
soaked in honey
slim and flaky.

And the jamez,
What a thing!
Life without it is
worth nothing!

Áblemámá
Our leavened bread
tastes better than
all matzo you've had.
Those who swallow it
even while dying,
return to life
and feel like flying.

Katzenjammer victims,
the suffering and ailing,
order our churut!
Your troubles are trailing.

On Armenian land thus,
wise are the politics
since gastronomy
is the main polemic.

Even today several dishes with an Armenian flavor are made throughout Transylvania. One of the most characteristic is *churut,* a special "solid soup" made from curdled milk fermented in a particular way, ground parsley, and the leaves of other vegetables; it is an ancestor of the bouillon cube. The making of *churut* has its own secrets as well as historical significance. The numerous wars, the constant traveling, the perpetual readiness to flee, and the changing economic and climatic factors taught the Armenians to produce foods that could be condensed and have high caloric value. These foods were still full of flavor after being reconstituted and could be easily enriched. They became expert at processing extraordinary materials rich in calories—

honey, poppy seeds, and nuts—and at preparing condensed, complex, and compact foods. Few people today know that the typical central European nut or poppy seed cake, which has been simplified to a "roll" recently, was created by the Armenians, albeit in a somewhat different form. Actually, in ancient times the Armenians discovered "modern" and superior preserving techniques, without the use of preservatives, tin containers, or glass jars. The Armenians indeed knew how to preserve milk, vegetables, and meats. Their famous soup, *ángáds-ábur,* a kind of meat broth enriched with *churut,* was filled with *piroshki* stuffed with ground meat; the stuffing was originally made with dried meat powder. Naturally, this required both the bold and skilled use of spices and a penchant for experimentation.

Herbs were also an essential element in the Armenian cuisine. King Hetum, who reigned in Armenia from 1289 to 1296, wrote in his book about the particular characteristics of the *penuna* flower; *churut,* poultice, and balm were prepared from this. According to the king's notes, it was an angel who called Moses' attention to the *penuna,* when he climbed to the top of Mount Sinai. Moses then used the *penuna* to try to cure his daughter-in-law, who had been bewitched by the devil. On the basis of this legend the Armenians attributed great powers to herbs. Herbs were also collected for religious purposes. The plant was dug up roots and all, since in this state it was most valuable. The centuries have not diminished the Armenians' belief that herbs will exorcise the devil, or the wicked spirit, from the bewitched person. Moreover, it keeps evil away from those already purged.

The Armenians' food specialties played an important role in their rites of passage, religious rituals, and holidays as are described below.

The Wedding

Weddings, the most important celebrations within the family, consisted of three parts. "Escorting" was the first step of the betrothal, in which the groom, along with all his male relatives, was entertained at the house of the eligible girl. It was celebrated with a sumptuous feast.

"Evening of morning," the next step, was the celebration held on the eve of the wedding. The groom took a basket of gifts to his bride. Among the gifts given to her was some *dákták hálvá,* as well as a bride's "farewell" milk loaf. According to tradition, the men and women dined separately at this time. Later on, only the men were permitted to participate in the "feast of mourning," a tradition that later became known as the bridegroom's farewell party.

The third part of the wedding was the marriage ceremony itself. It was prohibited for a large audience to participate in the actual nuptial ceremony; however, the guests were allowed to join in the festivities later. The consumption of meat spreads, turnovers, and baked goods and the use of silverware during the celebration were strictly controlled by the city fathers.

The Funeral

One of the integral parts of a funeral was the burial feast; on this occasion food was also distributed to the poor. At the feast—or, as the Armenians call it, the *hokuhac*—the most important course was a soup with noodles and meat dumplings, or *háku erustá,* dedicated to the spirit of the deceased. Since its preparation is easier than that of *án-gáds-ábur,* it still remains a popular dish in the Transylvanian Armenian cuisine. Interestingly, until 1900 it was customary to await the guests with strudel at the cemetery gate following the burial.

Mádágh

This celebration commemorated pagan animal sacrifices. Originally, on more important holidays, or days of a wake, an animal was slaughtered in the churchyard. The skin and fat of this animal were given to the priests. The meat was cooked on a spit or in a cauldron, distributed, and consumed there in the churchyard. This custom was gradually prohibited, until in 1727 it was decreed that whoever slaughtered a steer, sheep, or lamb on holidays and distributed it according to that terrible old custom would be obliged to pay twelve forints (a stiff fine) to the church.

New Year's

The delicacy for New Year's was *dáláuzi,* one of their best-known sweets, which is made of nuts and honey. This is a regional Moldavian-Transylvanian name, which is not known in the Far Eastern areas. During the holiday celebration it was never lacking from an Armenian home in Transylvania. Few people remember its old name now, yet it is still very popular in delicatessens. The Armenians offer it at their New Year's toasts, when they chant *"snochavor nor dari,"* or "Happy New Year," and sing this special song with an ancient melody:

ODE TO HONEYDEWED NUTS (DÁLÁUZI)
Nuts honeyed or honeyed nuts
Tasteth sweet for old or tots.
Thou tempteth our mouth
And giveth thy sweet,
Alluring a weak heart
Quickening its beat.
But futile is the hope thou giveth
That in sweetness we all liveth.
Or where happiness hath its seat:
Our hearts, thou can't make sweet.
And sorrow won't turn to merry
When heavy tears and honey marry.

Dolefully we say: No ifs and buts!
Magic ain't done by honey and nuts.
Stay what thou art: tasty and sweet,
A mere good bit for good folks to eat.

(Sung to the tune of an old Daluz song,
collected around 1836 by Gábrus Zachariás)

Another New Year's pastry, called *dari-ev,* was a type of milk loaf. There were even superstitions connected with it, which is why its preparation was eventually prohibited. Before baking, a silver coin was inserted in the dough. At Christmas, the head of the family would cut the loaf into as many slices as there were members in the family. If the person who received it was young, he would have good luck—but if the person was very old, it was an unfortunate sign.

The Transylvanian Armenians would cook a dumpling with a meat filling in the *ángáds-ábur* soup, while the Armenians from Galicia made a rectangular jam-filled dumpling. These dumplings, called *dolváth,* brought good luck to the recipient and indicated that he or she would get married in the new year.

Mardi Gras

On the days before Lent, in every Armenian household the guests were first served *kátá* and *páráhi,* sweet pastries.

Christmas

Christmas is preceded by eleven days of fasting. On days of strict fasting, one substantial food allowed was *machoch,* a mixture prepared from poppy seeds and peppermint. This poem describes its essence:

Áblemámá
machoch *for fasting*
if you eat this
—even if you are dying—
You'll revive!

The soup for Christmas Eve dinner was *ángáds-ábur.* The second course of this dinner consisted of various types of *dolmá*—cabbage stuffed with meat, pork, and roast capon. Besides this, stuffed fish would also be eaten.

On Christmas, bread was baked using the best flour and the loaves were sprinkled with anisette. Compote was served instead of soup and *dolmá* stuffed with rice and raisins was the main fare. The pastry served for Christmas was *páchláva*—an afternoon snack often made with rose petals picked from a wild rose hip bush.

The degree to which the spirit of Armenian cooking permeates the Armenian imagination is demonstrated not only by the poetry of their festive folk customs but also by their proverbs: "You only know a person when you have eaten seven loaves of baked bread with him." "It's much better to carry stones with a clever man than to eat *piláf* with a fool." "*Piláf* cannot be made with talk; butter and rice are needed." "When I was hungry, I didn't have any *piláf;* now I have *piláf* and I'm not hungry."

Armenians even use foods as affectionate nicknames. Poetic names for women include *Dolváth* (good luck dumplings), *Dsásu* (food), *Sakhár* (sugar), *Zátrig* (hyssop). Food plays a major part in typical Armenian humor—albeit a peculiar species of dry humor. For example, their most common hero, Garabeth, figures in their jokes. "What's sweet in the middle and woolly on the outside?" Answer: "Garabeth ate honey and a herd of sheep ran around him."

Despite the hardships these unique people have endured for centuries, they have kept their proud identity.

A GLANCE AT THE CUISINE OF MOSES' DISCIPLES

by Paul Kovi and István Szőcs

A HISTORICAL INTRODUCTION

Many years ago, a short essay by the best of the contemporary Transylvanian Sekler writers, Áron Tamási, fell into my hands. This short story, which appeared in a book entitled Bölcső *and* Bagoly (Cradle and Owl) *was about the origin of the Sekler people. This brief work sparked in me the flame of curiosity about Moses' disciples—the Jews and the Sekler Sabbatarians—and since then I have feverishly researched their most complex history. Here are a few lines and thoughts on my findings of the last twenty or thirty years.*

While I was researching the general and gastronomic history of the Transylvanian Jews, many factors and details remained unanswered. In no way could I explain their presence in Transylvania and Hungary at the beginning of the tenth century, even though I found many period references to their presence in the Carpathian Mountains. It seemed unlikely that the Jews came from Germany, France, and Italy, because the unsettled, "wild" Hungarians had conducted continuous raids and merciless wars in Western Europe, in which they plundered the rich cities of these countries and levied ransom from them. The south of the country was confined by the Byzantine Empire, and at this time there were no recorded persecutions that would have created an exodus of the Jews to Transylvania and northern Hungary.

Then I found a most important source that seemed to reveal the answers: a book entitled *The Thirteenth Tribe* (1976), by Arthur Koestler. It is a scholarly work, painstakingly researched, meticulously documented, and spellbindingly written by this eminent thinker and chronicler. The Hungarian-born author writes in his book that in southeastern Europe there existed from about the seventh until the eleventh century a Jewish land and kingdom, called Khazaria.

In the seventh and eighth centuries the Jews of the Byzantine Empire had been continuously persecuted and expelled from the country. Most of them moved to land along the northeast area of the Black Sea, in the region called Khazaria (now part of Russia). Their haven was located at the estuaries of the Volga and Dniester rivers, between the Caspian and Black seas, which extended to the natural border of the Caucasus Mountains in the south.

The Khazars, who originally came from an area farther east, close to China, were a relatively advanced and civilized people. They welcomed the talented Jewish immigrants with the thought that they would help them build their empire. (Some latter-day Western historians called the Khazars Scythians, a people well known for their artistry in gold objects.) Soon after the Jews settled, they assimilated into the ruling class. Finally, in about A.D. 740, the king of the Khazars (called the Kagan) embraced the Jewish faith and declared Judaism the official religion of the leading Khazar tribes. In Byzantine, Arab, and Hebrew literature there are numerous letters, travel notes, and references concerning this most unusual occurrence. Also, renowned British Orientalists have documented this particularly interesting period of history more than adequately.

From the beginning of the seventh century until the end of the ninth, the Hungarians lived under the suzerainty of the Khazars, just as the Khazarians had lived as vassals of the Huns in previous centuries. It must be clarified that the closely related Huns and Hungarians considered the Khazars a cousin race and nation. Later on, the Hungarians developed a beneficial relationship with the Khazars and became close allies; the Hungarians guarded the Khazars' northern border and collected war taxes from tribes living at their end of the Khazarian Empire.

The Khazars freely mixed with the Hungarians and supplied them with much-needed leadership and administration, commerce and trade. Because of the changes in the balance of power, the Hungarians began to move west. (In addition, they were being pushed from the east by wild, nomadic tribes and harassed from the north by incursions of the fierce Rus-Vikings.) Many of the Khazars chose to go with them; and three of the rebellious but important Khazar tribes, the Kabars, joined them in the search for a new homeland, thus forming the leading and most adventurous of the Hungarian tribes. By this time, the Khazar ruling classes, including the Kabars, followed Judaism; this is evidenced (in old writings) by the fact that there were many Jews occupying and ruling the eastern slopes of the Carpathian Valley in Hungary, where they still live today. The Kabars, who were the dominant tribe in Hungary, controlling trade and raids, settled in the middle of the south in this country and many of them in Transylvania, among some Avars, Huns, and a few ousted Khazar families. As in old Khazaria, they instituted the two-ruler system. The selected figurehead was Árpád, from the "Magyar" tribe, but the dominant leader who made the laws and decisions was Jula, or Gyula, from the Kabar tribes.

Since the Hungarians lived peacefully with the Jewish Kabars in Khazaria for many centuries, they did not have any animosity toward the Jews living amongst them. In fact, some historians believe that it was because of their Khazar origin that the Hungarians considered the Kabar Jews their equals or superiors and pointed to the Jews' craftsmanship and business acumen.

In the eleventh and twelfth centuries, the Khazars had been defeated by the Russians, their empire and power greatly reduced; shortly after, they were dispersed throughout eastern Russia, Lithuania, and Poland. But many of them chose the safe road through the mountain passes into the Carpathian Valley. They settled in the land called Transylvania, among their many "cousins"—the Kabars, Huns, and Hungarians—living and prospering there; the Kabars were especially successful, as they were known to be fine artisans and gold and silver smiths. Incidentally, in 1791 perhaps the most significant quantity of Scythian (Khazar) gold—even more than is now housed in the Hermitage Museum in Leningrad—was found in Transylvania, in the village of Nagyszentmiklós.

When my gastronomic research for original Jewish recipes led me to the northeastern Transylvanian frontier towns of Munkács, Mármaros-sziget, and Szatmár, I found that their ancient cooking methods and recipes were more of Far Eastern or Chinese origin, rather than Arab-Mediterranean.

I was even more surprised to discover that the Sabbatarians, or Jew-imitators, as they were (and still are) called in Transylvania, wanted to be more Jewish than Moses and the Old Testament put together. The Székely-Sabbatarians were a small group of Transylvanians who, in the sixteenth century, returned to the laws of the Old Testament and practiced Judaism. However, in my opinion it just might be possible that this was a hidden religion that came back from the underground, having been lost or hibernating for four or five centuries. And it might just be that the Sabbatarians are descendants of the Khazar-Kabar Jews. (Even today there is a great preference among Seklers for first names taken from the Old Testament, anything from Aaron to Moses, Abel to Isaac.) It could have happened that the gospel was passed on from father to son, and when the time was ripe, after the Renaissance in the wake of Protestantism, the old Judaic dreams emerged. This is only my theory, so I will leave the historical proof to the historians.

The originality, variety, and beauty found in both the Jewish and Sabbatarian cuisines contributed a great deal to this book. In the following two sections you will find a recollection of their lives, households, traditions, and eating habits. The research and writing for this study were done in conjunction with my good friend István Szőcs.

THE JEWS OF TRANSYLVANIA

On the colorful palette of Transylvanian cuisine, particularly strong hues belong to the culinary art of the followers of Moses' doctrines—the Jews (and also the so-called Sabbatarians, or Jew-imitators). Although the dietary customs of the Jews have long been erroneously viewed as little more than a series of prohibitions, their culinary art is amazingly rich and worthy of deeper study. Like the Mohammedans, they are forbidden to eat pork. They also must keep a *kosher* kitchen. (This word is of Hebrew origin and refers to the ritual purity of food.) Furthermore, they have to refrain from consuming meat that is considered *treif,* the opposite of *kosher. (Treif*—a variation of the Hebrew *therefe*—is a Yiddish word meaning "torn meat" and signifies something unclean.)

It has been documented, on the basis of literary legends and a great many oral traditions that have been passed down, that Jews resided in Transylvania prior to the sixteenth century. Hitherto scholars have not been able to confirm or to prove that Jewish tribes did live here during the times of the Dacians, in the third and fourth centuries, and helped in laying down the foundations of mining and viticulture in Transylvania. However, some legends from the Dacian period often refer to Jews and seem to suggest that they already lived in Transylvania during the reign of Xerxes, king of the Persians. According to other sources, the heroic king of the Dacians, Decebal, allowed the Jews to come to Dacia after the loss of their shrine in Jerusalem. This gesture was perhaps more of an expression of his opposition to Rome, and strengthened his empire. Decebal gave the Jews permission to found a town where they could mine and pan for gold.

The second and more documented fact of Jewish immigration to Transylvania occurred when the Kabar tribe from Khazaria joined the Hungarians in the ninth century in their search for a new homeland as the Hungarians departed from Etelköz (the land so named because it was between Volga and Dnieper rivers) in southern Russia. The Kabars followed the Jewish faith. They were gallant soldiers, and after the conquest of the country they were ordered to Transylvania to defend the frontiers and were, therefore, called *seklers,* meaning frontier guards. Thus, quite possibly the Seklers—later called Székelys—considered by Hungarian ethnographers the still existing seed of the ancient Magyars, could in fact be direct descendants of the Kabars, of the Jewish Khazar tribe.

Half a century after the Conquest (in the middle of the tenth century) a reliable source mentioned Jews residing in Hungary. It is also believed that the existing historical Transylvanian villages of Kozárd and Kozárvár were founded by the Khazars.

Following this early period there is documentation that the Jews were present in Transylvania at the end of the fifteenth century. These were primarily refugees from Turkey: Spanish or Turkish Sephardic Jews who joined the Greek and Serbian merchants (they were following the invading army of the sultan, and settled on the frontiers of the newly occupied territories). They were first referred to in a written document of the National Assembly held at Kolozsvár in 1578: "Greeks and Jews are prohibited from engaging in trade, except in their defined domicile." One of these "Locus depositionis" was the town of Gyulafehérvár, defined as the settlement and sphere of trading activity for the Jews.

This ban was lifted in 1623 by Prince Gábor Bethlen, the best-known ruler of Transylvania. He allowed the Jews to settle outside the town walls of Gyulafehérvár and other cities, and to wear their own distinctive clothing. However, this measure did not remain effective for very long. About twenty years later, György Rákóczi II withdrew the right of free settlement from the Jews. Yet despite intimidation by town authorities and Saxon traders, Jewish merchants continued to reside throughout Transylvania, although both their political and economic status remained ambiguous, as it did for about the next two hundred years.

In the 1620s the Jews of Transylvania paid taxes only to the prince—their benefactor—and only in exceptional cases contributed to the state treasury (collected by town authorities). Since a large number of Jews still lived in the defined ghetto alongside the walls of Gyulafehérvár and other towns, no taxes had to be paid to the town. It was this exemption that became the source of jealousy, intrigue, and hatred. But then, in 1662, the National Assembly ordered the entire permanent Jewish population of Transylvania to pay one tenth of their assets as taxes (temporary residents paid only one hundredth of their assets!). By this time many new Jews had immigrated from Poland and eastern Russia. They settled mainly in the northern trading centers. Although Jews had to suffer some minor assorted injustices in other areas, the elders and the nobility of Gyulafehérvár made their life most difficult. For instance, the town forbade the butchers to sell cattle to the Jews, thus making it impossible for them to slaughter the animals according to their *kosher* rituals. By the beginning of the eighteenth century, when Gyulafehérvár was destroyed, only seventy Jews (who were living within the inner walls of the town) were registered as paying taxes there.

In 1781, Emperor Joseph II reimposed Rákóczi's decree: Jews were limited to residence only in the confines of Gyulafehérvár. This ruling remained effective until about 1845.

At the 1839–40 National Assembly, Baron József Eötvös advocated the emancipation of the Jews, announcing that "in a state where the citizens are of different denominations, concord can be maintained only with the independence and reciprocity of the denominations. . . . Everyone living within the frontiers of our land should enjoy the blessings of the Constitution." His views were finally put into effect in 1867 with Article 17, which stated: "The Israelite inhabitants of the country are declared to be equal with Christian citizens in the exercise of all civil and political rights." One year later, Article 38 enabled the Jews to set up their own schools and allowed the parish community (the temple or synagogue) to become the basis of the Jewish organization.

The Gastronomy of the Transylvanian Jews

Like all their other rituals, the modern dietary customs of the Jews stem from an ancient civilization and were often based on reasons of health. There are several explanations, for example, of why pork had been declared impure. The Egyptians, for instance, regarded it as such because pigs were the sacred animals of Seth, the "negative god." Others refrained from eating it because allegedly the taste of pork resembled the taste of human flesh. (Modern microanatomical studies indeed indicate that there is a close relationship between human and porcine tissues.) While these views are subject to interpretation, it is commonly accepted that in excessively warm climates pork consumption is unhealthy—it adversely affects the liver, kidney, bile, and the intestinal tract (more than in cold climates). The apparent rationale for most of Moses' food restrictions seems to have been the desire to prevent food poisoning. That explains why Moses prohibited the consumption of the "tissue" most susceptible to poisoning—blood. This is the reason their meat had to be completely drained of blood, washed, and salted; and, by the same principle, unless the meat came from a freshly killed animal, it would never be used in a Jewish kitchen. Here is a pertinent quotation from the *Religious Book* by Simon Péchi, a leading Transylvanian Sabbatarian, written in 1630, advising his community of both propriety and ritual pertaining to meat processing:

> For those who wish to eat slaughtered cattle, game, or fowl: . . . the greatest care should be taken to ensure that the animal is not beaten to death or spoilt in an unseemly manner; with a very sharp, big knife, not a little one, which should be tried out with the fingernail, pulling it along to find out that it is sharp, otherwise, it would tear the animal and it should be considered torn—unclean, or *therefe!* The feather of the fowl and the fur of other animals should be cleaned away at the place where the first cut is made, so that the good, sharp knife should have a clear path. Then the blood should be drained until it has all flowed away, and the cut meat should be cleaned from blood with crude salt before the cooking and baking starts. . . .
>
>   . . . the blood of no type of animal should be eaten, but poured onto the ground, and no blood of a live animal should be drained for eating. . . .

This decree "borrowed" by Péchi from Jewish texts clearly and explicitly spells out these rituals.

The use of milk products was also restricted so far as their storage and serving were concerned. Since these foods also spoiled quickly, they had to be kept in separate dishes and never served along with meat.

For social reasons and because of political pressure, the culinary customs of Jews who settled in Eastern Europe were quickly assimilated with those of the surrounding non-Jewish communities. Some dishes, adapted by the Jewish gastronomy, were consolidated during history to such an extent that their origin was forgotten and they are now fully considered to be Jewish dishes. Such transformed meals, for instance, include *borscht* and mush or pancake, which originated in the Russian kitchen, and *mamaliga* or corn pudding (called *knédli* in Transylvania), which is of Rumanian origin. *Kneidlach* (potato dumplings) is a popular Lithuanian Jewish dish. *Compote,* which is eaten with meat dishes, may be of Polish, Rumanian, or Lithuanian origin, depending on the vegetable or fruit used.

Most Jews who settled in Eastern Europe were poor, and their cooking habits drew mainly on inexpensive ingredients. Their culinary repertoire consisted of the following:

Soups

Jews usually preferred the bitter or sour soup made from beets or sorrel as a starter. But frequently this sour *zoier—borscht* or sorrel soup—was their main course, served with bread or potatoes. In the spring, they ate sorrel soup with sour cream; in the summer, beet juice seasoned with potatoes and chopped onions was considered a special dish. Soups made from their favorite legumes included pea, lentil, and bean.

Meats

The most widely known Jewish meat dish adopted and embraced by Christians in Transylvania is *sholet* (called *cholent* by the Jews). This is a ritualistically prepared dish of generously seasoned baked beans with goose meat, various vegetables, and oil. Its cooking starts before the Sabbath on Friday, and the dish remains in the oven, baking on low heat, until Saturday night. The long, slow baking makes the meat exceptionally tender. The *sholet* has many variations, according to the proportions and types of beans, vegetables, and meat. A non-*kosher* version of *sholet* made in the county of Szatmar is prepared with the smoked shank of pork and tastes heavenly.

The meat restrictions of the Jews encouraged creativity and eventually enriched their cuisine instead of limiting it. Although there were few food items available that complied with their dietary laws, a variety of imaginative recipes emerged. The preparation of ritual dishes served during their several holidays grew into a fascinating and rich culinary tradition. Thus developed, for example, the innumerable variations of dishes made with goose and the imaginative use of mushrooms (as a meat substitute) among the Sabbatarians, who even used them in the traditional Transylvanian stuffed cabbage.

Bread

Also well known and widely accepted is the originally Jewish unleavened bread known as matzo. Today, ground matzo (matzo meal) is used as an ingredient in forming dumplinglike balls to be served either in soups or as an accompaniment to meat. In fact, the use of matzo is now international: scores of egg dishes, pastries, and other delicacies are made with it, including sweet cakes prepared with honey and spices. Such use of matzo might have been common even in ancient times, because the "manna falling from heaven" is described in the "books of Moses." Similar references are made in the Bible by King Solomon, who also recommends the consumption of honey in any form.

For the Sabbath and other holy days, Jewish women prepare *barches,* two large and one small braided milk loaves or kind of *challah,* sprinkled with poppy seeds. (The poppy seed is not an original Jewish condiment, but "borrowed" from the Greek-Roman cuisine.) The *barches* of the Ashkenazic Jews are also decorated with an additional narrow braid, and ornamented with rosettes, spirals, stylized hands, and other figures. (Sephardim, who are unfamiliar with *barches,* eat matzos at Passover and on the Sabbath, and common bread on other days.) The wealthier families prepared it from white flour, then brushed the dough with egg and sprinkled it with poppy seeds. Persian Jews call it *challah,* and theirs is of a flatter shape. Although the word *barches* is undoubtedly of German origin, neither the word nor the dish is known among German gentiles.

Originally the Ashkenazic Jews made the *barches* as a ceremonial food for marriages, since it symbolized the ritual shearing of the heads of the bride and groom before the wedding. It later became a traditional rather than symbolic food; this plaited egg and milk loaf became obligatory for every Sabbath meal, wedding feasts, and religious celebrations for the circumcision of an infant. But the *lechem mishne,* the two loaves, were no longer obligatory; one was sufficient.

Desserts

There are a number of original and tasty desserts, cakes, and pastries in the Jewish cuisine. It's surprising that the form or shape of the pastries, made for more than a thousand years by the highly moralistic and monogamous Jews, have always been symbolic of male fertility. Special pastries are prepared for the Sabbath and the holidays, most of which have symbolic meanings. The Sabbath breakfast consists of poppy seed horns and sweet cheese turnovers. The favorite Pesach breakfast pastry, the hoop-shaped *kraenz,* is a symbol of fertility. A ladder-shaped loaf symbolizes Moses climbing the ladder to Heaven to receive the Torah.

Then there are their pastas—broad ribbon-shaped noodles and long macaroni-shaped noodles—which are used in desserts such as noodle pudding. The symbolism of the latter most probably can be traced back to the ceremony of praying for rain: the shape of the macaroni represented a worm—to the farmer, a sign of the approaching rainy season.

The rolled-up pastry *Kindl,* of German origin (called *kindli* in Transylvanian Jewish cuisine), is a typical Purim sweet. *Fladen* or *fladni*—a multilayered pastry—is considered the symbol of an annual abundant yield. Honey, the basic sweetener, also symbolizes abundance. On the eve of the New Year, apple slices dipped in honey are served as a prayer to God for a happy and sweet new year.

Boys have always been privileged among the Jews. There were celebrations when they entered school and when they took their first exams. The pastry *resegruten* was made in their honor. A spicy dough was rolled into sticks, then tucked into a loaf of kneaded dough made with wine, sultanas, and nuts, and finally baked until the sticks were crispy.

The Sephardic Jews also prepared *mezonoth* for weddings, which is similar to the doughnut-shaped bun the bridegroom crumbles over the head of the bride in the Holy Land.

The fascinating gastronomic art of the Transylvanian Jews is further enhanced by the unique culinary habits of the other group of Moses' disciples: the Sabbatarians.

THE AMAZING SAGA OF THE SZÉKELY SABBATARIANS OR JEW-IMITATORS

The roughly twenty thousand Sabbatarians or Jew-imitators who emerged in Transylvania deserve special attention from a gastronomic point of view. While there were only four important Jewish communities of a few hundred members each during the sixteenth and seventeenth centuries, the Sabbatarians followed them in keeping the culinary rules as prescribed by Moses. Their revival came at the end of the fifteenth century, when small groups of Székelys (or Seklers) returned to the Laws of Moses and the Old Testament. They were called "persons of Jewish aberration" and in the beginning came to light as Unitarians with the advance of Protestantism. Later on they left the Unitarian Church completely and moved toward stricter Judaic religious practices. They believed in the existence of a single God, but denied the divine nature of Christ, and rejected all religious ceremonies, such as baptism, not mentioned in the "books of Moses." They marked out Saturday as their weekly day of rest, hence their name: Sabbatarians.

The spreading of Jew-imitation among Transylvanian Hungarians has various explanations. It is attributed by some to the political and social oppression the Székelys had to suffer, while others claim these people were remnants of the Jewish Kabars and Khazars, who came to Transylvania before and with the Hungarians in the ninth and tenth centuries.

Despite centuries of persecution, the Sabbatarians continued to imitate the Jews, as they were co-followers of Moses. In 1868, when religious freedom was granted in Transylvania, the Sabbatarians all converted to Judaism.

Political and Social Background

The political, social, and economic oppression of the Seklers spanned several historical periods.

In the principality of Transylvania, from the ninth century on, the Seklers lived alongside a small population of Huns, Avars, and Kabars who also fought for their survival. At the beginning of the eleventh century these groups were attacked and conquered by King Stephen of Hungary and were forced to practice Catholicism, which was by then the religion of the ruling Hungarian tribe, the Magyars. From then onward the Seklers lived in areas that they divided into seven tribal seats. A leader from each seat was elected on a yearly rotational basis, but they remained independent. This office of a separate Sekler bailiff was abolished in 1461 and the authority was consolidated in the Transylvania *voivod* (ruler) or *Vajda*, named by the king. On this date the sufferings of these courageous people began, marking the end of their political independence. Here are a few important dates in their history—landmarks of their continuous oppression.

In January 1542, the Diet of Torda elected a new prince, John Sigismund (son of János Zápolya, a large landowner), who began organizing Transylvania into an independent principality. This led to levying new taxes as a means of boosting treasury revenues. The rich nobility, who went to war on horseback, belonged to the order of the mounted, while those living the lives of commoners constituted the order of pawns. In 1556, the Diet ordered that all of the Catholic Church's estates be confiscated, and in 1558 it expanded tax payment obligations to the Seklers, as well as to the noblemen (neither had ever paid taxes before).

The order of pawns protested against taxation on several occasions, but the majority of the leaders and the mounted nobility helped tax collectors with a force of arms. However, when tax collectors began demanding more, and extorted money and food, the pawns, mostly simple farmers, mounted a widespread armed revolt in 1562. This was suppressed, and the prince asked that the Diet institute this resolution: "the leaders and the mounted should live the free lives of noblemen and the farmers (Seklers) should be their serfs." After István Báthori was elected prince in 1571, the Seklers submitted a written complaint about their plight and fought against their oppressors once more, but they were defeated.

When Zsigmond Báthori, István's son, was reelected prince in February 1601, he made a new promise to give the Seklers freedom in return for their unanimous support. This time the prince did not renege, and on New Year's Eve, 1601, he issued a charter that, in part, reestablished the old privileges of those Seklers in the seats of the counties of Csik, Gyergyó, Kászon, and Maros who had stood by him. While this document gave freedom back to the pawns, it failed to reestablish their equality, nobility, and property. Not even with a force of arms could they get their lands back from those who had appropriated them.

The hopelessness of the Seklers' situation provided the fertile ground for the spreading and development of Sabbatarianism.

Religious Background

The driving forces behind Sabbatarianism were the Renaissance and the Reformation. Luther's principles started to gain ground in Transylvania when the pope excommunicated János Zápolya for his alliance with the Turks in the 1630s. As a result,

Zápolya converted to the Protestant faith. His conversion set an example for the masses living on his vast estate, and they followed suit. In addition, the most ardent advocate and missionary of the Reformation movement in Transylvania was a Saxon named Ferenc Dávid. He was instrumental in establishing perhaps the most important religious landmark in Transylvanian history. In 1557, the Transylvanian Diet acknowledged Calvinism as an accepted religion and as such it was recognized by law. This first enactment of religious freedom in the world was mostly due to Dávid's charisma. Inspired by widespread religious polemics, in 1563 Dávid converted first to Calvinism, then to Unitarianism. Since he was, at the same time, the court minister of the prince, Parson of Kolozsvár, and Bishop of the Transylvanian Calvinists, Dávid could now spread his ideas freely.

The Seklers, the oldest inhabitants of Transylvania, since early in the ninth century had been persecuted by the Turks, the Tartars, the Germans, the Saxons, the Transylvanian Hungarians, and their own landlords. They were seeking salvation and found their "savior" in the Old Testament, perhaps because their own fate was similar to that of the besieged Jewish people. There was a core of fear within their psalms, with Jehovah as the framework—Jehovah could help them deal with their anger and despair. The Seklers readily identified with the people of Israel and Judah, as is evident in this Sabbath song:

> *We chose to abide by your law, because*
> *we like and appreciate Israel's camp;*
> *We have joined it ourselves, without*
> *fearing its miserable fate.*

(Thus the Sabbatarians were labeled Jew-imitators.) Sabbatarianism did not come to Transylvania from abroad but was born there, although later it also sprang up in Bohemia.

The number of Jew-imitators grew rapidly among the oppressed Unitarian and Calvinist Seklers because the ancient Jewish spirit found a very special place in their hearts. As early as 1595, a large community of Jew-imitators settled in the small town of Székelyvásárhely, and later in Székelykeresztúr. Some went to live in larger towns like Kolozsvár and Torda. Most of the Jew-imitators at Székelyvásárhely were tailors, furriers, goldsmiths, and other artisans.

Finally, when in 1868 Transylvania was reannexed from Austria by Hungary and religious freedom was granted to the Jews, the Sabbatarians converted to Judaism. The authorities first tried to prevent the conversions, but in 1869 the minister of religion prohibited persecution of any convert. In 1920 the newly signed Peace Treaty of Vienna listed the Jewish people as a national minority and decreed that all followers of the faith of Moses must state their nationality as Jews. But a tragic end came in 1940 when the Sabbatarians, who were considered entirely Jewish, were taken to concentration camps and exterminated. Only a few Sabbatarians remain today, and they live "underground" because of the persecutions of the new regime. Today, only historical works record the existence and religious activity of the once active and devoted community of Jew-imitators.

Gastronomic and Religious Rituals

Holidays

The Sabbatarians observed the Jewish holidays laid down in the Old Testament. Pesach or Passover was their most revered holiday, when they ate roasted lamb and unleavened bread with bitter herbs. There was only one Mosaic law the Sabbatarians could not keep, namely, the law that prohibited all agricultural work on the Sabbath. Adherence to that law would have exposed them as followers of the faith they practiced in secret.

The Sabbatarians did not baptize their children; nor was circumcision performed. Instead, they held name-giving celebrations, when, in most cases, their children received biblical names from the Old Testament.

Depending on their original denomination, their marriages were performed by Unitarian or Calvinist clergymen, but they also were secretly married according to the Jewish rite, in the house of the Sabbatarian who was entrusted with rabbinical duties. After the ceremony, the newlyweds ate fish and nuts—foods symbolizing fertility.

The Sabbath

The Sabbatarians followed Moses' commandments concerning the rites and eating habits on the Sabbath. On this day of worship and rest they put on their best clothes and ate copiously. However, it could not always be observed in public, especially during the persecutions, and so they hid behind the facade of Unitarianism.

All work, including baking and cooking, was forbidden on a Saturday. Meals for Friday nights and the following day were prepared on Friday after lunch, and with that done, all fires and lights were put out. When Saturday arrived the family gathered around the table, which was laid out with a bread or braided *challah* (covered with lace) and jugs of wine. The head of the family would light the candles and then spread his hands over the table as he said a blessing. After the prayer the *challah* was unwrapped and served, along with a fine stuffed fish dish, specially prepared for the Sabbath. Once this was consumed, everyone would sing a traditional Sabbath song, and then the soup and meat courses were served. To neutralize or eliminate the food odor, scented, spicy herbs such as basil and tarragon were brought in, either to fumigate the air or for eating after the rich meal.

The Rules of Eating

The prohibitions in the "books of Moses" were always observed, particularly concerning the consumption of meat. Accordingly, blood, pork, camel, rabbit, wild boar, snails, frog, birds of prey, and animals not freshly killed were forbidden; but the meat of the foreparts of cloven-hooved and ruminant animals were permitted.

The Sabbatarians killed the animals for food the same way as the Jews, but since they did not have *kosher* butchers, their leaders wrote detailed instructions in keeping with requirements of the ritual.

If you must kill cattle, game or bird for eating, you must make sure that the animals are not beaten to death, injured before being killed or torn to pieces. . . . And at the place where the first cut is made, the feathers of birds and the hair and wool of other animals should be cleared away to give way to a good sharp knife. Then you must let all the blood run off and wait until it is all cleared out. And when you prepare your chopped up meat for frying and cooking, you should use lumps of salt to soak up blood.

A Sabbatarian woman would never borrow pots and dishes from Christians, nor would she lend her own, lest they be used for cooking forbidden food. Some Sabbatarian women even ran Jewish *kosher* kitchens.

The Sabbatarians were reluctant to entertain strangers, especially for meals, not only because they were afraid their eating habits would give them away as Jew-imitators but also because they did not want their plates and spoons to become "unclean."

Meals

Sabbatarians substituted beef or mutton for pork, replaced lard with vegetable oil, butter, duck, and goose fat, and used cheese or cottage cheese where bacon was needed. They raised geese instead of pigs. Geese could be kept in flocks, and pastured; they were therefore viewed, with good reason, as "pigs with wings."

The Sabbatarians cooked their geese in as many different ways as other groups in the community prepared pork: they smoked its flesh, used its fat as shortening, and made sausages from it. When roasting a whole goose, they just rubbed its inside with sage, marjoram, rosemary, thyme, and juniper berries, and seasoned the stuffing with the same herbs. The bread used for the stuffing was made of rye or a mixture of wheat and rye or wheat and millet.

In addition to goose stew, they ate hen, mutton, and beef soups, usually on the Saturday Sabbath evening. Meat was mostly braised but in a slightly different way than done today. For instance, leg of mutton with garlic was first half roasted on a spit, then impregnated with garlic, sprinkled with black pepper, and braised with vegetables. This method of braising was also used for a leg of lamb, pheasant, partridge, wild pigeon, wild duck, leg of deer, certain cuts of beef, and smoked ox tongue. They had a preference for stuffed meats, such as pullet stuffed with mushrooms and veal, ox tongue with cheese and mushrooms, chicken with its own giblets, lamb with its liver and heart and mushrooms, pigeon with chicken livers and mushrooms, partridge with veal liver and its own giblets, and pheasant with apples and chestnuts or mushrooms. Sabbath meals often included fish, especially fish stuffed with nuts and mushrooms.

The Sabbatarians used garlic and onion excessively, even in soups and gravies. They would eat fried dough or toast with ginger or garlic, or a bread or pie of garlic soaked in wine.

Garnishes or complete dishes were also made of grains such as millet, barley, buckwheat, rye, and oats. A preparation made from grains that were finely ground into a smooth flour was called a "mash"; and a *kása* or grits was made from the coarsely ground grain. These were both cooked in water, with goose or duck fat, and mixed with cheese or cottage cheese. The mixture was then cut into thin slices, which were arranged in layers, and each layer was moistened with water and honey and sprinkled with poppy seeds. *Kása* was also made of "Turkish wheat" (corn). Sabbatarians often filled their short pastry or strudel dough with goose or pheasant meat, or fish. Their "cakes" made with honey, poppy seed, and nuts were sometimes several feet long.

Those not living in areas where wine was produced frequently made their own wine from local uncultivated grapes; and beer was also brewed at home from fermented barley or honeycomb. Another of their beverages, *boza,* which is still made in the Far East, survived nowhere else in Europe but in Transylvania. It is made of wheat or millet flour, which is kneaded into a dough, cut into small cakes, and baked in an open fireplace; then it is broken into pieces and put in large pots, and hot water is poured on top. In a few days, the *boza* ferments and becomes a pleasantly sour drink with a mild alcohol content. They also drank a type of vermouth that was usually treated with honey.

While the Sabbatarians had a cuisine that was based on the food restrictions of the Jewish religion, they created innovative dishes because of these limitations.

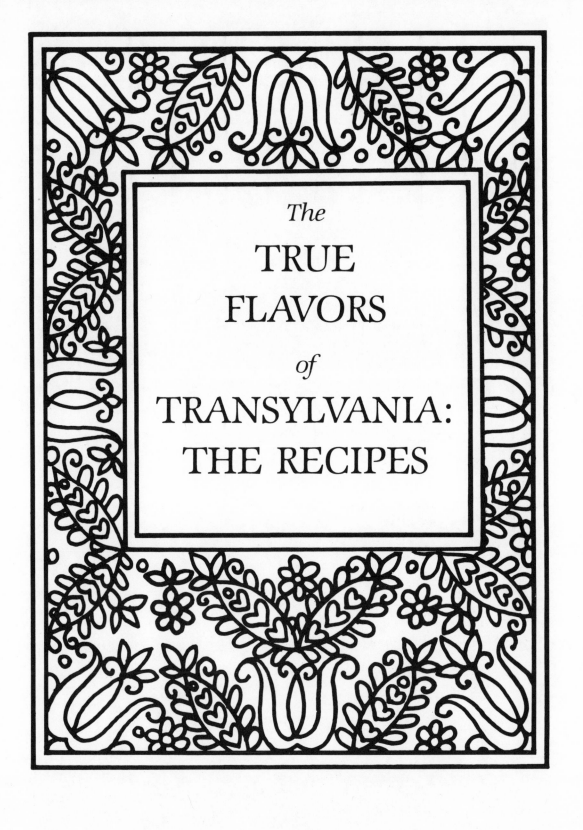

The
TRUE
FLAVORS
of
TRANSYLVANIA:
THE RECIPES

AN INTRODUCTION

As my work in preparing this book gradually progressed, I began to realize the earthy-peasant richness and the original virgin taste of the foods of this dreamy land, where the many ethnic groups contributed to the colorful variation of this special cuisine.

Then at one point I decided to research the recipes in depth—not unlike the way Bartók and Kodály collected their marvelous folk music—and I went from village to village, kitchen to kitchen, and hearth to hearth to find the nearly lost art of the original Transylvanian cooking and flavors. By the time I was ready to compile the work, I had in hand well over 20,000 recipes. I am referring here not only to old and new cookbooks, but also to many family culinary treasures handwritten into little booklets 100 to 150 years ago, which mothers handed down to daughters as part of the bride's dowry. Needless to say, many of the recipes were similar, but at the same time many contained very imaginative variations on the same "theme"; just an additional pinch of this, a sprinkling of that, elevated them from the ordinary.

I have selected the recipes in this book for their ability to capture the essence of the Transylvanian experience and style. Because of their nature, they have not all been tried or tested for this book, but they have been tasted and enjoyed throughout the centuries. It is important for the reader to realize that the recipes are largely reminiscent of the style of cooking practiced and enjoyed at the turn of this century. Great differences in technique and method of preparation abound, from the wood-burning oven (without reliable heat controls) to ingredients without preservatives or chemicals and even eggs of a different size from today's.

In my mother's house, as I was growing up, I had the privilege to taste most of these foods, participate in their preparation, and observe the meticulous process to achieve the best combination and concentration of flavors. Even today on my yearly visit home, my chore and obligation are to prepare, cut, and split firewood for the coming winter. My mother still cooks with a wood-burning stove and it would be futile to ask her the cooking temperature of the prepared dishes. This is one of the reasons specified temperatures do not appear with the recipes.

It will take *a good cook* with fine taste to bring out the best of flavors, colors, and textures from these carefully selected recipes. But even then, as well as now, cooking was a very individual expression. Please just remember these are not specifically detailed measured and remeasured recipes, but rather a collection of delightful and forgotten foods described and re-created in an old-fashioned manner. It should serve as a guide to an intuitive cook to rediscover these culinary secrets and specialties.

Some of the recipe booklets I "inherited" were written in a beautiful style and language used in Transylvania before and at the turn of the century. When I read them, they sounded like poetry to me, and it became a greatly satisfying experience to translate and remold them into contemporary English. The poems written as an introduction to some of the recipes are a reflection of the mood and the period in which they were conceived.

The recipes are grouped not as one might find in a contemporary cookbook; rather, they correspond well to the kitchens and eating habits of the Transylvanian people of the early 1900s and before. While some of the recipes fit perfectly into today's kitchens, others are difficult to reproduce, since the ingredients are just no longer available. And a few of these should be tried only by those who are well versed in re-creating recipes. Some will be added to your culinary treasures, and others I trust will convey the beauty of Transylvania's heritage through her gastronomic stories, tastes, and smells.

FIRST COURSES

APPETIZERS

Shepherds' Stuffed Mushrooms
(Bureţi Ciobăneşti)

Traditionally, this dish is served with cooked cornmeal, the basic staple of the Transylvanian mountain shepherds.

Children of the forest, when dead,
Set their mother to shedding tears
Of delicious golden dewdrops, the honeyed chanterelle
Oh that the sadness of the wood should live so sweet!
One shepherd of a liquid gaze
Picks (one half pound) and pulls off their stems
To dine this eve in lordly fashion.
Oh that the sadness of the wood should live so sweet!
First cooking crisp six ounces smoked bacon
Then blotting gently and crumbling it to bits
To fill each mushroom's bowl, together with a dab
Of cottage cheese (one half pound he needs)
Oh a happy night draws by!
Mushrooms bake on top of a charcoal grill
Their perfume rising above the oil, smoke, heather, and wool.
In cities they use ovens and hardened glass vessels
To bear the forest's second consumer function
But not a final pyre—serve them on a blanket
Of cooked cornmeal
Oh a happy night draws by!

6 ounces sliced smoked bacon
½ pound chanterelle or other
mushrooms, cleaned and
stemmed

Cook the bacon until crisp. Remove, drain on paper towel, and crumble.

Cook on top of a charcoal grill until done. If you are making the dish at home, bake mushrooms in a heatproof dish in a moderate oven or broil them. Season with salt and pepper.

½ pound cottage cheese
Pinch of finely chopped thyme or
savory
Pinch of salt and pepper

Fill each mushroom cap with a little bacon and cottage cheese. Sprinkle with finely chopped thyme.

Baked Eggs with Cheese and Chanterelle Mushrooms
(Sajtos Tojás Gombával)

Thin bread slices
½ cup butter
½ pound chanterelle
mushrooms, cleaned
Salt and pepper to taste

Lightly toast the bread slices. Butter on both sides and place them side by side in a baking pan, covering the bottom of the pan fully.

6 to 8 eggs, well beaten
¼ to ½ pound hard cheese,
coarsely grated
Pinch of ground caraway seeds

Sauté chanterelle mushrooms in the remaining butter. Spread mushrooms over toast.

Add salt and pepper to well-beaten eggs, pour over the toast and mushrooms, and top with grated cheese. Sprinkle with ground caraway seeds. Bake in a moderate oven until the top is reddish brown.

NOTE: Other mushrooms may also be used in this recipe.

Pike Roe Salad
(Csukaikra Saláta)

¼ pound pike roe
Salt and pepper to taste
½ cup oil

Juice of 1 lemon
12 green olives, pitted and halved
1 onion, chopped

Sprinkle roe with salt and pepper. Mix well. Add oil drop by drop, as in the preparation of mayonnaise, and beat until frothy. Add lemon juice.

Place roe on a plate and surround with olive halves. Serve chopped onion with it separately.

NOTE: This salad may be prepared from the roe of any freshwater fish.

Pike Dumplings
(*Csukagombóckák*)

2 pounds pike, cleaned, and head
 and tail removed
1 onion, finely chopped
5 tablespoons butter
2 rolls
½ cup milk

4 eggs, separated
5 sprigs of parsley, finely
 chopped
Pinch of salt and pepper
½ cup fine bread crumbs
½ cup oil

Cook pike in a pot of salted water on low heat until tender. Skin and bone it. Chop fish into small pieces. Set aside.

Sauté onion in butter in a frying pan until wilted. Crush the rolls and soak in milk. Drain excess milk from rolls and mix with onions.

In a large bowl beat the egg yolks. Add parsley, chopped pike, salt and pepper, and onion mixture. In another bowl, beat the egg whites until they form peaks. Gently fold in the beaten egg whites.

Form small dumplings from mixture and roll them in fine bread crumbs. Heat the oil in a frying pan; when the oil is hot, add the dumplings and fry them until brown.
Drain on paper towel and serve.

VARIATION

If desired, fresh roe may be added to the dumplings. The roe should first be seasoned with ginger and a bit of tarragon vinegar and marinated in white wine for half a day. Place a small amount in the center of each dumpling.

NOTE: The dumplings are served as an appetizer with an appropriate sauce, such as tarragon mayonnaise. They are also served as an accompaniment to clear fish soups.

Goose Crackling Pâté
(*Libatöpörtős Pástétom*)

This was the favorite dish of the Jews of the Szatmár county.

Ah gay and giddy, gallant goose
Gone, delicious, bereft thy juice
From thee we take two and one half cups
Crackling and five hard-boiled eggs
Ground twice and then to this paste
Add a little red vinegar, salt to taste,
One half onion and a pinch of thyme,
Blend and mold, and now it's prime
To decorate and refrigerate
And as guests await
As did many Jews in old Szatmár
One cuts strips, squares, circles, and stars
Of onions, radish, chive, peppers red
To lay about the goose crackling spread
Like diamonds from their starry bed.

2½ cups goose cracklings
   (page 208)
5 hard-boiled eggs
½ onion, chopped
1 tablespoon prepared mustard
1 tablespoon tarragon vinegar
Pinch of finely chopped fresh
   thyme or crumbled dried
   thyme

1 tablespoon goose fat (optional)
Salt and pepper to taste
Chopped chives, green onions,
   red radishes, and green and red
   peppers, cut into small
   decorative shapes, for garnish

Pass the goose cracklings and the
hard-boiled eggs through the grinder
twice. Place in a large bowl and mix in
the onion. Add the mustard, tarragon
vinegar, and thyme.

If it is too dry, add 1 tablespoon of goose fat. Add salt and pepper; mix well. Mold into desired form, garnish with the vegetables, and refrigerate before serving.

NOTE: This is a fine snack when spread on the traditional *challah* and sprinkled with paprika.

Eggs with Goose Liver
(Libamájas Tojás)

Libamájas Tojás was a traditional Saturday luncheon appetizer in Jewish households.

4 to 5 hard-boiled eggs, finely chopped
1 onion, minced
½ cup goose cracklings (page 208)
Salt and pepper to taste

¼ pound goose or duck liver, cut into ⅓-inch slices
Flour for dusting
½ cup goose fat
Paprika to taste
1 teaspoon chopped parsley

Combine eggs, onion, and goose cracklings. Add salt and pepper and mix well. Place mixture on a plate, shape into a mound, and decorate it using a fork.

Before serving, dust sliced goose liver with flour. Sauté it in goose fat until done and decorate top of chopped egg mixture with it. Sprinkle with paprika and chopped parsley. Chill slightly.

NOTE: Duck or chicken livers are often substituted for goose livers.

Sheep Cheese Spread with Paprika
(*Kőrözött Juhtúróból*)

The name *Kőrözött*, which means "rounded" in Hungarian, refers to the thorough mixing of ingredients. This is a popular snack item throughout Central Europe. Everyone seems to have a special variation and maintains that it is better than anyone else's. *Kőrözött* is delicious spread on black bread and is often accompanied by a large glass of beer.

Black bread alone, weighted with toil's burdens
Bread gnarled, pitted like the clay before spring rains
Cold and colder still with chilled beers
Black bread heavy as a man crawling across stubborn ground
Remembering to look at the clouds:
Between earth and sky the bright white mixture floats with ease
Between grass and sun graze goats and cows
Whose milk froths forth for butter and cheese
Take this then to spread on bread
One pound sheep curd cheese, one half pound butter,
One half pound cream cheese, swirled together
Lightly, to the smoothness of a circle
Kőrözött meaning rounded in Hungarian.
Between extremes, black and white, clay and clouds,
Bread and spread, lie many moments
Lie many tastes, each an event to be blended:
Raging paprika, stings of salt, bolts of mustard,
Flecks of ground caraway, perhaps a heel of onion
Some add chopped caper or mashed anchovy, stirred
With two ounces beer and one half ounce Cognac
Adding fire and life so that the final molded mixture
Must be chilled to hold back a yeasty leavening
Slight in one hour while the spread hardens
When the ground dries,
When the earth and sky bloom together
In gratitude garlanded with red tomatoes,
Green peppers, radish roses, and shining pickles.

**1 pound sheep curd cheese, feta
  or *brînză* (see Note)**
½ pound butter
½ pound cream cheese
Ground caraway seeds to taste

½ teaspoons dry mustard
Paprika to taste
Pinch of salt
½ ounce Cognac
2 ounces beer

Mix the sheep curd cheese, butter, and cream cheese together lightly until spread is smooth and without lumps.

Slowly add the caraway seeds, mustard, paprika, and salt. Continue mixing. Gently stir in the Cognac and beer until all is blended well together.

Mold into desired form and refrigerate for an hour, until the mold "sets." In the meantime, the beer starts off a light fermentation process and the *kőrözött* hardens slightly.

VARIATIONS

Minced young green onions or chives may be folded in for additional taste. Some recommend chopped capers or anchovy paste as flavorings. When ready, the *kőrözött* may be garnished with tomatoes, green or red peppers, radish rosettes, and small pickles. Alternatively, the spread can be stuffed into meaty, long green or yellow peppers, which, after refrigeration, may be sliced into small rings and served on bread.

NOTE: Brînză is a soft Eastern European sheep's-milk cheese.

Little Sheep Cheese Fritters
(Gogoşele de Brînză)

3 egg whites
1 cup sheep cheese or feta,
   finely grated
Salt to taste

½ cup well-sifted bread crumbs
1½ cups oil
½ cup butter

Beat egg whites until stiff peaks form.
Stir the cheese into egg whites.
Season with salt.

Make walnut-size little balls from this
mixture, roll in bread crumbs, and fry
in a skillet in hot oil and butter
mixture.

When slightly browned, remove the
fritters with a slotted spoon and drain
on paper towel to remove excess oil.
Place on a heated platter and serve
immediately.

Sheep Curd Cheese with Dill
(Kapros Orda)

1¾ cups *orda* (see Note)
½ cup butter
2 tablespoons thick sour cream

Salt to taste
2 tablespoons minced fresh dill

Strain the *orda* through a colander.
Set aside.

Heat butter in saucepan and stir with a wooden spoon until just melted; remove from heat. Add the *orda,* sour cream, and salt. Stir until creamy (but do not cook). Finally, stir in the dill.

Place the *orda* on a platter, garnish as desired, and keep in a cold place for 2 or 3 hours before serving. Serve with sliced country bread.

VARIATIONS

Chopped scallions or chives may be added. *Orda* is also very popular stuffed in thin pancakes (see page 317) and rolled. Place the stuffed pancakes side by side in a buttered fireproof dish. Brush the tops of the pancakes with a mixture of ½ cup sour cream and some chopped dill. Bake in a hot oven for about 15 minutes. Serve hot. In some provinces sugar is added to the *orda* and dill and salt are eliminated, in which case the pancakes are served as a dessert.

NOTE: Orda is a soft fresh sheep's-milk curd cheese. If it is not available, substitute fresh ricotta cheese or cream cheese.

Gourd Flower by Joseph Domjan

Calf's Liver Pâté
(*Májpástétom*)

2 pounds calf's liver
1 pound soup greens, cleaned
¼ pound sliced smoked bacon

¼ cup prepared mustard
Salt, pepper, ground cloves, and
marjoram to taste

Boil the liver and soup greens in a pot of lightly salted water until liver is tender. Drain. Fry the strips of smoked bacon until crisp. Drain on paper towels.

Pass the cooked liver through the grinder twice. Grind the bacon once. Mix the two together. Add the mustard, salt, pepper, cloves, and marjoram. Mix well, shape into desired form, and refrigerate.

VARIATION

A *roux* made with butter, flour, and red wine can be added to the liver while still hot. This interesting variation is prepared in the area around Arad.

Pancakes Filled with Anise and Calf's Brain
(*Ánizsos-Velős Palacsinta*)

1 calf's brain, blanched, cleaned,
and trimmed
1 small onion, finely chopped
1 teaspoon chopped parsley
1 cup rendered lard
5 ounces veal shoulder
1 cup butter

1 tablespoon sour cream
Salt and pepper to taste
Pinch of aniseed
12 thin pancakes (page 317)
2 eggs, beaten
½ cup bread crumbs

Sauté the brain, onion, and parsley in some of the lard until done.

Meanwhile, sauté the veal in butter until done and douse it with sour cream. Pass it through a meat grinder.

Chop the brain into small pieces. Mix it with the minced veal. Season with salt and pepper and aniseed.

Spread the pancakes with this mixture. Fold in the edges and roll them up. Dip the pancakes into the beaten eggs, then the bread crumbs. Fry them in the remaining hot lard in a skillet until golden brown all over.

NOTE: These pancakes may be served with slices of quince, soaked in wine and sautéed in butter.

Stuffed Bear's Foot
(*Töltött Medvetalp*)

Töltött Medvetalp is still such a sophisticated hunter's dish in the Székelys' (Seklers') land that the recipe is known only by a few individuals. Those two or three cooks who know the secret prefer to divulge only the basics. Thus, the quantities below are approximations, because they are based on very old descriptions of this dish.

1 bear's foot
Vinegar to taste
Salt, pepper, paprika, bay leaf,
   lemon peel, and juniper berries
   to taste

¼ pound mushrooms, sliced
½ pound cooked ham
2 eggs, beaten
Melted rendered lard
½ cup red wine

Blanch the bear's foot with boiling water. Repeat the blanching by dipping the foot into boiling water until the fur becomes pluckable. With a sharp knife cut around the foot and between the nails several times to clean properly.

To prepare the marinade, combine the vinegar, salt, pepper, paprika, bay leaf, lemon peel, and juniper berries in a pot. Boil the foot in this liquid for about 1 hour. Then let foot cool in it.

Remove the foot from the marinade. Reserve the marinade. Bone the foot and remove the nails. Combine mushrooms, ham, eggs, and salt and pepper and stuff the foot with this mixture. Grease the foot with melted lard, and wrap it in parchment paper.

Bake in a moderately hot oven until meat is tender. When meat is ready, remove the foot from the paper. Add red wine to the marinade, and pour the liquid over the foot before serving.

Armenian Meat Turnovers
(*Meszov-Párbáds or Örmény Húsosbéles*)

This meat-filled pastry is similar to the Polish, Rumanian, and Russian dishes called *pirog* or *pirozski*. It differs from them especially in its use of the characteristically Armenian flavoring, mint.

**1 recipe for strudel dough
(page 328)**

Filling
**1 onion, finely minced
1 tablespoon rendered lard**

**Salt and pepper to taste
1¼ cups cooked chopped beef
1 tablespoon finely minced
parsley
1 sprig of mint, finely minced
6 ounces sour cream**

Roll out dough and stamp out circles with a round biscuit cutter. Alternatively, the dough may be cut into squares. With a smaller cutter, cut out a hole in the center of half of the circles. In preparing the pastries, the circles with holes in the center will be placed on the full circles.

In a skillet, sauté the onion in the lard until wilted; add salt and pepper. Add the meat and cook for 5 more minutes. Add the finely minced parsley and mint. Stir in the sour cream.

Place a mound of filling on each circle of pastry, and cover with the pastry with the hole in center, sealing the edges together. Place on a baking sheet in a moderate oven and bake until golden brown.

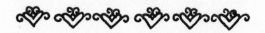

GARDEN RICHES:
STUFFED AND LAYERED

Stuffed Grape Leaves
(Töltike)

40 young grape leaves
About ½ cup rice
10½ ounces ground veal
10½ ounces ground pork
1 large onion, finely chopped
⅔ cup rendered lard

Salt and pepper to taste
15 to 20 grape tendrils, chopped
¼ cup plus 3 tablespoons flour
5 sprigs of fresh dill, chopped
Paprika to taste
½ cup sour cream

Pour boiling water over the grape
leaves and let soak for 15 to 20
minutes. Then drain and wash in cold
water.

Prepare the stuffing mixture. Cook the rice in 1 cup water until almost done and add the ground meat. Sauté the finely chopped onion in a frying pan in half the lard, and add it to the mixture. Season with salt and pepper. Place a mound of filling in each grape leaf, fold in the ends, and roll them up.

Arrange the stuffed grape leaves, rolled side down, in a pot. Shred any remaining unfilled leaves and place them and the tendrils in between the stuffed leaves. Add water to cover and place a plate on top to weight them down. Simmer leaves until tender.

Prepare a light *roux:* melt remaining lard in a saucepan. Mix in flour and cook, stirring constantly, until the flour is completely coated by the lard and the mixture is light golden and smooth.

Add a few tablespoons of the hot cooking liquid from the grape leaves to form a thick sauce, stirring constantly with a whisk to prevent lumps. Add chopped dill, paprika, and salt and pepper. Thoroughly stir the *roux* slowly into the liquid from the grape leaves and let mixture thicken.

Mix in sour cream, and bring to boil. Remove the grape tendrils before serving.

NOTE: The fourth step above explains the technique for making a *roux.* All recipes that call for a *roux* can utilize these instructions.

Savoy Cabbage Pâté from Torda
(Tordai Kelpástétom)

3 savoy cabbages, cored
½ cup rice
1 roll
¼ cup milk
2 pounds lean pork shoulder, minced
1 medium onion, minced
2 tablespoons rendered lard
1 garlic clove, crushed
2 eggs

Marjoram, salt, pepper, and paprika to taste
3½ ounces heavily smoked bacon, thinly sliced
½ teaspoon caraway seeds, crushed
1 to 2 cups chicken or beef broth
1 tablespoon flour (optional)
1 cup sour cream (optional)

Cook the whole cabbages in a pot with salted water to cover until half done. Drain, separate the cabbage leaves, and cut out thick ribs. Set aside.

In another pot, cook the rice in 1 cup water until done. Soak the roll in milk, squeeze out excess milk, and shred. Mix the rice with the shredded roll and minced pork.

Sauté onion in lard in a frying pan for about 5 minutes. At the last minute add garlic. Blend the onion into the rice and pork mixture. Add the eggs, marjoram, salt, pepper, and paprika. Mix thoroughly.

Cover the bottom of a round heatproof casserole dish with some of the smoked bacon slices, reserving the rest.

Cover the bacon slices with the largest cabbage leaves; use only one third of the cabbage. Place half of the meat mixture on top and pat it down. Add another one third of the leaves and press. Sprinkle with half of the caraway seeds.

Add the remaining meat mixture and finally cover with the remaining cabbage leaves. Sprinkle with the remaining caraway seeds. Arrange the remaining bacon slices on top.

Bake in a preheated moderate oven for 1½ hours. During baking baste two or three times with a few tablespoons of the broth. Turn out the cooked *pâté* onto a serving platter. Cut it as you would a cake.

The *pâté* may be garnished with a sauce made from the drippings and juice left in the casserole. Scrape up the particles from the bottom, and heat on top of the stove; add flour and stir for a few minutes. Add paprika to taste, and ½ cup water (or any remaining broth). Stir and boil for 5 minutes. Turn off heat and mix in sour cream. Serve the sauce with the *pâté*.

Layered Kohlrabies from Nyárád
(Nyárádmenti Rakott Karalábé)

Kohlrabi, patient slow-growing dweller
at the bottom of the garden
You know how time labors aloud in the garden
How the earth though tilled when soft will harden
Seeds crack and struggle to find the sun's pardon
Kohlrabi waiting at the bottom of the cellar
When you are baked in layers, the year becomes day:
Plows slicing into wet spring clay
Sound like the dicing of kohlrabies thin
For frying in butter and sugar;
Surely the sweet May air turns hot
And the diced roots will steam until tender
Other things happen, layers on layers
Beef is braised with salt and pepper
Rice is steamed as rice is rain's own twin
Weeds are shredded like the braised beef's lot
These things always occur together
Lard a casserole as bright as August weather
To plant the kohlrabies at the bottom again
Cover them and each layer in the pot
That follows, beef, rice, kohlrabi again
With thick white sour cream, layer on layers
As snow will soon blanket the garden
And time returns to jars in the cellar.

2 pounds kohlrabies, peeled and diced	**1 pound bottom round beef**
Salt and pepper to taste	**1 onion**
⅔ cup butter	**¾ cup rice**
1 teaspoon sugar	**1½ cups sour cream**
	Pinch of chopped summer savory

Season the kohlrabies with salt and pepper and sauté in butter in a skillet until tender. Then sprinkle with sugar. Set aside.

Salt and pepper the beef. In a pot, cook the beef and the whole onion in water barely to cover until tender. Reserve.

Boil the rice in 1½ cups water until tender. Dice the meat finely and mix it with the rice. Grease an ovenproof casserole with butter. Line the bottom with kohlrabies, then a layer of the meat and rice mixture. Cover with a layer of sour cream.

Repeat layering until all ingredients are used. The top layer should be of kohlrabies.

Place casserole in a hot oven and bake for 15 minutes. Before serving, season with chopped summer savory.

NOTE: Layered kohlrabies may be served with a tomato sauce if desired.

Kohlrabies Stuffed with Calf's Brains
(Velővel Töltött Karalábé)

9 ounces fresh green peas
7 tablespoons rendered lard
Salt and chopped fresh dill to
   taste
9 ounces calf's brains, blanched
   and cleaned

Pepper to taste
10 large kohlrabies, peeled and
   centers scooped out
1 cup sour cream
3 tablespoons grated hard cheese

In a frying pan sauté the peas in the lard, and when half done, season with salt. Add dill, cover, and steam until tender. Drain, reserving the liquid.

Cook the brain for 5 minutes in the reserved cooking liquid from the peas, drain (reserving the liquid again), then slice and add to the peas. Taste, then season with pepper, salt, and dill.

Stuff the kohlrabies with this mixture and place them in a shallow pan. Add the reserved liquid and enough water, if needed, to barely cover the kohlrabies. Cover the pan and cook. When kohlrabies are soft and the liquid has almost entirely evaporated, transfer them to an ovenproof casserole.

Cover with sour cream and sprinkle the top with grated cheese. Place the casserole in a moderate oven and bake until the top begins to brown.

NOTE: The leaves and stems of the kohlrabies can be added to the cooking liquid, to produce a more flavorful dish.

Stuffed Potatoes
(Töltött Pityóka)

1 pound pork shoulder, minced
Salt to taste
Dash of pepper, ground cloves,
   and ground caraway seeds
5 to 6 large potatoes, peeled, cut
   in half, and centers scooped out

2 or 3 bay leaves
½ teaspoon rendered lard
2 tablespoons flour
Vinegar to taste
1 cup sour cream

Season the meat with salt, pepper, cloves, and caraway seeds, and stuff the potatoes with this mixture.

Place the potatoes in a shallow pan, stuffed side up. Add bay leaves, and enough salted water to come up three fourths the height of the potatoes. Simmer potatoes until they are tender and the meat is cooked.

Remove potatoes from cooking liquid and set aside. Prepare a golden *roux* with the lard and flour. Thin it with some of the cooking liquid from the potatoes.

Add *roux* to remaining potato liquid, bring to a light boil, and let it thicken. Turn off heat and add vinegar and sour cream before serving. Remove bay leaves and pour sauce over potatoes.

Stuffed Whole Lettuce
(Töltött Saláta)

4 large heads of lettuce
1 pound pork shoulder, minced
¾ cup rice
Salt, pepper, savory, and dill to taste

1 teaspoon rendered lard or ½ cup milk
½ cup flour
Vinegar to taste
1 cup sour cream

Wash the heads of lettuce but do not remove the leaves. Combine the pork, rice, and salt and pepper. Carefully spread open the lettuce leaves and fill the spaces between them with the pork mixture. Close the outer leaves around the stuffing, and tie a piece of string around each head of lettuce to hold it together.

Put the lettuce heads in a pot and add enough salted water to cover them. Add savory and dill and cook until meat is done. Remove the stuffed lettuce and the herbs from the cooking liquid.

Prepare a golden *roux* with the lard and flour. Thicken the cooking liquid with the *roux.* Bring to a light boil. Turn off heat and stir in vinegar.

Carefully remove the string from the heads of lettuce and cut them into quarters. Pour the sauce over and serve with sour cream.

VARIATION

Stuffed savoy cabbage may be prepared in the same manner.

Stuffed Cucumbers in the Armenian Manner
(Thethum Dolmá)

4 to 5 medium cucumbers, peeled, halved lengthwise, and centers scooped out
1 pound pork or veal shoulder, minced

2 cups chicken broth
1½ cups sour cream
2 egg yolks
Lemon juice, chopped dill, and salt to taste

Stuff the cucumbers with the minced meat.

Place cucumbers in a shallow pan, stuffed side up, pour in enough broth to barely cover them, and cook at a simmer. When done, remove cucumbers and set aside.

Mix together well sour cream and egg yolks and add to the cooking liquid. Cook on low heat until it thickens, stirring constantly. Season with lemon juice, dill, and salt and pour over cucumbers.

NOTE: Tomatoes may be used to add a piquant sour flavor to the dish. In the summer, fresh pickled gherkins can be used instead of cucumbers.

Armenian Stuffed Onions
(Szoche-Dolmá or Töltött Hagyma)

6 large onions, peeled
1½ cups white wine
2 cups chicken broth
10½ ounces ground veal or pork shoulder
1 teaspoon sugar

Lemon juice, savory, and salt to taste
2 teaspoons flour
1 egg yolk
1¼ cups sour cream

Cut off one or two slices at the root end of the onions, so that all layers of the onion are visible.

Bring wine and broth to a boil in a pot. Add the onions, and cook them just long enough so that the layers can be separated. Drain, reserving the liquid.

Remove the inner layers of each onion, beginning at the center, being careful not to damage the outer layers. Leave the last two or three outer layers intact.

Loosely stuff the hollowed centers of the onions and arrange them in a shallow pan. Pour in enough of the reserved wine and broth mixture to barely cover the onions. Season with sugar, lemon juice, savory, and salt.

Cover and simmer until tender. Remove the onions. Blend flour, egg yolk, and sour cream together well. Add to the cooking liquid. Cook on low heat for 1 to 2 minutes, stirring constantly, until it thickens. Pour sauce over onions and serve.

Rumanian Stuffed Eggplant
(Vinete Umplute)

4 medium eggplants, washed, dried, and halved lengthwise
Salt and pepper to taste
⅔ cup butter
1 cup rice
1 bread slice
½ cup milk
14 ounces boneless pork leg

1 onion
½ cup mixed chopped fresh dill and parsley
2 egg yolks
3 or 4 tomatoes, peeled and sliced
4 tablespoons grated hard cheese
2 to 3 tablespoons sour cream

Scoop out and discard the centers of the eggplants, leaving ½ inch of flesh all around. Lightly season eggplants and brown slightly in butter in a frying pan. Set aside.

Cook the rice in 2 cups water so that it remains slightly hard. Drain excess water, if any. Soak the bread slice in the milk; drain any excess milk.

Pass the meat through the grinder twice, together with the milk-soaked bread and the onion. Then add rice, ¼ cup water, salt, pepper, chopped dill and parsley, and egg yolks. Blend thoroughly.

Stuff the eggplants with the meat mixture. Arrange them in a shallow pot. Cover eggplants with the sliced tomatoes. Pour in 1 cup water. Let simmer, covered, over low heat.

When the meat is done, place the eggplants in a baking pan. Sprinkle with grated cheese and spread on sour cream. Put in moderate oven and bake until brown.

Layered Eggplant
(Rakott Vinetta)

Salt to taste
3 pounds eggplants, peeled and thickly sliced
¾ cup plus 2 tablespoons flour
1½ cups oil or 10 tablespoons rendered lard

Sugar and pepper to taste
2 tomatoes, sliced
3½ to 4 tablespoons butter
¾ cup bread crumbs
3½ ounces hard cheese, grated

Salt the eggplant slices and dip in flour. In a skillet sauté the eggplant slices on both sides in the oil. When done, drain them on paper towel and set aside on a plate.

Grease a baking dish, and line it with a layer of eggplant slices. Sprinkle layer generously with sugar, pepper, and salt. Top with some of the tomatoes. Combine the butter and bread crumbs. Scatter the buttered bread crumbs on top of the eggplant.

Continue making layers with the eggplant, sugar, pepper, salt, tomatoes, and bread crumbs until all ingredients are used. The top should be covered with a thicker layer of bread crumbs. Sprinkle on cheese. Bake in a hot oven until top is crispy brown and serve.

VARIATION

This dish may also be prepared by including layers of sliced pork leg and sliced hard-boiled egg. The top should be spread with sour cream.

Pinto Beans with Basil
(Tarka Paszuly Bazsalikommal)

10½ ounces dried pinto beans
7 ounces rice or millet
1 pound soup greens, sliced
14 ounces beef sausage, sliced
1 onion, chopped
1 green pepper, chopped

1 bay leaf
Salt to taste
2 tablespoons oil
2 tablespoons flour
Chopped fresh basil to taste
1¼ cups sour cream

Soak the beans overnight in water to cover. The next day, drain the beans and put them in a pot with three times as much water as beans. Add rice, soup greens, sausage, onion, green pepper, and bay leaf and cook until all ingredients are tender.

Prepare a brown *roux* with the oil and flour. When the bean mixture is done, thicken it with the *roux.* Season with basil and bring to a light boil. Adjust taste with salt. Stir in sour cream before serving.

NOTE: The consistency of this dish may be made either thick, with the addition of the *roux,* or thin.

Mock Fish
(Falsch Fisch)

This dish is served cold on the eve of the Sabbath, if no fresh fish is available.

½ roll
½ cup milk
11 to 14 ounces poultry breasts or suckling veal breasts
1 carrot, peeled and sliced
1 parsnip, peeled and sliced

½ onion, peeled and sliced
2 small potatoes, peeled and sliced
Salt, pepper, and sugar to taste
1 egg (optional)
A few peppercorns

Soak the roll in milk. Mince it together with the meat. Then mince half of the carrot, parsnip, onion, and potatoes.

Combine these ingredients in a bowl. Add salt, pepper, and sugar and fold in the egg. Set aside.

Boil 1 quart water in a pot with a few peppercorns and the remaining sliced onion, carrot, and parsnip. Cook, covered, over low heat. When the carrot is almost cooked add the remaining potato slices to the pot, cover, and bring to a boil.

Shape meat mixture into small balls with wet palms, and put them in the boiling water. Cover and let simmer. Continue to cook until the potatoes are tender; by that time everything in the pot will be done.

Strain, reserving vegetables (except the onion); remove peppercorns. Arrange the vegetables in the center of a dish, surrounded by the meatballs. Pour in as much liquid from the pot as needed to cover the meat and vegetables.

VARIATIONS

In Máramaros, in the spring, the cooking liquid is slightly sweetened.

NOTE: According to some recipes an egg is added to the meatballs to hold them together better, so it is optional here.

POULTRY AND MEAT SOUPS, *CIORBĂS* AND *KÄCHENS*

Sabbatarian Cabbage Soup with Smoked Goose Meat
(Szombatos Káposztaleves Füstölt Libahússal)

10 ounces smoked goose meat
1 carrot, peeled
2 parsnips, peeled
1 celery root, peeled
1 quart sauerkraut juice
1 tablespoon goose fat
1 small onion, finely chopped

1 tablespoon flour
14 ounces sauerkraut, drained
Salt and pepper to taste
Juice of 1 crushed garlic clove
Finely chopped basil to taste
½ cup sour cream

Put the meat in a pot with enough water to cover and let it boil lightly. When it begins to get tender, add the vegetables and sauerkraut juice and simmer. When done, remove the meat and vegetables from the pot. Chop the meat and slice the vegetables; set aside.

In a saucepan, melt the goose fat and add the chopped onion; cook until soft but do not let it brown. Then add the flour and make a light brown *roux.*

Thin the *roux* with a little cold water and add it to the soup. Add the sauerkraut, stir, and cook for 10 minutes.

Add salt and pepper, the juice of the crushed garlic clove, basil, and sour cream. Return the chopped meat and sliced vegetables to the soup. Bring to a boil and serve.

Stringbeans by Joseph Domjan

Lentil Soup with Partridge from Mezőség
(Mezőségi Lencseleves Fogollyal)

2 cups lentils
3 pounds veal bones
2 carrots, peeled
2 parsnips, peeled
1 celery root, peeled
1 small onion
1 bay leaf
Salt and ground pepper to taste

2 large or 3 small partridges,
  cleaned
¼ cup rice
2 egg yolks
1½ cups heavy cream
1 cup finely chopped mushrooms
¼ cup rendered lard

Soak the lentils in water to cover overnight; drain. Set aside.

Combine bones, carrots, parsnips, celery root, onion, seasonings, and 2 quarts water in a pot; simmer until soup is done. Strain soup and cook partridges in this liquid until tender.

Strain soup again and reserve. Bone the birds, then skin them, and cut into small pieces. Set aside until ready to serve soup.

Cook lentils in the strained soup over a low flame until tender. Meanwhile, cook rice in another pan in ¾ cup of the soup. When tender, add to the cooked lentil soup.

Combine egg yolks and cream, then stir into soup. Cook on low heat, stirring constantly, until it thickens soup.

In a frying pan, sauté mushrooms in lard. Add mushrooms and partridge meat to soup and serve immediately.

NOTE: In more simple homes, partridges were served cut in half rather than boned and cut into pieces.

Soup for a Transylvanian Wedding
(Székely Lakodalmi Tyúkleves)

**1 fat hen or 2 chickens, cut into
serving pieces
Salt and pepper to taste
1 small onion
10 sprigs of parsley
5 ounces mushrooms
2 small turnips, peeled and
julienned**

**1 small celery root, peeled and
julienned
1 small kohlrabi, peeled and
julienned
1 cup peas
4 ounces egg noodles
Finely chopped parsley to taste**

Put chicken in a pot with cold water to cover and bring to a slow boil over low heat. When boiling begins, spoon off the foam and add a touch of salt and pepper. Put onion, parsley, and mushrooms in a linen bag or piece of cheesecloth tied with a string and add to the pot. Bring to a slow boil again.

Add the vegetables, except the peas, to the pot 30 minutes after the soup begins to boil. Cook the soup on a slow and even flame until chicken is tender. Then add peas and cook for 5 more minutes.

Strain the soup, reserving the chicken and vegetables, and cook egg noodles in it until done. The soup must be golden yellow and semitransparent. Serve chicken pieces and vegetables separately and the noodles in the soup, sprinkled with finely chopped parsley.

NOTE: It is an old Székely custom to season the soup with ginger and saffron. The Saxons in the south have a very similar wedding soup; however, they add beef and use rice instead of pasta.

Pork Orja Soup
(Orjaleves)

The soup takes its name from the pig's meaty backbone (actually, the neck and shoulder parts), or *orja.* It is one of the primary main courses of the *disznótor,* the feast held in country households to celebrate the pig slaughtering. In some Transylvanian households fresh vegetables such as leeks and green peppers are preserved for winter use by storage in sand. By the middle of winter, they have a very concentrated flavor.

Soup

10 to 12 pounds pork bones,
   cleaned, washed, and blanched
2½ tablespoons salt
1 tablespoon peppercorns
1 fresh ginger root (about 3
   inches), peeled and cut in half
1 onion
4 carrots, peeled
2 celery roots, peeled
2 kohlrabies, peeled
½ head savoy cabbage, cut in half
1 pork *orja* (neck and shoulder),
   blanched
½ pig's head, cleaned and
   blanched
2 leeks, halved lengthwise and
   thoroughly cleaned
2 green peppers, seeded

½ pound turnips (with their
   young leaves, if possible),
   peeled
½ pound pork meat
1 teaspoon saffron
½ teaspoon sweet paprika
Salt and pepper to taste

Noodles

2 cups flour
3 eggs
1 teaspoon melted butter or oil
Pinch of salt and pepper
1 cup lukewarm milk or water
   (optional)
Pinch of ground nutmeg

Vinegary horseradish, assorted
   pickles, and mustard for
   garnish

Put bones in a large pot of water and bring to a boil. Add the salt and peppercorns. When it begins to boil, reduce the flame. Cook for approximately 1 to 1½ hours, depending on the size of the bones. Skim off the top from time to time.

Seasoning the soup should be done in the following manner: add the ginger to the soup. Then put the whole onion, carrots, celery roots, and kohlrabies in the soup. Bring to a boil, then lower heat and cook at a simmer.

After 20 minutes add the cabbage, *orja,* and half pig's head to the soup. Continue cooking over a low flame, occasionally removing the foam on top.

After another 20 minutes add the leeks, green peppers, turnips, and pork. Skim the top of the soup and continue cooking over a low flame.

Dissolve the saffron in some of the soup in a separate saucepan. Boil it for 1 minute, then set aside to cool. After a while add the paprika to the saffron, let it dissolve, then stir this mixture into the soup.

Continue cooking for 15 to 20 minutes. According to this timing, the vegetables and meats will be finished at approximately the same time. Adjust seasoning if necessary.

Prepare the noodles: Form the flour into a mound on a board and make a well in it. Drop the eggs, butter, salt and pepper, and nutmeg into the well. Work the mixture into the flour, adding milk if necessary, until the dough can be rolled into a ball and doesn't stick to your hands.

Knead the dough for about 10 minutes. Roll out dough thinly, then roll up the sheet of dough and cut into ½-inch-wide noodles, or any size you desire. (To cut into vermicelli, slice rolled-up dough into thin julienne strips.) Before serving, cook noodles separately in 2 quarts of soup until done.

To serve *orja* soup, ladle the basic soup into a tureen through a double layer of cheesecloth. Serve the cooked meats and the vegetables on separate platters. Serve the soup and the noodles together. Garnish with horseradish, assorted pickled dishes, and mustard.

NOTE: If a smaller quantity of soup is desired (and if, for instance, there is no *disznótor*), substitute whole pieces of beef for the pork parts; this can also add a strong flavor to the soup.

Prune Soup with Smoked Orja
(Szilvás Leves Füstölt Orjossal)

1 pound smoked *orja* (pig's back-bone—shoulder and neck)
11 ounces prunes
1 onion, chopped
1 cup rendered lard

¼ cup flour
1 egg
½ cup sour cream or milk
Pepper and vinegar to taste

Soak the *orja* and the prunes in water to cover overnight. The next day, drain the meat and prunes; put the meat in a pot and set the prunes aside. Simmer the meat and the onion in 2 quarts water.

When the meat is half cooked, add the prunes to the soup. When prunes and meat are done, prepare a light *roux* with the lard and flour.

Stir the *roux* into the soup, whisking constantly to prevent lumps, along with a mixture made of the egg and sour cream. Adjust flavor with pepper and vinegar. Bring to a quick boil on low heat to let it thicken, and serve.

Variations

Grated horseradish may be substituted for prunes. When using horseradish, 3 medium sliced carrots may be added to the soup. As with the prune soup, the flavor of the soup may be adjusted with vinegar and sugar before serving. Tarragon can be substituted for the horseradish, in which case the soup is called *kaszás* and served with toasted croutons.

An Armenian Soup to Save a Dead Soul
(Háku Erustá)

Háku Erustá is a traditional Armenian soup for a wake. It is served, along with the traditional sweets, after the funeral at the home of the mourning family.

Soup

4 quarts beef broth
1 tablespoon chopped lovage
1 tablespoon chopped balm or lemongrass

Meat Dumplings

½ pound ground beef, cooked
½ pound ground pork, cooked
4 hard-boiled eggs, chopped
1 onion, finely chopped
Salt and pepper to taste

Chopped sage, peppermint leaves, marjoram, and rosemary to taste

Noodles

1 cup flour
2 eggs
½ teaspoon butter or oil
Small pinch of salt and pepper
½ cup lukewarm milk or warm water (optional)

Prepare the soup: Season beef broth with lovage and balm and bring to a boil.

Prepare meat dumplings: Combine beef, pork, eggs, onion, salt and pepper, sage, peppermint, marjoram, and rosemary. Mix well and form into dumplings.

Prepare the noodles: Make dough with flour, eggs, butter, seasonings, and milk, if necessary (see page 83). Roll out dough until very thin and cut into fine noodles.

Cook the meat dumplings and noodles in the boiling soup until done. Serve.

Armenian Soup with Stuffed Pasta "Ears"
(*Ángáds-Ábur*)

Ángáds-ábur soup is a very popular Armenian dish that is prepared on Sundays. On meatless days, such as during Lent, the *ángáds* (or stuffed pasta "ears") are cooked in vegetable broth instead of meat soup. Also, in that case, the pasta is stuffed with a mushroom omelette instead of meat. This dish achieved immortal literary remembrance in Klára Kriszta's short story entitled "Oh, That Is the *Ángáds-ábur* Soup," published in 1891. This recipe also appeared in post–World War I Hungarian cookbooks. The *churut*—similar to a bouillon cube—which is the essence of the soup, is made primarily in August and September, in preparation for the winter.

Churut

3 quarts milk
3 bunches of parsley

1 bunch of celery greens
1 bunch of watercress
1 sprig of thyme

Stuffed Pasta

3 cups flour
2 eggs
1 teaspoon melted butter or oil
Pinch of salt and pepper
1 cup lukewarm water (optional)
1 small onion, finely chopped
2 tablespoons butter
1½ pounds ground veal
Pinch of sage
Salt and pepper to taste

The *churut* should be prepared at least 4 weeks in advance.

Let it age for 3 to 4 weeks. Stir once a day and skim off the top if necessary. After 4 weeks, when the milk smells bitter and the taste is very sour, test to see if it is ready. Boil 3 ounces of it; if it does not curdle, it is ready.

Soup

4 quarts strong beef broth
1 onion, finely chopped
½ pound mushrooms, finely chopped
2 tablespoons chopped balm or lemongrass
2 tablespoons chopped parsley

Sour cream

Prepare the churut: Boil half of the milk in a pot. Reduce heat and simmer for about 30 minutes. Let cool and mix in the remaining unboiled milk. Pour into a bottle. Keep in a cold spot.

Pass the parsley, celery greens, and watercress separately through a meat grinder until very finely ground. Pour the fermented milk into a pot and add 3 tablespoons of the ground parsley, 1 tablespoon ground celery greens, and 1 tablespoon ground watercress. Bring the pot of milk to a boil and add the thyme. Reduce heat and simmer for 30 minutes. Remove pot from burner and let cool until milk is lukewarm.

Remove thyme, and add the remaining ground parsley, celery greens, and watercress to the pot. Put pot back on heat and cook over low flame, stirring constantly, until reduced to a thick consistency similar to jam.

Next, let mixture dry completely in the pot in a cool spot. Then form it into conical shapes 1½ to 2 inches in size. This is the *churut*. Set aside.

Prepare the stuffed pasta: Prepare a simple pasta with the flour, eggs, butter, seasonings, and water, if necessary (see noodles, page 83). Cut dough into rectangles ¾ inch to 1 inch wide.

For the stuffing, sauté the onion lightly in butter in a frying pan. Add veal, sage, and salt and pepper. Stir and cook a little longer. Cool.

Stuff each pasta rectangle with a small amount of the mixture. Fold opposite corners of stuffed pasta on top of each other so that each resembles an ear shape.

Prepare the soup: In a pot, simmer the beef broth with onion, mushrooms, balm, and parsley until they are cooked. Then cook the stuffed pasta ears in the soup until done. Grate the *churut* and mix it, together with some sour cream. Add to soup just before serving. Do not cook again.

NOTE: Today, many cooks digress from the original Armenian recipe by putting ground meat in the pasta ears. Also, some do not dry the *churut* into a cone form during preparation. Rather, they pour it into small bottles and use it more quickly.

Vegetable Soup with Meat Dumplings and Cracked Wheat
(Borş de Perişoare or Húsgomsbócleves Korpaciberével)

1 celery stalk	**1 tablespoon rice**
1 turnip, peeled	**1 bunch of parsley**
2 carrots, peeled	**Salt and pepper to taste**
1 celery root, peeled	**2 cups sour bran soup (see Note)**
1 kohlrabi, peeled	**2 tablespoons sour cream**
1 parsnip, peeled	**(optional)**
1 pound top round of beef	**1 egg yolk, beaten (optional)**
2 onions	**Chopped dill to taste (optional)**
1 egg yolk	

Cook whole vegetables in a pot with 2 quarts salted water until crisp. Strain and reserve vegetable broth.

Grind beef together with onions; then add the egg yolk, rice, parsley, and salt and pepper.

With wet hands, shape meat into dumplings. Simmer them in the vegetable broth for 30 minutes.

Bring sour bran soup to a boil and add to vegetable broth. The sour bran may first be blended with the sour cream and egg yolk, if desired, and then simmered, stirring constantly, rather than boiled. Add the chopped dill and serve.

NOTE: Cibere, the fine cracked wheat or sour bran soup, has a characteristic and unique taste. It is also rich in various vitamins. It is prepared in the following way, according to an ancient Transylvanian recipe: in a large jar or clay pot (about 10 quarts), combine 1 pound cracked wheat and ½ cup fresh corn. Add 1 slice of brown bread, 2 or 3 slices of lemon, and 1 sour cherry tree twig (with leaves). Add 5 quarts boiling water, stirring with a wooden spoon. Cover jar or pot and keep in a warm place, being careful to stir it at least two more times in the next 2 hours. After 24 hours, the cracked wheat will become sour. Strain, pour into smaller jars, and keep in a cold place for 8 days. Always retain a cupful of the mixture to use as a fermentation starter base for the next batch.

Dill Soup with Veal
(Kaporleves Borjúhússal)

11 ounces veal
2 pounds veal bones
Salt and pepper to taste
10 tablespoons butter
¾ cup flour

10 sprigs of fresh dill, minced
4 egg yolks
¾ cup heavy cream or sour cream
Croutons made from 3 rolls

Cook veal and bones in a pot with 2 quarts water, skimming it from time to time. Strain soup; dice meat and reserve. Add salt and pepper to soup.

Prepare a golden brown *roux* with the butter and flour. Thin it with some of the soup, whisking constantly to prevent lumps. Add the dill to the *roux* and cook for a few minutes, then thicken soup with it.

Just before serving beat together the egg yolks and cream. Pour this mixture into the soup and blend well. Add the diced meat to soup. Cook on low heat, stirring constantly, until heated through. Serve with croutons.

Sour Bran Soup with Lamb
(Cibereleves Bárányhússal)

Head and 2 legs of 1 spring lamb, washed and cleaned
Bunch of spring onions or chives, minced
6 young garlic cloves, minced
1 quart sour bran soup (page 90)
1 onion
3 tablespoons rice or millet
A few sprigs of dill, chopped

A few sprigs of parsley, finely chopped
A few sprigs of lovage, finely chopped
Salt and pepper to taste
1 egg yolk
½ cup heavy cream and 1½ teaspoons sour cream, mixed together

Put the lamb's head and legs in a large pot with water to cover and bring to a boil. Skim the boiling liquid, add the spring onions and garlic, and continue to simmer.

In another pot bring to a boil the sour bran soup and a whole onion. When the meat is half done, add the rice, sour bran soup, dill, parsley, and lovage to that pot. Continue to simmer over a low flame for 20 minutes, or until the meat is done.

Strain the soup and reserve the meat. Slice the meat and set aside. Season soup with salt and pepper. Combine egg yolk and cream–sour cream mixture. Before serving, add the egg yolk mixture to soup and cook on low heat, stirring constantly, until it thickens, then add meat.

Lamb Soup with Tarragon
(*Tárkonyos Bárányleves*)

**4 pounds (total) lamb's breast and
   shoulder, boned (reserve
   bones), meat cut into pieces
   and blanched
Salt to taste
1 onion
Bunch of tarragon, chopped
A few peppercorns
2 carrots, peeled and sliced**

**2 parsnips, peeled and sliced
1 cup butter
½ cup flour
Tarragon vinegar or white vinegar
   to taste
½ cup sour cream
½ cup heavy cream
2 egg yolks**

Cook the lamb bones in a pot with water to cover until they make a good strong broth, skimming as necessary. Strain.

Add the lamb meat and salt to the strained broth. Put whole onion, some of the tarragon, and the peppercorns in a linen bag or piece of cheesecloth tied with a string and add to soup. Bring to a boil and simmer.

When the meat is half ready add the carrots and parsnips and cook until ingredients are done. Take the soup away from the burner.

Prepare a light brown *roux* with the butter and flour. Add the chopped tarragon and thicken soup with the *roux,* whisking constantly to prevent lumps. Bring to a simmer.

Season the soup with tarragon vinegar and add sour cream. Bring to a simmer again. Before serving, combine cream and egg yolks and add to soup. Cook on low heat, stirring constantly, until heated through.

Lamb Head Soup from Szilágyság
(Szilágysági Bárányfejleves)

So little lamb I see you again
Torn this time by still large and worldly events
A head, neck, and lung in a big pot of salty water.
Well, I sympathize
Throwing in black peppercorns to the
Dirgelike rolling of the water;
I believe the earth is patient with us—
Here is some parsnip, kohlrabi, carrot, bacon
Washed and cut for the pot—
Yes, unlike man.
The liver is thrown in shortly before the sinews loosen,
Then out comes the meat to be boned, cut up;
A sturdy black iron pot, sizzling with melting fat
Doused with flour to gild the bottom
Oh you deserve this Ali Baba's cave,
Here are garnets of paprika, emeralds of parsley!
In flows the broth, and the vegetables and meat,
So little treasure, as you simmer
Life's justice is done simply.

Head, neck, and lungs of 1 lamb,
  well cleaned
½ teaspoon peppercorns
1 parsnip, peeled and diced
2 kohlrabies, peeled and diced
1 carrot, peeled and diced
1 potato, peeled and diced
½ pound smoked bacon, diced

1 lamb's liver
1 tablespoon rendered lard or oil
1 tablespoon flour
1 tablespoon paprika
5 sprigs of parsley, finely
  chopped
Salt and pepper to taste

Put lamb's head, neck, and lungs in a large pot with 3 quarts lightly salted water (or water to cover). Bring to a slow boil. Add peppercorns. Reduce heat to simmer and skim off top.

Add the vegetables and the diced bacon to the lamb. Cook until the meat is done—when it almost falls off the bones. Add the liver only 5 minutes before the meat is done.

Remove all the meat from the pot and slice it; discard the bones. Set aside.

Prepare a golden brown *roux* with the lard and flour. Add one small ladleful of the soup and whisk it constantly until smooth. Add paprika and parsley; mix well. Thicken the soup with the *roux*. Add the sliced meat to the soup. Bring to a simmer. Season with salt and pepper. Serve.

NOTE: Shepherds leave the whole lamb's head and neck in the soup, and cut the meat when serving.

Transylvanian Ciorbă
(Ciorbă Trănsilvaneană)

1 pound smoked pork or meaty bacon
1 onion, chopped
12 ounces (total) cabbage and tender kohlrabi leaves, blanched and chopped

2 tablespoons rendered lard
2 tablespoons flour
Salt to taste
1 tablespoon chopped dill
2 or 3 garlic cloves, crushed
Buttermilk to taste

Cook pork in a pot with about 2 quarts cold water. In a frying pan, sauté onion, cabbage, and kohlrabi leaves in 1 tablespoon of the lard until tender. Set aside.

Prepare a golden brown *roux* with the remaining lard and the flour. Thin it with a little water and whisk the *roux* constantly until smooth. Let the *roux* bubble up a few times. Combine with the sautéed vegetables and add it to the soup.

Add salt, dill, garlic, and buttermilk. Let simmer a few minutes before serving.

NOTE: The Transylvania Rumanians use garlic with great frequency and pleasure. Every household has a wooden mortar, called *piulica,* just for this purpose. When crushed, its flavor gets absorbed more easily in the cooking process and makes for a tastier dish.

Veal Ciorbă
(Ciorbă de Mînzat)

1¼ pounds breast of veal, cut into bite-size pieces	**1 parsnip, diced**
1 veal shank	**2 medium potatoes, diced**
Salt and pepper to taste	**1 celery stalk, diced**
½ cup butter	**Juice of 2 lemons**
1 large onion, minced	**1 tablespoon chopped dill**
3 carrots, diced	**6 tablespoons sour cream (optional)**

Put veal breast and shank in a kettle. Add 3 quarts water and salt and pepper. Cover and simmer over low heat for approximately 1 hour. Skim as necessary. Add additional 1 or 2 cups water if amount of liquid decreases too much.

Heat butter in a frying pan. Add the onion, carrots, parsnip, potatoes, and celery. Sauté until vegetables are cooked through but still firm.

Add vegetables to veal and cook slowly for 1 more hour. Flavor with lemon juice, and add salt and pepper if needed.

When soup is done, take the veal shank out and cut the meat into bite-size portions. Return meat to soup. Sprinkle with dill and, if desired, top each serving with 1 tablespoon sour cream.

Lamb Pot Soup in the Rumanian Manner
(Ciorbă de Miel or Tavaszi Báránycsorba)

2 carrots, sliced
1 celery root, sliced
Bunch of spring onions or chives, sliced
1 tablespoon rendered lard
2 pounds boneless leg of lamb, cut into bite-size pieces

½ cup rice
5 sprigs of tarragon, finely chopped
½ cup sour cream
2 egg yolks
Salt and vinegar to taste
5 sprigs of parsley, chopped

In a pot, sauté the vegetables in lard. Add 2 quarts water, then simmer.

When the vegetables are half done, add the meat. Continue to simmer until ingredients are almost done. Cook the rice in 1 cup water in a separate pan until tender. Then add it to the soup and mix in the tarragon.

Remove soup from heat. Mix the sour cream and egg yolks together. Add to the soup and stir well. Cook on low heat, stirring constantly, until soup thickens. Season with salt and vinegar and sprinkle with chopped parsley. Serve.

Herb Bouquet by Joseph Domjan

A Saxon Soup for a Hangover
(Ehestandskächen or Szebeni Mazsolás Leves)

Ehestandskächen was the luncheon dish served on the second day of ancient Saxon village celebrations. It is known as a hangover remedy in Saxony because of its spicy and creamy quality.

There must be a chicken left somewhere in here
Last night's walloping dancing still pounds in the ears
Dully cut carrots and turnips . . . oh yes celery
These misshapen cubes to stop a salty pot's raillery
There must be a little pot around that's clean
Everything's full of dried sauce, crumbs, bones, old greens
In a bit of water will raisins and grapes simmer
Mesmerizing wisps of steam soothe an ill humor
Now another vessel for steaming gooseberries
With lemon, cinnamon, and Eastern emissaries
That seize the aches with spicing bold
As the berries finish and turn to gold
The morning is throbbing quickly past
The vegetables, soft, are set aside at last
The soup when thickened with a buttery roux
Takes in the raisins and gooseberry goo
Let it boil, turning as in a dream
To some distant container of sour cream
Echoes of czardas from phantom bows
Vanish as lemon juice steams through the nose
Add cream and drop in any leftover meat
Guests drag themselves out on sore tingling feet
Now more swilling toasts and boasts can they make
Waiting for the fire-hot soup to blast them awake.

1 fat hen
3 carrots, peeled
2 parsnips, peeled
1 celery root, peeled
Salt to taste
½ cup raisins
½ cup small seedless grapes

1 cup gooseberries
2 (1-inch) pieces lemon peel
1 cinnamon stick
3½ tablespoons butter
2 tablespoons flour
1 cup sour cream
Lemon juice to taste

Put the hen and whole vegetables in a pot with 3 quarts lightly salted water. Cook slowly until ingredients are tender. Strain, and reserve hen, vegetables, and liquid. Carve hen into small slices or pieces and set aside.

In another pan, cook gooseberries, lemon peel, and cinnamon stick in lightly salted water barely to cover until gooseberries acquire a golden yellow color. Press gooseberry mixture through a sieve and reserve.

Add the cooked raisin-grape mixture and gooseberries to the soup and bring to a boil. Stir in sour cream, and add sliced meat; simmer. Flavor with lemon juice and serve hot.

Cook raisins and grapes until soft in a pan with a little water. Set aside.

Prepare a light *roux* with the butter and flour. Pour in a ladleful of soup and whisk constantly until smooth; add thinned *roux* to soup and cook until it thickens.

Saxon Sauerkraut and Chicken Pot Soup
(Szász Káposztaleves Tyúkhússal or Kriläwend)

Kriläwend is considered a delicacy of Transylvanian-Saxon ecclesiastical cuisine. A late-winter specialty, it is prepared primarily for festive occasions.

1 fat hen or 2 chickens, cut into
   serving pieces
3 carrots, peeled and sliced
2 parsnips, peeled and sliced
1 celery root, peeled and sliced
1 small onion, chopped
2 cups sauerkraut

½ cup butter
1 cup white wine
1 teaspoon flour
1 quart sauerkraut juice
3 egg yolks
1 cup sour cream
2 teaspoons grated horseradish

Braise the chicken, vegetables, and sauerkraut in butter on low heat in a thick-bottomed pan, occasionally adding a spoonful of hot water and wine to keep the chicken meat from drying out. When the meat is tender, sprinkle it with flour.

In a separate pan, combine 2 quarts water and the sauerkraut juice. Boil for 10 minutes and while still hot pour over meat; mix well until smooth and continue to simmer.

Blend the egg yolks with the sour cream. Then slowly pour mixture into the simmering soup while constantly stirring. Simmer for another 5 minutes, or until it thickens the soup. Serve with grated horseradish.

Variation

In some regions the grated horseradish is added to the soup at the same time as the boiling diluted sauerkraut juice.

Saxon Horseradish Soup
(Krinaläwend or Szász Tormaleves)

2 pounds fatty pork
2 carrots, peeled and sliced
1 parsnip, peeled and sliced
1 onion, peeled and sliced
2 sprigs of rosemary
Salt to taste

2 cups grated horseradish
1 tablespoon rendered lard
2 tablespoons flour
1 cup sour cream or heavy cream
Pepper and vinegar to taste

Cook the pork, vegetables, and rosemary in a pot with lightly salted water to cover until tender. Strain, and reserve the meat, vegetables, and liquid. Slice the meat.

In the same pot, sauté the grated horseradish in lard until wilted. Sprinkle with flour, then gradually pour in the strained liquid, whisking constantly to prevent lumps.

Cook together well and add sour cream. Add pepper and vinegar. While still hot, pour over meat slices and vegetables and serve.

VARIATIONS

Lamb or meaty bacon may be substituted for pork. Also, beef, pork, and veal brains, or even blood sausage, may be used instead of pork.

In certain regions, the soup is cooked with sauerkraut diluted with water. Quarters of potato may also be cooked in the soup.

Tarragon Pork Pot
(Pfefferkraut Kächen or Tárkonyos Kächen)

2 pounds pork (a fatty cut or the shoulder)
2 pounds pork or veal bones
1 medium onion
3 carrots, peeled
2 parsnips, peeled
1 medium celery root, peeled
Salt
Peppercorns

8 to 10 sprigs of tarragon, stemmed, washed thoroughly, and finely minced
1 teaspoon chopped parsley
Vinegar to taste
1 teaspoon butter
1 tablespoon flour
2 teaspoons sour cream

Put pork, bones, and whole vegetables in a pot with 3 quarts water, a little salt, and a few peppercorns. Cook until meat is tender, skimming off the top as necessary.

Strain soup, reserving the meat and vegetables. Slice the meat. Place the meat and vegetables in a soup tureen or serving dish, discarding the onion and bones.

In another pan cook tarragon in a small amount of the soup until tender. Add the cooked tarragon and the chopped parsley to the soup; bring to a boil. Add vinegar.

Prepare a light *roux* with the butter and flour. Add sour cream. Add *roux* to soup while whisking constantly until it is smooth and thick. Cook for 5 minutes, then pour the hot soup over the meat and vegetables in the soup tureen. Serve hot.

VARIATIONS

This dish may also be prepared using lamb or beef instead of pork. If beef is used, add 1 ounce bacon per person. In the spring the dish may be prepared with a lamb, including the lamb's head; the lamb's brain, tongue, and face meat are special delicacies.

At the turn of the century, this dish was served with thin slices of bread placed in the tureen beside the meat.

NOTE: In the winter, when fresh tarragon is not available, this dish should be prepared with tarragon preserved in vinegar. Chop the tarragon and cook it in the soup. The vinegar from the tarragon will give the soup a sour flavor and it may not be necessary to add more vinegar.

Gooseberry Kächen from Schessburg
(Schessburger Aegrisch'kächen or Segesvári Egresleves)

2 pounds bottom round of beef
3 carrots, peeled
2 parsnips, peeled
1 small celery root, peeled
1 medium onion
Salt to taste
3 to 4 cups gooseberries, cleaned
and washed

1 tablespoon finely chopped
parsley
3 tablespoons flour
1 teaspoon butter
¾ cup sour cream or heavy cream
Sugar to taste (optional)
Toasted thin bread slices

Simmer beef and whole vegetables in a pot with 3 quarts lightly salted water until meat is tender. Strain the soup; reserve the meat.

Cook the gooseberries in 1 quart of the soup until they become yellow. Be careful not to overcook the berries, or they will burst. When done, add the finely chopped parsley and pour gooseberry mixture back into soup.

Combine the flour, butter, and sour cream and stir until smooth. Add to soup and cook on low heat, whisking constantly until smooth and thick. Sugar may be added if desired.

Slice the meat and arrange it in a soup tureen surrounded by toasted bread slices. Cover with the hot soup. A thin slice of toasted bread should be placed in each individual soup bowl as well.

VARIATIONS

In certain provinces the gooseberries are first pressed through a sieve and then added to the soup. In other regions three fourths of the gooseberries are sieved and the remaining are added whole to the finished soup. This *kächen* may be prepared with currants or small, sour grapes instead of gooseberries.

BEAN SOUPS
AND POTATO SOUPS

Sekler Pinto Bean Soup
(*Székely-Alfalusi Paszulyleves*)

½ pound dried pinto beans
1 pound smoked pork (ham or
    loin)
Salt
1 head of iceberg or lamb's
    lettuce, shredded

1 teaspoon finely chopped fresh
    dill
¼ cup rendered lard
½ cup flour
Paprika to taste
½ cup sour cream

Soak the beans overnight in water to cover. Drain. The next day cook them in a pot with the smoked meat, in three times as much water as beans, until both are tender.

Salt the lettuce, then rinse it and dry it on a towel. Add it to the soup, along with the dill.

Prepare a light *roux* with the lard, flour, and paprika. Thicken the soup with the *roux*. Add sour cream. Let it simmer and serve.

Sabbatarian Bean Soup
(*Szombatosok Paszulylevese*)

2 pounds dried white beans
5 quarts vegetable–bone broth
(made with meat bones rather
than poultry, if possible)
2 pounds smoked beef tongue or
2 smoked goose breasts and 2
smoked goose drumsticks
1 onion, chopped
¼ cup goose fat

1 garlic clove, crushed
½ cup flour
1 teaspoon chopped fresh
tarragon
Salt and pepper to taste
2 cups fresh (not dried) egg
barley (page 267)
1 cup sour cream

Soak beans overnight in water to cover. The following day drain the beans and cook them in a large pot with the vegetable–bone broth. Add the smoked tongue. Bring to a boil.

In a frying pan sauté half the chopped onion in half the goose fat until golden brown. Season with crushed garlic and mix into the boiling soup. Then cook soup at a simmer.

When the beans and the meat are tender, sauté the remaining chopped onion in the remaining goose fat, add the flour, and prepare a light *roux*. Season with tarragon and salt and pepper. Thicken the soup with the *roux*.

Cook the egg barley in the soup until tender. Add sour cream, heat for a few more minutes, and serve.

NOTE: If fresh tarragon is not available, soak ½ teaspoon dried tarragon in a little water for an hour.

The best pasta to use for this soup is egg barley, which should be freshly made, not dried. The Hungarians call it *csipetke* or pinched pasta; also, theirs is a bit larger.

White Bean Pot with Smoked Pork
(Weisse Bohnenkächen mit Geselchtem Schweinefleisch)

1 pound dried white beans
2 pounds smoked pork (ham or loin)
1 small onion, finely chopped

1 cup rice
Vinegar, salt, and pepper to taste
1 cup sour cream
Chopped parsley to taste

Soak the beans overnight in water to cover and drain the next day. Put them in a pot with 3 quarts water. Add the pork and the onion. Simmer until all ingredients are tender. Remove meat when done and set aside.

Pour 2 cups of the cooking liquid from the soup into another pot and cook the rice in it. In the meantime, strain the beans and the remaining soup through a sieve. Combine this mixture with the cooked rice.

Add vinegar to taste and salt and pepper only if needed. Mix in sour cream. Cook the soup until hot. Sprinkle with chopped parsley. Cut the meat into thin slices or cubes, put in a soup tureen, and pour the hot soup over them.

VARIATIONS

This dish may also be prepared with beef, lamb, or veal. The Saxons, however, prefer it with smoked ham. The liquid used to cook the ham can be used in preparing this dish, even if another type of meat is added. In the Seklers' regions the soup is seasoned with tarragon.

NOTE: Be careful in adjusting the soup with pepper and especially with salt, as the smoked pork might make it salty enough.

Green Bean Pot
(*Fisolen-Kächen*)

2 pounds beef bones
2 pounds bottom round of beef
3 carrots, peeled and sliced
2 parsnips, peeled
1 celery root, peeled
Salt to taste
½ pound smoked slab bacon
2 pounds green beans, trimmed,
  and cut in half if very long

Vinegar to taste
1 medium onion, chopped
1 tablespoon finely chopped
  parsley
2 tablespoons rendered lard
3 tablespoons flour
1 cup sour cream

Cook bones, beef, and whole vegetables in 2 quarts salted water. When meat is half done, add bacon and cook until meat is tender. Strain and reserve meat and bacon.

Add beans to a pot of 1 quart boiling water and cook until tender but still crispy. When done, drain and add a little vinegar. Set aside.

Sauté the onion and parsley in the lard, add flour, and prepare a light *roux*. Thin the *roux* with some of the soup, whisk until smooth, and add to soup. Simmer soup until it thickens.

Slice the meat and bacon and arrange in a soup tureen with the beans. Mix sour cream into the hot soup and cook until heated through. Pour soup over the meat, bacon, and beans and serve.

Saxon Potato Pot
(*Kartoffelkächen*)

**2 pounds top round of beef, cut
into pieces
3 carrots, peeled
2 parsnips, peeled
1 celery root, peeled
1 medium onion, peeled
1 pound potatoes, peeled and
sliced or diced**

**1 tablespoon finely chopped
parsley
Salt and vinegar to taste
1 tablespoon rendered lard
2 tablespoons flour
Mixed heavy cream and sour
cream to taste**

In a pot with 3 quarts lightly salted water, cook the beef and whole vegetables (except the potatoes) until tender. Strain; reserve the meat and vegetables. Cook the potatoes in the strained soup until tender. When the potatoes are done, add parsley and salt and vinegar; set the soup aside.

Prepare a brown *roux* with the lard and flour and add to the soup. Bring the soup to a boil, stirring constantly, until it thickens. Lower the flame and add the cream mixture.

Slice the meat and vegetables and arrange in a soup tureen. Cover with the hot soup. Serve immediately.

VARIATIONS
The soup can also be prepared from mutton or pork. In some regions, where the soup is made with beef, a few slices of bacon are added when the meat is half done.

Potato Soup with a "White Ruffled Petticoat"
(Fehér Rokolyás Pityókaleves)

As plowmen strain throughout the land
And herders plod high meadows grand
The aunts all morning in the kitchen stand
And a daughter brings a kettle in hand
The well's icy water set to boil
Potatoes lasting through winter's soil
Peeled—how lucky they didn't spoil
Diced—now beaded with the bubbles' coil
Two of the many hands will make a roux
Two lumps of butter with flour to stew
Thrown in with vinegar and sugar too
The pot's seething grows as the days toil through
Bay leaves and bones are saved for flavoring;
At last round the rim comes a frothy ring
As when the horsehair bites into a string
And women whirl with their hems to fling
Showing white skirts in bright lacy rings
Then soup's off the fire and in they'll fling
Two egg yolks and sour cream, which brings
A finished soup before those mudstained kings.

2 pounds potatoes, peeled and diced
Salt to taste
3 tablespoons butter
2 tablespoons flour
Vinegar to taste

Small bunch of tarragon, tied together, or 1 tablespoon dried tarragon
Sugar to taste
2 egg yolks, beaten
Heavy cream to taste

Boil 3 quarts water in a kettle. Drop in the potatoes, add salt, and cook them until tender.

When the potatoes are done make a light *roux* with 2 tablespoons of the butter and the flour. Take a ladleful of the potato soup and thin the *roux* with it, whisking constantly until smooth. Then stir it into the soup.

Bring soup to a boil while stirring constantly until it thickens. Season with vinegar, tarragon, and a little bit of sugar. Let soup come to a boil again.

Remove from heat and stir in beaten egg yolks. Stir in a liberal amount of cream and the remaining butter. Remove tarragon and bring to a boil—this will create a white foam at the edge of the soup; hence the name.

VARIATIONS

Two or 3 bay leaves may be substituted for the tarragon. If available, add some smoked ham bones.

Dill by Joseph Domjan

HERB, VEGETABLE, AND FRUIT SOUPS

Herb Soup for St. Paul's Day
(Szentpálnapi Füves Leves)

2½ pounds veal bones
1 small piece fresh ginger
Paprika, salt, and pepper to taste
10 sprigs of parsley, finely
    chopped
4 celery stalks, finely chopped
10 to 15 sprigs of dill, finely
    chopped

5 sprigs of tarragon, finely
    chopped
1 onion, finely chopped
7 tablespoons butter
½ cup flour
2 egg yolks
½ cup sour cream
Croutons made from 2 rolls

Rub the veal bones with ginger and simmer for about 1 hour in 2 quarts water, lightly spiced with paprika, salt, and pepper.

In a frying pan, sauté the parsley, celery, dill, tarragon, and onion in half the butter. Sprinkle with flour and let the mixture brown slightly. Set aside.

Remove the bones from the soup. Add a little soup to the herb mixture and stir it until smooth. Add to the remaining soup and simmer until it thickens. Season with salt and pepper.

Combine egg yolks, sour cream, and remaining butter; beat well. Add mixture to soup and cook on low heat, stirring constantly, until it thickens. Serve immediately with croutons.

Caraway Seed Soup
(*Köménymagleves*)

1 onion, grated
1 teaspoon caraway seeds
Pinch of pepper
2 teaspoons oil

2 teaspoons flour
Salt to taste
1 cup egg barley (page 267)
A little finely chopped parsley

Sauté the grated onion, with the caraway seeds and pepper, in the oil until it becomes brown. Add flour and make a light *roux.* Thin the *roux* with 2 quarts of cold water, to make a soup, and simmer. (If desired the soup may be strained in order to remove the caraway seeds before serving.)

Season with salt and cook egg barley in the soup until tender. Stir in chopped parsley before serving.

VARIATION

Croutons may be served with the soup instead of egg barley.

NOTE: This is the standard breakfast soup of the young recruits in the army.

Cream of Sorrel Soup
(*Sóskaleves*)

Soup

**1 cup sorrel, cleaned, washed,
   and finely chopped**
2 tablespoons oil or butter
Salt and pepper to taste
2 tablespoons flour
**1 quart meat or chicken broth or
   water**
1 cup heavy cream

Spaetzle

½ cup flour
1 egg
1 egg yolk (for *spaetzle*)
**1 teaspoon sour cream (for
   spaetzle) or ½ teaspoon melted
   butter or oil (for noodles)**
**Small pinch of salt, pepper, and
   nutmeg**
¼ cup lukewarm milk

Sauté sorrel in hot oil until completely soft, stirring constantly. Add salt and pepper and the 2 tablespoons flour; continue stirring.

Slowly add broth, stirring constantly until smooth and thick. Simmer for a short while, then stir in cream.

To prepare spaetzle *(German dumplings):* Combine the flour, egg and egg yolk, sour cream, and seasonings, adding milk as necessary to form a dough. Take off small bits of the batter with a spoon, or put it through a colander, sliding cutter, or pastry bag, and cook in the simmering soup until done.

NOTE: To make the noodles, see the recipe on page 83.

Sweet and Sour Beet Soup
(*Céklaleves*)

**1 pound beets, washed and
  peeled**
Salt to taste
Pinch of sugar, plus more to taste
Pepper to taste
Pinch of chopped fresh tarragon
Juice of 1 lemon

1 tablespoon butter
1 tablespoon flour
½ cup milk
Vinegar to taste
¾ cup heavy cream
1 egg yolk, beaten
1 cup buttered mashed potatoes

Cook beets until tender in a pot of
lightly salted water to cover, with a
pinch of sugar. Strain and press the
beets through a sieve into the cooking
liquid. Adjust salt and add pepper and
tarragon. Flavor with lemon juice.

Make a light *roux* from butter and
flour. Thin it with milk, whisking
constantly to make it smooth, and stir
into soup. Bring to a boil and cook
until thick. Adjust sourness with a little
vinegar and add sugar to taste. Turn
heat down to low.

Mix cream with the egg yolk and stir
into soup. Place mashed potatoes in
the soup plates. Cover with soup and
serve.

Cold Cucumber Soup with Dill
(Supă Rece cu Castraveți Cruzi)

1 pound veal bones
2 carrots, peeled
1 onion, peeled
½ celery root, peeled
6 cucumbers, peeled and diced

Salt and pepper to taste
1½ cups sour cream
Chopped fresh dill to taste
2 sprigs of fresh tarragon,
  chopped

Make a broth the day before preparing the cucumber soup: cook the veal bones and the whole vegetables, except the cucumbers, in 2 quarts water. Let it come to a simmer, then skim the top, and add 4 of the diced cucumbers. Season with salt and pepper.

Simmer until the vegetables are tender but still firm, let cool, and strain the soup. Refrigerate overnight until well chilled.

Skim the top thoroughly, and carefully pour the soup into a soup tureen without disturbing the sediment, if there is any. Pour a little soup into a saucepan and cook the remaining 2 diced cucumbers for 10 minutes. Cool, then add to the soup.

Blend in sour cream, dill, and tarragon. Stir gently. Serve cold.

VARIATION

The soup can also be seasoned with chopped chives.

Rumanian Leek Soup with Pancakes
(*Supă de Praz cu Clătite*)

Soup

1 carrot, peeled and diced
1 parsnip, peeled and diced
1 small celery root, peeled and
   diced
1 quart milk
4 large potatoes, peeled and
   chopped
3 to 4 leeks (white part only),
   cleaned and sliced

¾ cup butter
Salt and pepper to taste

Thin Pancakes

1 egg
⅔ cup lukewarm milk
1 cup flour
¼ teaspoon salt
Bunch of chives, finely chopped

In a saucepan, cook the carrot, parsnip, and celery root in milk until tender. Strain, and return soup to pan. Cook the potatoes and leeks in the soup.

When the potatoes and leeks are tender, add 4 tablespoons of the butter. Season with salt and pepper.

Prepare pancakes: In the meantime, mix egg, milk, flour, salt, and chives (see page 317). Use the remaining butter to fry the pancakes. Roll up the pancakes, cut them into ¼-inch strips, and add to soup when serving.

Apple Soup from Kükül̋ő
(*Kükül̋őmenti Almaleves*)

**2 pounds tart apples (such as
  Granny Smith), peeled, cored,
  and cut into small cubes**
Lemon juice
Salt to taste
1 teaspoon cinnamon
2 or 3 cloves

2 lemons, sliced
**½ cup fruity white wine, plus
  more if necessary**
2 egg yolks
½ cup sour cream or heavy cream
1 teaspoon chopped parsley
Sugar (optional)

Place the apples in a mixture of lemon juice and water to keep them white; reserve. Combine salt, cinnamon, cloves, lemon slices, and wine in a pot with 2½ quarts water. Bring to a boil, then add the apples.

When apples are cooked, remove pot from heat. Mix egg yolks with sour cream and add to soup, stirring constantly while on low heat until it thickens. Add chopped parsley.

If necessary, adjust flavoring with more lemon juice and wine and sweeten with sugar. Let soup come to a simmer and serve.

VARIATION

Rhubarb soup is prepared in the same manner. Wash the rhubarb, peel it to remove its strings, if necessary, and cut into small pieces before proceeding as above.

NOTE: Like all fruit soups, this one may be served cold.

Sour Cherry Soup
(*Meggy Leves*)

Whispered under quiet eaves in morning
That angels fly to come and pry
Open blossoms in the trees abounding.
Soon the flowers fade yet swell to cherries
That farmers pick to wash and pit
So boiling water receives the berries.
When shortly set aside and touched with salt
The lady sweetens and egg yolks beaten
With cream will brace a soup for heaven's vault.

2 pounds sour cherries, cleaned,
   washed, and pitted
½ cup sugar
Salt to taste

Juice of 1 lemon, or to taste
2 egg yolks
1 cup light cream

Boil 2 quarts water in a pot and add cherries. Cook for 10 minutes, gradually adding the sugar, salt, and lemon juice.

Mix the egg yolks with cream and add to the soup. Heat soup on low, stirring constantly until it thickens. Serve soup hot or chilled.

VARIATION

This soup can also be prepared from red currants. In many homes half of the currants are passed through a sieve into the soup.

NOTE: In finer kitchens, in order to bring out the deep and rich flavor of sour cherries, they add a well-reduced liquid made from cherry pits, water, cinnamon, cloves, and vanilla. The soup is garnished with sweetened, beaten egg whites and sliced, toasted hazelnuts.

ASSORTED SOUPS

"Tailor's Collar" or Stuffed Pasta in Broth
(Szabógallér vagy Tűrt Laska Leves)

Stuffed Pasta
1¼ cups flour
1 egg
½ teaspoon melted butter or oil
Pinch of salt, pepper, and nutmeg
½ cup lukewarm milk or water
   (optional)
1 onion, finely chopped

Prepare pasta: Make a noodle dough with the flour, egg, butter, seasonings, and milk, if necessary. Roll out the dough when ready to cook so it will not get dry.

¼ cup rendered lard or oil
1 teaspoon paprika
Salt to taste

Soup
4 quarts chicken broth
1 teaspoon chopped parsley

Cook the onion in lard until wilted. Sprinkle with paprika and salt.

Heap small mounds (about a scant ½
teaspoon) of the onion mixture in
straight lines on half of the rolled-out
dough, spacing them 2 inches apart.
Fold the other half of the dough over
the stuffing.

Using a spatula, press the two pieces
of dough down gently around the
edges to seal them together. Also,
press the spatula around the mounds
of stuffing, outlining the dough into
squares. Cut the squares with a knife
or with a pastry cutter (just like
ravioli), being careful not to allow the
stuffing to leak out.

Bring the chicken broth to a boil and
cook the stuffed pasta in it until done.
When ready, sprinkle soup with
chopped parsley and serve.

NOTE: The stuffing was prepared differently in every home. Sometimes it contained
freshly cooked roasted meat or leftover meat, mushrooms, young kohlrabies, wild carrots, and herbs.

Sour Cream Soup
(*Tejfölösleves*)

1 teaspoon butter	**3 cups sour cream**
1 small onion, chopped	**3 cups chicken or vegetable broth**
½ teaspoon caraway seeds	**Nutmeg, allspice, and salt to taste**
Pinch of pepper	**Toast or croutons**
1 tablespoon flour	

In a small pot, melt the butter. Sauté the chopped onion, caraway seeds, and pepper in it. Add the flour and let it brown.

Stirring vigorously, blend in the sour cream, then the broth. Bring to a simmer for a very short time, then season with nutmeg, allspice, and salt.

Serve with toast or croutons.

NOTE: Tiny fried dumplings may also be served on top of the soup.

Tripe Soup with Lemon
(*Savanyú Pacalleves*)

In the past, since tripe was inexpensive it was the dish of poorer people. Today, gourmets are pleased to discover sour tripe soup on the menu of Kolozsvár's restaurants. (In Hungary, the tripe stew or *pacal-pörkölt* is a much-sought-after delicacy in country inns.) Tripe soup with lemon was a favorite luncheon dish and a hangover remedy.

4 pounds tripe
Salt or coarse cornmeal
2 pounds beef or veal bones, blanched
2 onions, peeled and sliced
2 parsnips, peeled and sliced
2 carrots, peeled and sliced

1 celery root, peeled and sliced
4 egg yolks
10 sprigs of parsley, chopped
1 or 2 teaspoons vinegar or lemon juice
Salt and pepper to taste

Since tripe takes a long time to cook, it should be started well in advance. Wash the tripe several times in water, rub it with salt, then rinse again in water.

Put the tripe in a pot and cook in 4 quarts water for 30 minutes. Drain. Add another 4 quarts water, salt it lightly, and simmer for 3 to 4 hours.

Add the bones and vegetables to the tripe soup. Continue to simmer until the tripe is cooked, about 2 to 4 hours more. It is ready when it can be torn by hand. Add more water if too much of the liquid evaporates.

Strain the soup and discard the bones. Keep the vegetables, if desired. Slice the tripe and return the slices to the soup.

Beat the egg yolks in the bottom of a soup tureen and carefully mix in the hot soup. Add chopped parsley and vinegar, and correct seasoning.

NOTE: Experienced cooks know to put wine vinegar and freshly grated horseradish on the table as an accompaniment, so that the guests can serve themselves.

It takes 6 to 8 hours to prepare this soup, depending on the age of the tripe.

Lung Soup
(*Lingli*)

The Saxons serve this soup as a first course for Friday-evening supper.

**1 pound veal or beef lung,
   cleaned and washed thoroughly**
2 carrots, sliced
2 quarts beef broth
1 tablespoon goose fat or oil

1 tablespoon flour
1 egg yolk, beaten
1 garlic clove, crushed
Chopped chives to taste

In a pot, cook the lung and carrots in the beef broth until tender. When ready, strain soup (reserve carrots) and pass the lung through a meat grinder; set aside.

Prepare a light brown *roux* with the fat and flour. Stir in the egg yolk and crushed garlic. Add the ground lung to the *roux* and mix well.

Thin the *roux* with some of the soup, while whisking constantly on low heat, until it has the consistency of a thin sauce. Add to soup and bring to a light boil, stirring constantly until it thickens. Add reserved carrots. Sprinkle with chopped chives and serve.

VARIATION

The soup can also be made with chicken gizzards cut into small pieces.

Sour Bran Soup with Cheese Dumplings
(*Korpacibere Leves*)

Soup

2 carrots, peeled and chopped
1 parsnip, peeled and chopped
2 celery ribs, chopped
1 kohlrabi, peeled and chopped
¼ head of cabbage, chopped
¼ cup rendered lard
¼ cup flour
Salt, pepper, peppermint,
    marjoram, and lovage to taste

Dumplings

½ cup rendered lard
¾ cup cottage cheese, feta, or
    brînză
¼ cup sour cream
Finely chopped dill to taste
2 eggs
½ cup flour

2½ cups sour bran soup (page 90)
1 onion

In a skillet, sauté the carrots, parsnip, celery, kohlrabi, and cabbage in ¼ cup lard until tender. Sprinkle with ¼ cup flour and ¼ cup water and continue cooking. Add more water as needed (about 1 quart), and season with salt, pepper, peppermint, marjoram, and lovage. Simmer until ready.

Prepare dumplings: In a bowl, beat lard until foamy. Add the cottage cheese, sour cream, dill, eggs, flour, and enough water to make a good batter for dumplings.

Drop the pieces of dough into the soup and cook until done.

When the dumplings are ready, cook bran sour soup with a whole onion in a separate pan. When onion is cooked, skim off foam, discard onion, and stir sour soup into the basic soup. Serve.

Rumanian Fish and Sour Bran Soup
(Borş de Peşte or Halleves Korpaciberével)

2 pounds carp or bass, filleted and cut into chunks
Salt to taste
1 onion, finely chopped
1 tablespoon lard
2 carrots, peeled and sliced
1 parsnip, peeled and sliced
1 green pepper, cored, seeded, and sliced
1 stalk celery, sliced

1 small leek (white part only), sliced
1 celery root, peeled and sliced
1 pound tomatoes, peeled, seeded, and sliced
2 cups boiling sour bran soup (page 90)
½ teaspoon chopped parsley or chopped lovage

Rub fish with salt. Set aside.

In a pot, sauté the onion in hot lard, then add the carrots, parsnip, pepper, celery, leek, and celery root. When lightly browned, pour in 2 quarts water.

Let soup boil, and when ingredients are half cooked add the tomatoes. When the vegetables are done, pour in the boiling sour bran soup, and then add the fish chunks. Cook over a low flame until done.

When soup is nearly ready, sprinkle the top with chopped parsley or lovage.

Sour Bran Soup with Mushrooms
(Cibereleves Gombával)

2 carrots, peeled and sliced
1 celery root, peeled and sliced
1 parsnip, peeled and sliced
1 pound field or parasol mushrooms (or any kind of mushrooms), cleaned and sliced
1 cup sour bran soup (page 90)

1 cup rice or millet
1 tablespoon oil
1 tablespoon flour
1 egg yolk, beaten
1 teaspoon finely chopped lovage
1 teaspoon chopped parsley
Salt and pepper to taste
Pinch of ground ginger

Place the carrots, celery root, and parsnip in a pot with 2 quarts lightly salted water and bring to a boil. When the soup begins to boil, add the mushrooms. When vegetables are tender, add the sour bran soup and rice. Continue cooking for 15 minutes.

Prepare a golden brown *roux* with the oil and flour. Thin it with some of the soup, whisking constantly, then add the *roux* to the basic soup and cook until it thickens.

Stir in the egg yolk, lovage, and parsley. Cook the soup on low heat until smooth and thick, whisking it constantly. Season with salt, pepper, and ginger. Serve.

Mushroom Cream Soup
(*Gombakrém Leves*)

½ small onion, grated
1 cup butter
1 pound forest mushrooms (or any kind of mushrooms), cleaned and sliced
Salt and pepper to taste

Small bunch of parsley, chopped
1 quart chicken or beef-bone broth
1 tablespoon flour
3 egg yolks
1 cup heavy cream or sour cream

In a pot, sauté the grated onion in all but 2 tablespoons of the butter until glossy. Add the mushrooms and sauté them as well. Season with salt and pepper and parsley, then simmer until mushrooms are tender. Add broth and bring to a boil.

Meanwhile, make a light *roux* with 1 tablespoon of the reserved butter and the flour.

Combine cream and egg yolks in a bowl, and mix in 1 to 2 tablespoons soup. Blend until smooth.

Add the cream mixture and the *roux* to the mushroom soup. Heat soup, whisking constantly until it thickens, and season with salt and pepper.

Put the remaining 1 tablespoon butter in a soup tureen, pour the soup over it, and serve hot.

Armenian Sweet Soup
(*Anusabur or Örmény édesleves*)

4 ounces raisins
4 ounces almonds
4 ounces walnuts
4 ounces hazelnuts
4 ounces pitted prunes
½ cup dry white wine

8 ounces millet
Cinnamon, ground cloves, and
grated lemon rind to taste
2 tablespoons oil
1 tablespoon flour
1 tablespoon honey

Soak the raisins, almonds, walnuts, hazelnuts, and prunes in a pot with 1½ quarts water for 2 hours. Add wine, then cook over low heat for about 2 hours.

Add the millet and continue to cook for 20 to 25 minutes. Add cinnamon, cloves, and lemon rind.

Prepare a light *roux* with the oil and flour. Add to soup, stirring constantly with a whisk, until smooth and thick. Sweeten soup with honey before serving.

NOTE: Anusabur is usually prepared as a soup for New Year's and is made especially for children. It is also served as a sauce at Lent; in that case it should be made with half the quantity of water.

Sauerkraut Soup with Prunes
(*Szilvás Káposztaleves*)

2 pounds sauerkraut
1 quart sauerkraut juice
9 ounces pitted prunes
1 onion, finely chopped
¼ cup rendered lard or oil
Salt to taste

½ cup flour
Pinch of finely chopped tarragon
1 tablespoon paprika
1 cup sour cream
1 egg
Pepper to taste

Rinse the sauerkraut to get rid of the excess salt and wring it out. Put in a pot containing sauerkraut juice and 1 quart water. Bring to a boil. When the sauerkraut is almost cooked, add the prunes and simmer for 15 minutes.

In a saucepan sauté the onion in lard until it becomes glossy. Season with salt. Add flour and prepare a light *roux*. When done, add the finely chopped tarragon.

Remove pan from heat, add a ladleful of soup, and whisk constantly until it is a smooth and thick sauce. Add the paprika, then stir the *roux* slowly into the soup. Bring to a quick boil and let it thicken.

Blend the sour cream and egg together in a bowl; mix in a tablespoon of the soup. Stir sour cream mixture into soup, and cook on low until heated through. Season with salt and pepper. Serve.

SOUP GARNISHES

Cottage Cheese Dumplings with Dill
(*Kapros Túrógombóc*)

¼ cup plus 2 tablespoons cottage
  cheese
2 eggs, separated
1 cup semolina

½ teaspoon butter
Pinch of salt
2 sprigs of fresh dill, finely
  chopped

Break up the cottage cheese curd with
a fork and blend in the egg yolks,
semolina, butter, salt, and dill.

Beat the egg whites separately until
foamy and fold into mixture.

Shape small dumplings from this
mixture. Drop them into lightly
boiling soup and cook until done.

Sabbatarian Sour Cream Dumplings
(*Szombatos Tejfölös Galuska*)

½ **tablespoon goose fat**
2 eggs
1 cup sour cream

Salt and pepper to taste
Semolina or flour

Whisk goose fat until frothy. Add eggs, sour cream, salt and pepper, and enough semolina to make a light dough. Mix it well.

Continue to beat mixture, then let stand for 15 minutes. Scoop up pieces of dough with a spoon and roll them into small egg shapes. Drop the dumplings into lightly boiling soup.

Bring it down to a simmer and cook for 15 minutes.

NOTE: Do not interrupt the simmering of the soup for any reason, or the dumplings will become hard.

Matzo Dumplings
(*Pászka vagy Maceszgombóc*)

4 eggs
4 tablespoons melted goose fat
**Salt, pepper, ground ginger, and
    chopped parsley to taste**

**4 tablespoons matzo meal or
    semolina**
**3½ ounces matzo (2 crackers),
    crumbled**

In a large bowl mix together the eggs, ¼ cup water, goose fat, and salt, pepper, ginger, and parsley. Then add matzo meal and the crumbled matzos. Mix well and let stand for 1 hour.

With wet palms, roll mixture into walnut-shaped dumplings or into small egg shapes. On a low flame, lightly boil the dumplings in a large quantity of soup for 15 minutes.

Do not interrupt the boiling, or the dumplings will become hard. Serve immediately in the soup.

Goose Crackling Dumplings
(*Libatöpörtős Galuska*)

½ pound goose cracklings (page 210), minced
2 eggs

Salt, pepper, and marjoram to taste
2 or 3 tablespoons bread crumbs

Mix goose cracklings with the eggs, salt, pepper, marjoram, and enough bread crumbs to make a kneadable dough.

Shape into small nut-size dumplings, and cook them for a few minutes in lightly boiling soup.

Rice Dumplings with Marjoram
(Majorannás Rizsgombóc)

**1 cup rice or millet
1 teaspoon goose fat
½ onion, finely chopped
Salt, pepper, and marjoram to
taste**

**2 cups hot beef broth
3 egg yolks
1 whole egg
2 tablespoons butter
½ cup flour**

Soak rice or millet in warm water for 15 minutes to soften. Drain. Heat the goose fat in a pan, add onion, and sauté until glossy. Mix in the rice and season with salt, pepper, and marjoram. Pour in the hot beef broth and simmer until rice is tender.

Whisk together the egg yolks, egg, butter, and flour. Mix well with rice. Shape into small dumplings. Cook dumplings in additional lightly boiling beef broth until ready.

Buckwheat Dumplings
(Hajdinagombóc)

**10 ounces buckwheat flour
Bone broth
½ pound goose fat or goose
    cracklings (page 210), diced
1 onion, finely chopped**

**10 sprigs of parsley, finely
    chopped
5 eggs
Salt to taste**

Let the buckwheat flour soak in a large amount of boiling water for 2 or 3 hours, until it swells. Drain. Cook the buckwheat flour in twice the volume of broth until it becomes a thick gruel. Let it cool.

Meanwhile, heat the goose fat in a frying pan and sauté the onion and parsley in it until glossy. Combine onion with the buckwheat gruel. Beat in the eggs, add salt, and blend well together.

With wet palms, shape mixture into small balls. Drop dumplings into lightly boiling soup and cook until ready. Serve.

Semolina Dumplings with Spinach
(*Daragombóc Parajjal*)

7 tablespoons butter
4 eggs
2 cups semolina
Salt to taste

Small bunch of spinach, cleaned, washed, blanched, and cut into small pieces

Cream the butter. Slowly add the eggs, then the semolina, salt, and spinach. Mix well.

Bring the soup (broth) to a boil. Test to see if the dumplings are ready for cooking by gently dropping one small dumpling into the lightly boiling broth.

If the test dumpling falls apart, add a little more semolina to the mixture. If the dumpling holds its shape, form more small dumplings and cook them in lightly boiling broth until ready.

NOTE: During poultry slaughtering season a fowl's blood may be retained (in a bowl) and used in the dumplings; it first must be lightly salted to prevent coagulation. Mix it with the semolina and salt while stirring constantly. Then blend together with butter–egg mixture and spinach.

Goose Liver Pie
(*Ludmáj Lepény*)

1 goose liver (at least 1 pound)
5 tablespoons butter
4 eggs
2 rolls
1 cup milk

Salt, pepper, chopped
** peppermint, and chopped**
** parsley to taste**
1 small onion
1 teaspoon marjoram
1 garlic clove, crushed
1 tablespoon bread crumbs

Press the raw goose liver through a sieve. Set it aside.

Whisk butter until creamy. Separate 2 of the eggs. Mix the egg yolks (reserve the whites) and the 2 whole eggs with the butter. Soak the rolls in milk, crumble them, and add to the mixture.

Add reserved goose liver, salt, pepper, peppermint, parsley, onion, marjoram, garlic, and bread crumbs. Mix well.

Beat the reserved egg whites until stiff and fold into the mixture. Pour into a buttered baking pan. Bake in a moderate oven until done, cut into squares, and serve with hot soup.

Cottage Cheese Pockets with Onions
(*Thelpác or Túrós Derelye Hagymásan*)

Dough

1 cup flour
1 egg
Pinch of salt and pepper
1 cup lukewarm milk or water
  (optional)

Cottage Cheese Filling

¾ cup plus 2 tablespoons cottage
  cheese
Salt and sugar to taste

4 eggs, separated
Finely chopped dill and
  peppermint to taste

Onion Filling

3½ to 5 ounces smoked slab
  bacon, diced
1 onion, finely chopped
Dash of paprika
Salt and chopped peppermint to
  taste

Prepare the dough: Make a hard dough with flour, egg, salt and pepper, and milk, if necessary. Roll out dough thinly just when ready to cook, so it will not dry out.

Prepare cottage cheese filling: Press cottage cheese through a sieve and season with salt and sugar. Mix in egg yolks (reserve the whites) and dill and peppermint.

Prepare onion filling: Fry the bacon until the fat is rendered. Brown the onions in the drippings. Season with paprika, salt, and peppermint.

Then heap small mounds (about a scant ½ teaspoon) of each of the mixtures in straight lines on half of the rolled dough, spacing them 2 inches apart.

Brush the reserved egg whites around the mounds and the edges of the dough. Fold the other half of dough over the stuffing.

Press the two pieces of dough gently down around the edges to seal them together, using a spatula. Also, press the spatula around the mounds of stuffing, outlining the dough into squares.

Cut the squares with a knife or with a pastry cutter (just like ravioli), being careful not to allow the stuffing to leak out. Cook the filled dumplings in soup (preferably vegetable) and serve.

LUNCHEON DISHES
or
SECOND COURSES

Mushroom Dishes, 140

Cabbage Dishes, 150

Innards, 165

Fish Courses, 180

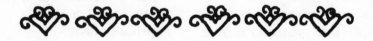

MUSHROOM DISHES

Morels Stuffed with Veal
(Töltött Kucsmagomba)

1 pound morels, cleaned
½ pound veal (from the leg), cut
  into small pieces
1 tablespoon chopped parsley,
  plus more to taste
1½ tablespoons butter
Salt, pepper, and ground nutmeg
  to taste

1 roll
¼ cup milk
2 egg yolks
2 cups sour cream and 1 cup
  heavy cream, mixed together
½ cup bread crumbs
Paprika to taste

Dice the smaller or broken morels,
reserving the larger ones.

Lightly sauté the veal, diced
mushrooms, and parsley in 1
tablespoon of the butter. Add salt.

When lightly browned, chop all
ingredients finely once again. Season
with pepper and nutmeg.

Soak the roll in milk, crumble, and add to the veal–mushroom stuffing. Mix in egg yolks. If the stuffing seems too thick, thin it with some of the sour cream mixture.

Remove the stems from the larger morels and reserve. Stuff the caps with the stuffing mixture, then place the stems on top. Arrange the stuffed mushrooms in a buttered baking dish. Top them with bread crumbs and parsley to taste and sprinkle with paprika.

Cut the remaining butter into pats and place on top. Cover generously with the sour cream mixture.

Place dish in a hot oven, bake for 15 minutes, and serve.

Mushrooms with Nutmeg
(*Gomba Szerecsendió virággal*)

¾ **pound mushrooms, cleaned and sliced**
1 **tablespoon finely chopped parsley**
1 **tablespoon butter**
1 **teaspoon flour**

½ **cup bone or vegetable broth**
1 **cup sour cream**
Pinch of ground nutmeg
Dash of paprika
Salt and pepper to taste

Sauté mushrooms and parsley in butter, then sprinkle with flour. Stir constantly until the mixture is completely coated with the butter and is smooth.

Pour in broth and whisk constantly (to prevent lumps) until a thin sauce is made. Mix in sour cream, nutmeg, and paprika.

Bring to a light boil, stirring constantly. Season with salt and pepper and serve.

NOTE: Serve these mushrooms over toasted bread or rolls.

A Mushroom Dish for Lent
(*Rizikegomba Böjtre*)

**1 pound chanterelle mushrooms
(or cultivated mushrooms),
cleaned
2 bay leaves
Salt**

**1 medium onion, chopped
2 tablespoons oil or butter
Pinch of summer savory
Pepper to taste**

Layer the mushrooms in a large jar, sprinkling each layer with salt and pressing down each layer as you go. Put a bay leaf on top of two of the layers.

Cover the last layer with salt, then seal the top of the jar with plastic wrap. Store in a cool place.

To use the preserved mushrooms,
soak them in water to wash the salt
off, rinse, and dry. Sauté mushrooms
with chopped onion in oil or butter.

Season with savory, salt, and pepper
and serve.

NOTE: Collect the mushrooms in the summer and carefully clean them. Once they are
preserved, they will last throughout the winter.

Serve these sautéed mushrooms with buttered roast potatoes.

Sabbatarian Mushroom Omelette
(*Szombatos Gombás Tojás*)

14 ounces mushrooms, cleaned
1 teaspoon chopped parsley
½ cup butter
Marjoram to taste
3 or 4 eggs, beaten
Salt and pepper to taste

1 tablespoon goose fat
1 tablespoon flour
1 cup sour cream
3 to 4 tablespoons grated hard
   cheese

Sauté the mushrooms and parsley in
butter. Season with marjoram when
done.

Line the bottom of a buttered baking
dish with half the mushrooms. Cover
the mushrooms with the beaten eggs,
seasoned with salt and pepper.

Put the pan in a slow oven for a few minutes to keep it warm, then make the following sauce. Prepare a light *roux* from the goose fat and flour. Add sour cream and grated cheese and blend well.

Pour half the sauce on the mushrooms and eggs. Cover with the remaining mushrooms, then top with the remaining sauce. Bake in a hot oven for a few minutes and serve immediately.

Mushroom Gulyás with Marjoram
(*Majorannás Gombatokány*)

2 onions, grated
1 teaspoon chopped parsley
2 tablespoons goose fat
1 cup bone or vegetable broth
1 pound mushrooms, cleaned
　and sliced

Salt and pepper to taste
½ cup *spaetzle* (page 115) or egg
　barley (page 267)
Pinch of marjoram

Sauté the onions and parsley in the goose fat until onions are wilted. Add broth and mushrooms and simmer. Season with salt and pepper.

Just before the mushrooms are done, bring the broth to a boil and cook the *spaetzle* or egg barley in it. Season with marjoram. Cover and simmer a short time, until done. Serve.

Armenian Mushroom Patties
(Örmény Gombaétel)

1 onion, chopped
3 tablespoons rendered lard or oil
Dash of paprika
About ¼ cup chicken or vegetable
 broth
1¼ pounds mushrooms, cleaned
 and chopped
1 tablespoon butter
3 eggs, beaten

5 tablespoons flour
Salt and pepper to taste
1 teaspoon chopped parsley, plus
 more to taste
Ground ginger and rosemary to
 taste
1 cup milk
Vinegar to taste
½ cup sour cream

In a frying pan sauté the chopped onion in 1 tablespoon lard until wilted. Add paprika, broth (water is used on Lenten days), and mushrooms and cook.

When mushrooms are done, combine them with the butter, eggs, 4 tablespoons flour, salt and pepper, and 1 teaspoon parsley. Season with ginger and rosemary. Shape flat patties from this mixture.

Heat another tablespoon of lard in the pan and fry the patties until golden. Cut the fried patties into smaller squares.

Make a light *roux* with the remaining 1 tablespoon lard and 1 tablespoon flour. Thin the *roux* with the milk, whisking constantly until smooth.

Add the vinegar, salt, and chopped parsley. Lightly boil for a few minutes until it thickens. Add the sour cream and heat, but do not boil. Pour the sauce over the mushroom patties, or serve separately.

VARIATION

The Transylvanian Armenians preferred to make this dish with boletus mushrooms.

Kohlrabies Stuffed with Mushrooms
(Karalábé Gombával Töltve)

8 young kohlrabies, peeled
2 tablespoons butter, plus more cut into pats
¼ pound mushrooms, cleaned and chopped
1 teaspoon chopped parsley
1 egg

1 tablespoon bread crumbs, plus more for sprinkling on dish
1 onion, grated
Salt and chopped dill to taste
2 tablespoons sour cream, plus more for topping

Scoop out the centers of the kohlrabies and chop finely. In a skillet, sauté them in half of the butter along with the mushrooms and parsley. Remove skillet from heat.

Combine the mushroom mixture with the egg, bread crumbs, and grated onion. Add salt and dill, and stir in sour cream.

Stuff the hollowed kohlrabies with this mixture. Arrange the kohlrabies in a buttered casserole and top each with a pat of butter and some sour cream. Sprinkle with bread crumbs and bake in a moderate oven until tender.

NOTE: Any remaining stuffing can be shaped into little balls and placed between the kohlrabies.

Carrots Stuffed with Mushrooms
(Gombával Töltött Murok)

7 or 8 large carrots, peeled
**5 ounces mushrooms, cleaned
  and chopped**
**1 cup *tarhonya* (egg barley)
  (page 267)**
3 tablespoons butter

Chopped parsley to taste
**Salt, pepper, and marjoram to
  taste**
1 tablespoon flour
1 cup sour cream
1 cup melted butter

Parboil the carrots in a pot with salted water to cover. Drain. Scoop out the centers, reserve half of them, and dice finely. Set aside.

Brown the egg barley in 2 tablespoons of the butter in one skillet and sauté the mushrooms and parsley in the remaining butter in another skillet.

Combine the mushrooms with the egg barley. Add the diced carrot centers. Season with salt and pepper and marjoram.

Stuff the carrots with the mushroom mixture and arrange them in a buttered baking dish. Make little round balls from any remaining stuffing and roll them in flour. Arrange them among the carrots.

Mix the sour cream with the melted butter and pour it over the carrots. Bake in a hot oven for 15 minutes.

NOTE: For this dish, the garden variety of sugar carrots is the most appropriate. In the heart of the Székely region, wild carrots were used.

Chanterelles with Squash
(*Rókagomba Tökkel*)

1¼ pounds young yellow squash, sliced
¼ cup butter
1 teaspoon finely chopped fresh dill
Paprika to taste

1 pound chanterelles (or cultivated mushrooms), cleaned and sliced
1 teaspoon grated onion
Salt and pepper to taste
1 teaspoon chopped parsley
Juice of 1 lemon

Parboil the squash in plenty of salted water (do not overcook, to keep it crisp). Drain. Melt half the butter in a frying pan, add the squash, and sauté slowly until golden but not soft. Sprinkle with dill and paprika.

Meanwhile, in another pan sauté the mushrooms and onion in the remaining butter. Season with salt and pepper and parsley.

Arrange the squash in the middle of a serving dish, sprinkle with lemon juice, and surround with the sautéed mushrooms. Serve.

Mushroom and Bean Scones
(*Gombás Paszulypogácsa*)

1 cup dried white beans
2 carrots, peeled
1 parsnip, peeled
5 ounces mushrooms, cleaned
 and very finely chopped
2 tablespoons butter

1 tablespoon flour
4 eggs, beaten
Salt, pepper, and chopped parsley
 to taste
Bread crumbs
Oil or rendered lard, for frying

Soak the beans overnight in water to cover. The next day drain and rinse them. Put the beans, carrots, and parsnip in a pot with three times as much lightly salted water and cook until done. Pass beans and vegetables through a sieve.

In a frying pan, sauté the mushrooms in butter. When done, add the bean-vegetable purée, flour, and 2 of the eggs. Season with salt, pepper, and parsley. Let the mixture cool.

Form mixture into flat scone shapes, dip them in the remaining 2 eggs, and roll them in the bread crumbs. Fry them on both sides in hot oil until golden brown. Drain and serve.

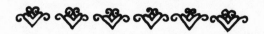

CABBAGE DISHES

Layered Sauerkraut as Made in Kolozsvár
(Kolozsvári Rakott Káposzta)

This is one of the old, popular Transylvanian dishes. It is mentioned in the very first gastronomic writings, such as Miklós Misztótfalusy-Kis's book written in 1695. Naturally, it has gone through many variations since then. The original recipes call for the inclusion of poultry or game birds. In some regions it is still done that way. In the past centuries, it was often flavored with ginger, summer savory, or any other popular flavoring item, including coffee.

4 pounds sauerkraut, drained (some juice reserved)
¾ cup rice
2 tablespoons rendered lard
1 cup beef broth
1 large onion, chopped

1¼ pounds lean minced pork
1 teaspoon paprika
10 ounces smoked sausage, sliced
½ cup sour cream and ½ cup heavy cream, mixed together
4 ounces sliced smoked bacon

Heat the sauerkraut with some of its juice; when done, press out all the juice.

In a skillet, sauté the rice in 1 tablespoon lard until glossy. Add broth, and cook until nearly done but still firm.

In another skillet, sauté the chopped onion for 5 minutes in the remaining 1 tablespoon lard. Add the minced pork and brown it for 15 minutes, stirring the mixture with a fork. Then remove from heat and add paprika.

In a greased ovenproof casserole, place one third of the hot sauerkraut, half the rice, half the pork mixture, and one third of the sausage. Sprinkle with half the sour cream mixture.

Make another layer the same as above, then cover with the remaining sauerkraut. Decorate the top with remaining sausage slices and the bacon.

Top with the remaining sour cream mixture. Cover and bake in a preheated moderately hot oven for 15 to 20 minutes.

Goose with Sauerkraut and Basil
(*Káposztásruca Bazsilikommal*)

1 goose or duck
Salt to taste
Pinch of marjoram
4 to 5 Golden Delicious apples,
    peeled, cored, and sliced

2 tablespoons butter
2 pounds sauerkraut, drained
Pinch of basil

Season the goose inside and out with salt. Rub the inside with marjoram. Sauté the apples quickly in butter.

Stuff the goose with the apples and sew up the opening (pull up the skin flap and sew it to the bird to seal in the stuffing). Put it in a roasting pan in a preheated hot oven and roast until half cooked. Drain off some of the drippings.

Cover a buttered baking dish with sauerkraut and sprinkle it with basil. Place the goose on top. Return to the oven and continue cooking at moderate heat, basting frequently with the drippings, until done.

When ready, remove the apples from the inside. Slice the goose and serve it garnished with the sauerkraut and the apples.

Sauerkraut with Roe
(*Káposztás Ikra*)

This dish shows an undeniable Chinese influence, because of the mixture of sauerkraut (pickled cabbage), fish roe, and lard, which is found only in this cuisine.

1 pound sauerkraut, drained (juice reserved) and rinsed
1 onion, halved
½ cup rendered lard

10 ounces fish roe (see Note)
1 cup dry white wine
Pepper to taste
Dash of saffron

In a skillet, sauté the sauerkraut and onion with the lard. Remove the onion when the sauerkraut is almost done. Then spread the roe over the sauerkraut and heat it for a few minutes.

In a saucepan, heat the wine and reserved sauerkraut juice with the pepper and saffron. Reduce to two thirds the amount.

Pour this liquid over the sauerkraut and roe mixture. Stir lightly, let it come to a boil, remove from heat, and serve.

NOTE: The roe of any type of freshwater fish can be used, except that of the barbel, which is poisonous!

In old descriptions of this recipe ginger was used instead of saffron.

An Old Saxon Cabbage Pot
(*Kohl Kächen*)

2 pounds whole pork leg
2 to 3 heads cabbage, cored, outer leaves removed, and quartered
1 or 2 garlic cloves
2 large potatoes, peeled and cubed

1 tablespoon butter
2 tablespoons flour
Vinegar, sour cream, and salt to taste

In a large pot, bring 3 quarts salted water to a boil and cook the meat. When done, remove the meat from the liquid and cut off the fat. Set aside. Put the cabbage in the pot, add garlic, and boil for 15 minutes.

Then add the potatoes to the pot and continue boiling until both the cabbage and potatoes are done.

Prepare a light *roux* from butter and flour. Add it to the pot, whisking constantly to prevent lumps, until it thickens the liquid. Discard the garlic.

Add a little vinegar, sour cream, and salt, if necessary. Slice the boiled pork and arrange it in a serving dish. Pour the hot cabbage and potato sauce over the slices. Serve hot.

"Slushy" Cabbage
or
Boiled Cabbage with Pork
(Lucskoskáposzta)

The wind yelled at the cabbage, the pig is fat.
The wind slyly told the farmer, the pig and cabbages are ready.
The wife heard her spouse and watered a vat;
So two cabbages were quartered, and the pig, and that was that.
The wind caught the pot's steam, from the cabbage and some pork
Laced with salt, savory, and dill, and begged the lady:
Enough already, throw in some flour and take your fork,
Wait for thickening and free from the fire;
Leach the herbs and set meat to plate moist and heady.
A show of vinegar, clops of cream I desire
Spoke the broth awaiting pork a cabbage to soak.
So when the family gobbled this filling and hot
Plate, said the wind, the power of that bloke!

**2 small heads of cabbage, cored,
    outer leaves removed, and cut
    into ⅓-inch strips
2 pounds pork shoulder
6 to 8 slices smoked bacon
1 onion, finely chopped
½ teaspoon black peppercorns
12 leaves of fresh summer savory
    (or ½ tablespoon dried)**

**5 sprigs of fresh dill (or ½
    tablespoon dried)
3 or 4 tomatoes, skinned, seeded,
    and chopped
1 tablespoon rendered lard or oil
1 tablespoon flour
½ cup sour cream
1 egg yolk
1 tablespoon tarragon vinegar
Salt to taste**

In a pot, boil cabbage in lightly salted water to cover, then remove and drain; reserve the liquid. Set aside cabbage.

Boil the pork meat in the same liquid until it is almost done, about 1 hour. Remove the pork and save the cooking broth again. Slice pork meat and set aside.

Cover the bottom of a large heavy pot with the bacon slices. Cook over medium heat until bacon renders some fat, then add the onion. Let the onion get glossy.

Then add about a 1-inch-deep layer of cabbage to the pot. Sprinkle on a few peppercorns. Cover with a layer of sliced meat. Tie the savory and dill together in several small bunches and place one bunch on top (if you use dried herbs, sprinkle them on generously).

Make another layer of cabbage, peppercorns, meat, and herbs, saving enough of the ingredients for another layer.

Add tomatoes. Put remaining meat, then cabbage, peppercorns, and herbs on top. Pour on the reserved cooking liquid; it should cover the layers completely. Cover and cook over low heat until meat and cabbage are tender.

Make a golden brown *roux* with the lard and flour. Beat in sour cream, egg yolk, and vinegar and 4 spoonfuls of the liquid from the cabbage. Mix it until smooth, then pour it into the pot. Add salt and slowly simmer for another 10 minutes, until it thickens.

Variation
Spare ribs or smoked pork chops can be substituted for the shoulder.

Cabbage in Tomato Sauce
(Mezőségi Paradicsomos Káposzta or Varză Murată cu Carne)

2 onions, chopped
½ cup rendered lard
¾ pound pork shoulder, diced
¾ pound veal shoulder, diced
Dash of paprika
Salt to taste

2 pounds cabbage, shredded
1 cup tomato purée
1 cup sour cream
½ pound smoked sausage, thinly sliced
Chopped dill and savory to taste

In a skillet, sauté 1 chopped onion in half of the lard. When glossy, add the diced meat and sauté until meat starts to brown. Take off heat and season with paprika and salt.

Sauté the other onion in the remaining lard until glossy, then add the cabbage. Add a little warm water occasionally when mixture becomes too dry. When cabbage is done, add it to the meat.

Stir in the tomato purée, sour cream, sausage, and dill and savory. Heat for a few more minutes before serving.

Ladó's Sloppy Stuffed Cabbage
(*Ladó's Lucskos Töltött Káposztája*)

This recipe is from a famous grand lady of old Háromszék, Mrs. Ferenc Porubszky de Poruba, wife of the county governor of Transylvania in the 1930s. Her household was famous all over the three Sekler counties. After World War I, Maria, the Queen of Rumania, always made a point to stop at her house while traveling through Transylvania. Ladisla Deér of Egervár—her maiden name, but addressed as Ladó by friends and admirers—still keeps one of the best "tables" despite her age, which is now 85.

2 pounds smoked pork knuckle, cleaned
2 medium-size cabbages, outer leaves removed
1½ pounds lean minced pork
1 cup rice
2 cloves
Salt and pepper to taste
1 teaspoon paprika

Finely chopped green pepper to taste
8 sprigs of savory
8 sprigs of dill
½ onion, finely chopped
½ teaspoon black peppercorns
1 tablespoon rendered lard
2 tablespoons flour
2 tablespoons tarragon vinegar
3 cups sour cream

Rinse the pork knuckle twice in water, then boil it in a pot of water until done. Set it aside and reserve the cooking broth.

Prick the cabbages in several places with a knife before cooking them, so that the hot water reaches the inside leaves as well, without the cabbage leaves falling apart. Then steam the cabbages until done.

For the stuffing, mix together the minced pork, rice, cloves, salt, pepper, paprika, and green pepper. Add as much water or reserved cooking broth as needed to hold the mixture together; it should not be dry.

One by one, remove all the cabbage leaves from their cores. Thin down the thicker veins of the leaves with a knife, leaving a thinner vein but one that will keep the two sides of the leaf from falling apart. Cut the cabbage cores into quarters, lengthwise.

Form 20 to 25 balls of duck-egg size from the stuffing and wrap them in the cabbage leaves. Fill the leaves loosely with the stuffing so that the cooked swollen rice won't burst the leaves open.

Grease the inside of a cooking pot or casserole and line the bottom and sides evenly with a layer of cabbage leaves that were not stuffed. Add half of the savory and dill and sprinkle with the onion.

Line up the stuffed cabbage leaves on one side of your pot and the cabbage cores on the other. When you are ready, cover the pot's contents with the remaining reserved broth.

Add salt to taste, and the black peppercorns. Put the remaining sprigs of savory and dill on top. Cover with more cabbage leaves.

Bring to a boil and simmer it for two hours over low heat. It can also be cooked in a moderate oven until done.

From time to time, shake the pot gently in a circular motion, so that the cabbage leaves will not get scorched. This is best achieved if the leaves were placed evenly into the pot.

Make a light *roux* with the lard and flour. Stir it into the stuffing along with the tarragon vinegar. Bring it to a boil again for two or three minutes.

When the stuffed cabbage is done, take a cup of liquid from the top of the pot and place it in a saucepan. Add the sour cream and cook over low heat until it is heated through. Serve this sauce separately, with the stuffed cabbage. Slice the knuckle and serve it as a garnish.

Stuffed Cabbage in a Different Way
(Töltött Káposzta más módra)

1 cup rice
1½ pounds ground pork
½ pound ground beef
2 eggs
1 onion, finely chopped
2 teaspoons paprika
2 tablespoons minced savory
Salt and pepper to taste
1 large cabbage, cored and outer
 leaves removed

4 tablespoons rendered lard
2 pounds cabbage, cored, outer
 leaves removed, and shredded
1 quart sauerkraut juice, diluted
 with 1 quart water or vegetable
 broth
1 cup sour cream and heavy
 cream, mixed

Make the stuffing: cook the rice in 2 cups water for 10 minutes, until about half cooked. Drain. Combine rice with the ground pork and beef, eggs, and onion. Season with half the paprika and savory, and the salt and pepper. Set aside.

Remove the leaves of the cabbage and blanch in boiling water, or steam them for 5 minutes. Cut out the thick veins, then stuff each leaf with a large spoonful of the meat mixture. Roll the leaves up and fold in ends to seal in stuffing.

Grease a large heatproof earthenware baking dish with the lard. Scatter one third of the shredded cabbage over the bottom, then place the stuffed leaves on top; sprinkle with the remaining savory. Make two more such layers. The top should be covered with shredded cabbage.

Pour in enough diluted sauerkraut juice to cover the cabbage. Sprinkle with some ground pepper and the remaining paprika. Cook on top of stove over low heat, without stirring, or in a moderate oven, until the stuffing appears tender when pierced with a fork.

Cover with the sour cream mixture and let simmer for 10 minutes. Remove from heat, spoon the shredded cabbage into the bottom of the serving dish, and carefully place the stuffed leaves on the bed of cabbage.

Variations

In Transylvania almost every family has its own recipe for stuffed cabbage. Perhaps the few things these variations have in common is that they are prepared from cabbage and/or sauerkraut, pork, and beef. Most cooks add salt, pepper, paprika, and other spices, such as caraway seeds, marjoram, and savory. According to some recipes, minced sauerkraut is added to the meat.

There are various methods of arranging the ingredients in the earthenware baking dish. For example, the bottom of it is often lined with smoked bacon rind or smoked pig's bones and then the cabbage is placed on top. A pig's trotter, smoked ribs, thin flank, or even smoked sausage may also be used.

NOTE: Add the sour cream mixture only to that quantity of cabbage that will be consumed at one meal. Without the sour cream the remainder can be kept awhile in a cool place, even without refrigeration. According to an old saying, stuffed cabbage is best when it has been reheated for the seventh time.

Cabbage Stuffed with Goose Breast
(Káposzta Libamellel Töltve)

6 pounds cabbage, cored and
** leaves removed**
¾ cup rice
1 onion, chopped
2 tablespoons rendered goose fat,
** plus more for greasing pan**
1½ pounds goose breast, with its
** fat, minced**
7 ounces round of beef, minced

2 eggs
Dash of ground pepper
1 teaspoon marjoram
Salt to taste
1 garlic clove, crushed
2 smoked goose drumsticks,
** boned and sliced**
2½ cups dry white wine

Reserve the larger leaves of the cabbage for stuffing and chop the remainder finely. Set aside.

Cook the rice in 2 cups water until half done. Drain. Sauté the onion in the fat quickly.

Combine the rice and onion with the minced meats, eggs, pepper, marjoram, salt, and crushed garlic. Blend well, then stuff each cabbage leaf with an egg-size quantity of the mixture. Roll up the leaves.

Grease the bottom of a large pot with some goose fat. Cover it with a third of the chopped cabbage and the sliced goose drumsticks. Place more chopped cabbage on top, then the stuffed leaves, and cover with the remaining chopped cabbage.

Pour in enough wine (and water, if necessary) to cover. Cook over very low heat until cabbage is tender.

Stuffed Savoy Cabbage from Hargita
(*Hargitai Töltött Káposzta*)

6 boned pork chops
2 tablespoons rendered lard
2 small onions, chopped
¾ pound fatty pork shoulder, minced
½ pound sausage, sliced
2 pounds savoy cabbage, cored and outer leaves removed
4 ounces smoked bacon, diced

2 pounds sauerkraut, drained
2 to 3 cups beef broth
1 tablespoon flour
1 cup sour cream
Salt to taste
Pinch of crushed caraway seeds or 1 bunch of fresh dill, chopped

In a frying pan, sear the chops in 1 tablespoon lard until browned all over. Remove chops from pan. Then sauté half the chopped onions and the fatty pork in the same pan, stirring, for 10 minutes. Add the sausage and fry for a few minutes.

Remove 12 large leaves from the cabbage and blanch them in boiling water, then drain. Top each chop with the onion mixture and wrap it in 1 or 2 cabbage leaves. Tie a piece of string around it to hold it together.

Sauté the remaining chopped onion in diced bacon and add the sauerkraut. Distribute half of the sauerkraut over the bottom of a greased earthenware baking dish. Place the wrapped chops in the dish, then cover with the remaining sauerkraut. Pour on broth and cook in a slow oven for 1¼ hours.

When ready, lift out the wrapped chops. Mix the flour with the sour cream and add the mixture to the sauerkraut; season with salt and blend well.

Cook over low heat on top of stove for another 10 minutes. Sprinkle with crushed caraway seeds or chopped dill before serving.

INNARDS

Armenian Blood Sausage for Country Fairs
(*Hütyü*)

This characteristic Armenian black blood sausage was sold at country fairs. A pig of approximately 200 pounds was butchered and the sausage was produced from its entrails and other parts; most of the pig's meat was used for different purposes. The sausage was stuffed with inexpensive ingredients, hence it was the foodstuff of poor people. In Károly Kós's book entitled *Népélet és Néphagyomány (Folklore and Folklife),* he wrote: "The Armenian women of Szamosujvár were selling *hütyü* from metal-plated kettles." The vendors were named the *"hütyü* women."

Blood, lungs, heart, and spleen of
   1 pig (about 200 pounds), cut
   into 2-inch pieces
5½ pounds pork meat (small cuts
   left over after dividing up
   whole pig), cut into ¾-inch
   pieces

8 bacon strips, fried and
   crumbled
Pepper, paprika, ground cloves,
   marjoram, ground dill seeds,
   and thyme to taste
Pig's intestines or sausage casings
3 pounds rice
½ pound rendered lard

In a saucepan, heat the pig's blood to a boil. Let cool, and strain through a sieve. Let it settle.

Clean the lungs, heart, and spleen. In a pot with 3 quarts water, boil the lungs, heart, spleen, and pork meat. Test them with a fork: if it comes out smoothly, the meats are done.

Remove from liquid, let cool, and grind them. Reserve the cooking liquid.

Cook the rice until done in the reserved cooking liquid; save any leftover liquid. Combine the ground meats and rice with the crumbled bacon and one third of the blood.

Mix the remaining blood with any leftover lukewarm cooking liquid and add the spices and herbs. Add salt only if needed, as the blood is already salty.

Combine both mixtures. Stuff the mixture loosely into the casings. Twist the casings to close, piercing the sausages with a pin as you go along.

Cook the sausages in simmering water on a low flame for about 20 minutes, or until a greasy liquid spurts out of the sausage when pricked. Remove from water and let cool completely.

Sauté the sausages in lard before serving.

NOTE: Beef blood can be substituted for the pig's blood. No salt is called for in this recipe because the blood from the freshly slaughtered pig is kept from coagulating by the addition of a good handful of salt.

The sausage stuffing is very juicy and loose.

Lung Ragout
(*Szászvárosi tüdőtokány* or *Lungen Tokana*)

1 large onion, chopped
5 tablespoons rendered lard
Lungs and heart of a lamb or calf,
   cleaned, briefly washed and
   soaked, and diced
1 teaspoon paprika

Salt and pepper to taste
2 tablespoons flour
Chopped thyme to taste
Spaetzle (page 115) or boiled
   potatoes

In a saucepan, cook the onion in 4 tablespoons of the lard until wilted, but do not let it brown. Add the diced lung and heart. Stir constantly, letting them simmer in their own juices.

Season with paprika and salt and pepper. Add 1 cup water and simmer for about 1 hour, or until tender. Stir it from time to time.

Prepare a light *roux* with the remaining lard and the flour. Add to the ragout, whisking constantly to prevent lumps.

Add thyme and simmer for another 10 minutes, until it is smooth and thick. Serve with *spaetzle* or boiled potatoes.

VARIATIONS

In some recipes 2 bay leaves and a teaspoon of tarragon or a dash of cayenne pepper are added at the same time as the water. Some cooks dilute the ragout with dry white wine instead of water. Vinegar and sour cream may be added just before serving.

Calf's Brains with Rosemary and Mushrooms
(*Gombás Velő*)

1½ pounds calf's brains or pig's brains, soaked in cold water for 1 hour, cleaned, membranes removed, and blanched
Salt to taste
3 sprigs of rosemary

10 ounces mushrooms, sliced
1 onion, finely chopped
2 tablespoons butter
Pepper to taste
½ cup white wine
Lemon juice to taste

Cook the brains until done in lightly salted water to cover flavored with the sprigs of rosemary. Cut into slices and arrange them in a circle on a platter. Keep the platter warm in the oven.

In a saucepan, sauté the mushrooms and onion in the butter. Season with salt and pepper. When the juices have evaporated, add wine and let it cook lightly until the liquid is reduced by half. Flavor with lemon juice.

When done, heap the mushrooms in the center of the platter and pour the juices over the sliced brains.

Calf's Brains with Eggs
(Tojásos Borjúvelő)

In the town wherein we live and labor
Some brainy things really do find favor.
Find three of the calf's kind, hopefully free;
Rinse coldly, drying shortly as you'll see
A use better than matters scholarly;
Who frankly thinks while trimming them and dicing
Or frying onions gold after slicing
Requires one to have an advanced degree
Adding brains and minced parsley lib'rally
Sprinkling in marjoram, salt, pepper three?
While this fries, beat some eggs to sunshine foam
Pour in skillet with the cerebral loam
Scrambling them up and gold'ning carefully
To be enjoyed without math or geometry.

3 calf's brains (about 1½ pounds), soaked in cold water for 1 hour, cleaned and membranes removed
1 medium onion, finely chopped
6 tablespoons rendered lard or butter
Small bunch of parsley, finely chopped
1 teaspoon salt
Pinch of ground black pepper
Pinch of marjoram
10 eggs, well beaten
1 teaspoon paprika

Blanch the brains in boiling water for 1 or 2 minutes. Dry them on a cloth, trim, and peel off any thin skin that is left. Cut the brains into small pieces.

Sauté the onion in lard in a frying pan until glossy. Add the parsley and the brains, then season with salt, pepper, and marjoram. Sauté for 5 to 6 minutes, stirring occasionally.

Pour the eggs over the mixture and cook them like lightly scrambled eggs, stirring and folding the mixture over from time to time. Just before they are ready, sprinkle with paprika, mix once more very gently, and serve.

Brain Sausages
(*Velős Hurka*)

2 large or 3 small pig's brains or 3 pounds calf's brains, soaked in cold water for 1 hour
2 onions, finely chopped
1 cup rendered lard
2 pounds lean ground pork

1 pound lightly smoked bacon, rind removed, cut into small pieces
Salt, pepper, chopped marjoram, and ground cloves to taste
2 cups millet or rice
Sausage casings
Butter

Steam the brains lightly over water and remove the membranes. Pass them through a sieve. Set aside.

In a skillet, sauté the onions in lard. Add the ground pork and cook until lightly browned, stirring constantly.

Add the bacon to the pork–onion mixture. Cook for another 10 minutes. Season with salt, pepper, marjoram, and cloves. Set mixture aside.

In a pot, cook the millet in 4 cups water until done.

Add the sieved brains and the millet to the pork mixture. Stir well. Stuff sausage casings with this mixture, twist the casings to close, and prick the sausages with a pin.

Steam or simmer the sausages in water for 20 minutes. Remove them from steamer or cooking liquid and put in cold water to cool off. Air-dry them in a cool place and leave in a smokehouse for 2 days. Bake or sauté in butter before serving.

NOTE: These sausages are perishable and should be consumed as quickly as possible, preferably within 10 days after smoking.

Roasted Sweetbreads from Szeben
(*Szebeni rostonsült borjúmirigy or Hermanstädter Bries*)

4 calf's sweetbreads (2 pairs)
2 onions, cut in half
1 celery root, cut lengthwise
2 carrots, cut lenghwise

2 parsnips, cut lengthwise
Salt and pepper to taste
4 tablespoons butter

Rinse the sweetbreads well. Soak them in cold water for 1 hour. Then blanch them for 2 to 3 minutes in boiling water. Firm them in cold water. Drain.

Cook the sweetbreads, onions, celery root, carrots, and parsnips in boiling water to cover. When sweetbreads are half done, let them cool in the liquid.

When cool, remove the sweetbreads and discard the vegetables. Cut them in half, and trim the waste (cartilage, membranes, etc.) from all the pieces. Season with salt and pepper.

In a buttered baking pan brown the sweetbreads in a moderately hot oven (or sauté them in butter in a frying pan). Then place them on a hot skewer and roast over a wood fire until tender.

VARIATIONS

The sweetbreads may also be rolled in bread crumbs and sautéed in hot butter in a frying pan. Serve with tartar sauce.

Tomatoes Stuffed with Chopped Liver
(*Májjal Töltött Paradicsom*)

8 large tomatoes
1 onion, finely chopped
5 tablespoons butter
10 ounces liver, cut into small pieces
2 slices bread, soaked in ½ cup milk and drained

Salt and pepper to taste
2 eggs, separated
½ cup red wine
Finely chopped basil to taste
½ cup sour cream and ½ cup heavy cream, mixed together

Cut off the top of the tomatoes. Scoop out the insides and reserve, seeds and all. Turn tomatoes upside down and let drain.

In a frying pan, sauté the onion in 2 tablespoons of the butter. Add liver to the onion and cook until it browns.

Mince together the liver mixture and bread. Season with salt and pepper and stir in 1 tablespoon of butter and the egg yolks until the mixture cools off. Beat the egg whites until stiff and fold them into the mixture. Fill the tomatoes with this mixture.

Place the tomatoes in a baking dish. Cut 1 tablespoon of butter into pats and lay a pat of butter on top of each tomato. Bake in a low oven until done.

Simmer the insides of the tomatoes in a small pan and press through a sieve. Melt the remaining 1 tablespoon of butter in a saucepan and add the tomatoes, wine, and basil. Bring mixture to a boil and reduce to two thirds the amount. Remove from heat and stir in half of the sour cream mixture.

Pour sauce over the tomatoes. Cook in the oven for a few more minutes, until the sauce boils up again. Pour on the remaining sour cream mixture just before serving.

Liver and Lung Sausages
(*Tüdős-Májas Hurka*)

2 pounds pork liver
2 pounds pork lungs, cleaned
Salt to taste
1 cup plus 1 tablespoon rice, well
   rinsed
1 pound meaty bacon
2 onions, finely chopped
1 cup plus 2 tablespoons
   rendered lard

2 teaspoons ground pepper
Marjoram, savory, and ground
   ginger to taste
½ teaspoon ground cloves
2 teaspoons paprika
2½ yards beef casings
Lard for frying

Put the liver and lungs in a pot with lightly salted boiling water to cover. Cover, and cook until tender. Remove from the liquid; reserve this cooking liquid.

Cook the rice until done in 2 cups of the reserved cooking liquid. In a separate pan cook the bacon until done in some of this liquid.

In a frying pan, sauté the onions in lard over low heat.

Grind the liver, lungs, and bacon. Add the rice, onions, salt, pepper, marjoram, savory, ginger, cloves, and paprika. Mix well.

Fill the casings loosely with the help of a sausage stuffer. Prick them with a pin in a couple of places. Tie the sausages every 8 inches with some string.

Cook the sausages in lightly boiling water for 15 minutes, or until the sausages rise to the top of the water. Hang the parboiled sausage loosely side by side in a cool dry place for at least 2 days.

Heat some lard in a skillet, add the sausages, and fry over a low flame until done, piercing them occasionally with the point of a sharp knife.

NOTE: To make more flavorful sausages, cooks in certain areas smoke them for 1 or 2 days before frying. In that case, they can be eaten as is, without being fried first.

Beef Tongue with Cabbage
(*Limbă cu Varză or Káposztás Nyelv*)

1 beef tongue or 4 pig's tongues, well scrubbed
3 sprigs of dill
Salt to taste
1 cabbage, cored, outer leaves removed, and shredded

½ cup oil
1 cup sour bran soup (page 90)
1 cup dry white wine
Pepper to taste

In a large pot, cook the tongue and dill in boiling salted water to cover. Simmer until tender. Remove the skin, gristle, and bones and cut into ⅓-inch-thick slices.

Sauté the cabbage in oil until tender or golden brown. Add the sour bran soup, wine, salt, and pepper. Put the cabbage on a platter and arrange the tongue slices on top. Serve.

VARIATIONS

Some cooks use smoked bacon drippings instead of oil to cook the cabbage. Chopped or julienned pickles may be substituted for the sour bran soup.

Stewed Tripe with Lemon
(Citromos Pacal)

This stew was a particularly popular dish at the Hotel New York in Kolozsvár, a meeting place for theater and entertainment figures and the local intelligentsia.

2½ pounds tripe, trimmed, soaked, and washed thoroughly in cold water
Salt to taste
Beef broth or water
1 teaspoon salt
2 veal knuckles or veal bones, cleaned and blanched
5 tablespoons rendered lard
2 ounces bacon, diced

¾ cup plus 2 tablespoons flour
1 garlic clove, crushed
Pinch of chopped basil and tarragon
Small bunch of parsley, finely chopped
Grated lemon peel to taste
Juice of 2 or 3 lemons
Pinch of black pepper
Steamed rice or boiled potatoes

Boil the tripe in a pot with plenty of salted water. Reduce heat after 30 minutes and let it simmer for 3 to 4 hours. Take out tripe and cool it in cold water. Cut into strips 2½ to 3 inches long.

Put tripe in a pot and pour in enough beef broth to cover. Add salt and the veal knuckles. Cook for 3 to 4 hours, till tender. Drain. Discard the veal knuckles.

Melt the lard in a saucepan, add the bacon, and fry slowly until the bacon is crisp. Sprinkle with the flour, and when it has turned a light yellow, add the garlic, basil, tarragon, parsley, and lemon peel. Stir well.

Add a little cold water and stir sauce with a whisk until smooth and thick. Then add the cooked tripe, lemon juice, and pepper. Continue to cook, stirring constantly, for 15 minutes. Serve with steamed rice or boiled potatoes.

NOTE: The veal knuckles or bones make this dish particularly gelatinous and smooth.

Chicken Giblets in Paprika Sauce
(Csirke-Zúza Paprikás Mártásban)

7 tablespoons rendered lard
5 ounces onion, finely chopped
½ teaspoon paprika
Chicken broth (optional)
1 pound chicken gizzards, cleaned, rinsed in several changes of water, thick skin removed, and cut into medium pieces

1 teaspoon salt
2 ounces bacon, cut into small cubes
1 pound chicken livers, rinsed and cut into large pieces
7 ounces green peppers, chopped
1 large fresh tomato
***Spaetzle* (page 115)**

Heat lard in a saucepan and sauté the onion until half done. Add paprika and a little chicken broth or water. Add the gizzards. Season with salt.

Cover and let stew on low heat, occasionally adding a little water as juices evaporate. Cook until tender, then reduce the pan juices until thick. Set gizzards aside.

Fry bacon cubes lightly in a skillet. Add livers to the pan and cook for another 2 to 3 minutes. Combine the sautéed bacon–livers mixture, peppers, and tomato with the gizzards. Let mixture stew until livers are tender.

Should the sauce be too thick, thin it with a little water or chicken broth. Serve dish hot, together with *spaetzle*.

Kidney Gulyás
(*Vese Pörkölt*)

1 onion, minced
4 tablespoons bacon fat
1 small beef kidney or 2 veal or lamb kidneys, soaked in cold salted and vinegared water for 1 hour and well cleaned, skinned, deveined, and cut into small strips
Salt and pepper to taste

1 or more bay leaves
½ teaspoon paprika
Flour-and-water paste (1 part flour to 2 parts water, mixed together)
Vinegar to taste
Sour cream to taste
Hominy or rice

In a medium saucepan, brown onion lightly in bacon fat. Add kidneys. Cook for 5 minutes, stirring constantly. Season with salt and pepper.

Add bay leaves, paprika, and enough water to cover. Cover and cook slowly until the kidneys are tender. Take out bay leaves.

Stir flour-and-water paste into pan and heat until it thickens slightly, stirring constantly. Add vinegar and sour cream. Serve with hominy or rice.

Fennel by Joseph Domjan

FISH COURSES

Stuffed Pike in the Style of Mármaros County
(Töltött Csuka Mármarosi Módra)

A favorite Jewish holiday dish.

2 rolls, soaked in 1 cup milk,
   drained
4 tablespoons butter
2 or 3 beef marrow bones,
   cooked, marrow removed and
   chopped
3 tablespoons grated hard cheese
¼ pound mushrooms, chopped
   and sautéed in butter
2 egg yolks

Salt and pepper to taste
½ teaspoon grated fresh ginger
1 teaspoon savory
2 (5-pound) whole pikes,
   cleaned, gills removed, heads
   and tails intact
½ cup oil
2 lemons, sliced
2 bay leaves
1 cup dry white wine

Combine the rolls, butter, bone marrow, cheese, mushrooms, and egg yolks. Season with salt, pepper, ginger, and savory. Stuff stomach cavities of the fish with this mixture and sew up the opening.

Arrange the fish in a baking dish, well greased with some of the oil, and cover with lemon slices and bay leaves.

Bake in a medium oven for 25 to 30 minutes. Baste frequently and generously with the remaining oil, wine, and pan juices. When fish are done, strain the liquid in the baking dish and serve as a sauce with fish.

NOTE: This delicious dish can also be made from carp, wels, or sturgeon.

Pike with Horseradish and Chestnut Dumplings
(Csuka Tormával és Gesztenyegombóccal)

Salt to taste
2 pounds whole pike, cleaned
2 onions, quartered
2 carrots, cut into large pieces
2 parsnips, cut into large pieces
A few whole peppercorns
1 garlic clove
2 pounds chestnuts
Pepper to taste

A few drops of lemon juice
½ cup bread crumbs
3 egg yolks
2 tablespoons butter
1 quart boiling milk
1 cup grated horseradish
Chopped dill to taste
1 tablespoon cornstarch

Salt the pike, and then set it aside for 30 minutes. Then cook the fish, in enough salted water to cover, along with the onions, carrots, parsnips, peppercorns, and whole garlic clove, until done. Take out garlic.

Meanwhile, put the chestnuts in some boiling water and then simmer. When done, clean them and chop very finely. Season with salt and pepper. Add a few drops of lemon juice, the bread crumbs, egg yolks, and 1 tablespoon of the butter. Mix well.

Form mixture into walnut-size dumplings, drop them into boiling milk, and cook until done. Remove dumplings from milk; reserve milk. Set aside the dumplings.

Melt remaining 1 tablespoon of butter in a saucepan and sauté the horseradish and dill. Then pour in half of the hot milk and let it cook. When almost done, add 1 tablespoon of the boiling liquid from the fish. Dissolve the cornstarch in a little water, add to milk mixture, and cook until it is a thick sauce.

Remove the fish from its cooking liquid, place it on a serving dish, and pour the sauce over it. Serve with the chestnut dumplings.

Layered Pike with Mint
(*Fodormentás Rakott Csuka*)

2 pounds whole pike, cleaned
Salt and pepper to taste
2 onions, chopped
4 tablespoons butter

1 bunch of mint leaves, finely chopped
3 tablespoons bread crumbs
2 cups sour cream
½ cup milk

Blanch the pike with boiling water, re-move the bones, and cut the fish into small pieces. Season with salt and pepper.

Sauté the onions in half the butter until golden brown. Set aside.

Place ½ tablespoon of the remaining butter, cut into pats, in a buttered baking dish, then arrange one third of the seasoned fish slices on top. Cover with one third of the sautéed onions. Sprinkle with a third of the mint leaves and bread crumbs. Blend together the sour cream and milk. Then top fish with a third of this mixture.

Repeat this layering two more times, until all the ingredients are used. Put the remaining ½ tablespoon butter, cut into several pats, on top of the last layer. Put the dish in a medium oven and bake until the fish is tender.

NOTE: This dish is traditionally garnished with a pickled crab apple salad or cooked beets.

Pike Stuffed with Walnuts
(Csuka Dióval Töltve)

There are few fishermen in wooden boats
Who sport and weave across the local streams,
Crystal lines dropped from distant mountain streams,
Catching the sly pike of the bony coats
Banked by fan-vault elms hiding pastured goats;
Rub with salt the skinned flesh, split downside seams
Await the soaking of a roll in cream's
Blend of yolks, whipped whites, and marjoram motes;
Mix now with crushed nuts which once felt a breeze
Carry them into a net of cane ply,
So to the river comes ground from the trees,
Into the belly stuff this mix and tie;
The meat's sweet wood scent will certainly please
So in hot butter let fish crisply fry.

Salt to taste
3 pounds whole pike, cleaned
Juice of ½ lemon
1 roll, soaked in 1 cup milk,
  drained
½ cup walnuts, roughly chopped

1 teaspoon chopped fresh or ½
  teaspoon dried marjoram
2 eggs, separated and whites
  stiffly beaten
Pepper to taste
½ cup butter, cut into pats
1 cup sour cream (optional)

Salt the fish and sprinkle with lemon juice.

Combine the following ingredients: the roll, walnuts, marjoram, egg yolks, and stiffly beaten egg whites; flavor with pepper to taste. Stuff the fish's stomach cavity with this mixture and sew it up.

Place half of the pats of butter in a baking pan. Add the fish and cover with the remaining butter.

Bake the fish in a moderately hot oven until both sides are crisp. Slice the fish before serving. Mix the pan juices with sour cream and serve with the fish.

NOTE: Carp or perch can be substituted for the pike used in this recipe. This dish was a particular favorite in finer Jewish households.

Gefüllte Fish from Szatmár
(Szatmári Gefüllte Fisch)

A festive dish, served at special events, such as weddings, bar mitzvahs, etc. Considered a distinguished delicacy, it is one of the genuinely traditional Jewish dishes. This recipe is unusual in that the ground fish mixture is stuffed inside the whole fish's skin and then cooked.

- 1 (4- to 5-pound) whole pike, cleaned
- 2 rolls, soaked in 1 cup milk and drained
- 6 shelled walnuts
- 3 onions, sliced
- Salt, pepper, and sugar to taste
- 1 parsnip, sliced
- 1 carrot, sliced
- 1 celery root, sliced
- 2 eggs (optional)
- Matzo meal (optional)
- Fruity white wine or fish broth (optional)
- 2 or 3 potatoes, peeled, boiled, and sliced

Scale the fish and blanch it in boiling water. Make an incision at the bottom of the head and skin the fish in one piece (be careful not to tear the skin). Reserve. Remove the head. Gently scrape off any flesh remaining on the skin. Bone the fish and reserve the backbone.

Grind the fish meat with the rolls, walnuts, and 1 onion. Season with salt and pepper. To remove the slightly bitter taste of the fish, add some sugar diluted in a little water to the fish mixture—pour on only as much liquid as it can absorb.

Boil the parsnip, carrot, celery root, remaining 2 onions, and fish's backbone in a pot containing 1 quart water.

Meanwhile, stuff the fish skin with the fish mixture and sew up the skin. If any of the mixture is left over, add the eggs and some matzo meal and form them into little balls.

When the vegetables are half done, add the stuffed fish to the boiling liquid (add the fish balls later). Add wine and some more water to cover the vegetables and fish. Simmer over low heat until all ingredients are tender.

Remove pot from heat and let fish cool in the liquid. Carefully lift the fish from the pot, place it on a serving dish, and remove the string used to sew up the fish. Discard the backbone. Garnish the serving dish with the cooked vegetables and fish balls.

Reduce the cooking liquid until thick (about half the original amount), then pour it over the fish. Serve fish with sliced potatoes.

NOTE: Most often this dish is served cold, but it can also be eaten hot.

Carp in Wine and Basil Sauce
(*Ponty bormártással or Crap cu Sos de Vin*)

2 pounds carp, cleaned, washed,
   and carefully dried
Salt and pepper to taste
1 bunch of fresh basil, cleaned
1 small onion, coarsely chopped
2 carrots, coarsely chopped
1 celery root, coarsely chopped

2 parsnips, coarsely chopped
4 to 6 peppercorns
2 garlic cloves
1½ cups dry white wine
1 tablespoon tomato purée
2 tablespoons butter, cut into pats
1 lemon, sliced

Sprinkle the fish inside and out with salt and pepper. Stuff the fish with half the basil.

Arrange a layer of the vegetables, some peppercorns, and the whole garlic cloves in a buttered baking dish. Pour in the wine and tomato purée. Place the fish in the dish.

Scatter a few pats of butter and a few slices of lemon on top of the fish and bake in a moderate oven. Baste frequently with its own juices until tender.

When cooked, place on a platter. Drain the juices into a saucepan and add the remaining basil. Bring to a boil. Adjust seasoning. Serve this sauce with the fish.

VARIATION

Sour cream may also be added to the sauce, if desired.

Carp Filled with Mushrooms
(Ponty gombával töltve or Crap Umplut cu Ciuperci)

2 to 3 pounds whole carp,
    cleaned, washed, and carefully
    dried
Salt to taste
1 pound mushrooms, thinly
    sliced
1 cup butter
½ pound onions, grated

2 garlic cloves, crushed
Pinch of ground nutmeg
1 bunch of parsley, finely
    chopped
Pepper to taste
1 tablespoon flour
1 tablespoon tomato purée

Season the fish with salt and set aside.

Sauté the mushrooms in half of the butter, together with the onions, garlic, nutmeg, parsley, salt, pepper, flour, and tomato purée. Stuff the carp's belly cavity with this mixture and sew up the opening.

Place the fish in a greased baking pan and top with the remaining butter, cut into pats. Pour 2 or 3 tablespoons of water over the fish and bake in a moderate oven for 1 hour. Baste fish occasionally with its own juices.

When done, arrange the fish on a serving dish and remove the string used to sew up the stuffed cavity. Pour the pan juices over the fish and serve hot.

Carp in Aspic
(*Pontykocsonya*)

Jewish families serve the carp in aspic as an entrée at family celebrations during the summer or on the Sabbath.

4 pounds various whole small freshwater fishes, cleaned
Sugar to taste
1 (4-pound) whole carp, cleaned, washed, dried carefully, and cut into thick slices (head and tail reserved)

Salt to taste
2 onions, sliced
1 carrot, sliced
1 celery root, sliced
1 parsnip, sliced
Pepper to taste

In a pot, simmer the small fishes in lightly sugared water to cover for 2 hours. Strain the fishes through a sieve, kind of gently pressing them through, and reserve this liquid.

Make a strong fish broth from the reserved head and tail and water to cover. Add to cooking liquid from small fishes.

Season the carp with salt. Set it aside.

Simmer the onions, carrot, celery root, and parsnip in the reserved cooking liquid. When the vegetables are half done, add the carp slices and the salty juice from the fish.

Continue to simmer over low heat, without covering the pot, for about 60 to 90 minutes, or until the liquid becomes sticky and jellylike. Season with salt, if necessary, and pepper.

Remove the pot from heat and let fish cool in the liquid. When it is cold, carefully lift out the fish slices and arrange them in a deep serving dish. Garnish with the vegetables. Strain the liquid over the fish, then refrigerate until it sets. Serve.

Carp in Sour Cream and Paprika Sauce
(*Paprikás ponty, tejfölösen*)

Salt to taste
2 pounds whole carp, cleaned, washed, dried carefully, and cut into ¾-inch slices
1 or 2 leeks (white part only), finely chopped
1 teaspoon lard
1 green pepper, seeded, deribbed, and cut into thin strips
1 red pepper, seeded, deribbed, and cut into thin strips

1 yellow pepper, seeded, deribbed, and cut into thin strips
1 tablespoon paprika
1 teaspoon tomato purée or 1 ripe tomato, peeled and seeded
1 cup dry white wine or Champagne
½ cup strong fish broth
½ cup sour cream mixed with ½ cup heavy cream

Salt the fish and let it stand for 1 hour.

In a pot, sauté the leeks in lard until glossy. Then add the peppers and sauté them together for 1 or 2 minutes. Remove the pot from heat and let cool a little.

Add the paprika, tomato purée, wine, and fish broth. Bring to a slow boil and add the fish.

Return to heat, cover, and simmer slowly until fish is cooked. When tender, pour on the sour cream mixture and heat again. Serve.

NOTE: Leeks have a more subtle taste than onions and are better suited to the light-tasting fish.

Other white-fleshed, meaty fish such as striped bass or red snapper may be substituted for carp.

Fried Trout in Garlic Sauce
(*Sült Pisztráng fokhagymamártással or Peşte cu Mujdei*)

**3 (1¾-pound) whole trout,
    cleaned, boned, and cut in half**
1 lemon, halved
Salt and pepper to taste
1 cup flour

1 cup oil
1 garlic clove, ground in a mortar
Tarragon vinegar to taste
½ onion, grated

Rub the fish pieces with the lemon halves, season them with salt, and let them stand for 1 hour. Sprinkle with a little pepper.

Heat the oil in a skillet until hot. Dip the fish pieces in the flour and fry them on both sides in the hot oil until done. Drain on paper towel.

Meanwhile, in a bowl, combine the garlic with a little tarragon vinegar, onion, and salt. Serve this sauce with the trout.

NOTE: Garnish with boiled unpeeled new potatoes.

Other white, nonfatty freshwater fishes, such as pike, perch-pike, and largemouth bass, can be substituted for the trout.

Trout with Parsley Sauce
(*Vajas Pisztráng*)

5 (1-pound) whole trout, cleaned
½ cup vinegar
Salt and peppercorns to taste
2 bay leaves
½ lemon, sliced

1 bunch of parsley
2 tablespoons butter
1 teaspoon finely chopped
parsley

Soak the trout briefly in the vinegar. Bring a pot of water seasoned with salt, peppercorns, bay leaves, lemon slices, and the bunch of parsley to a boil. Simmer the fish in this liquid.

When done, heat the butter in a saucepan. Sprinkle with finely chopped parsley. Place the fish on a platter and pour the butter sauce over it. Serve.

VARIATIONS

Salt the trout lightly and place it in a pan in a moderate oven (without the herbs and spices above). Baste with melted butter. When half done, douse with sour cream and white wine and bake until done.

Trout Baked on Stones (Kövönsült Pisztráng): It is prepared over an outdoor fire and is especially delicious. Cut the fish in half but do not salt them. Wash some large flat stones, lay them on top of each other, and set a fire above them. In a small pan, boil ½ cup water with 3 ounces diced smoked bacon and 1 teaspoon paprika. Set aside. When the stones are very hot, remove the embers. Sweep the ashes off the stones. Place the fish pieces on the stones and bake them on both sides. (The pieces may be rubbed with some smoked bacon before cooking.) When done, dip the pieces in the bacon-paprika mixture before eating.

NOTE: Other freshwater fish may be used instead of trout.

Eels with Cabbage
(Csikos Káposzta)

The flavoring of ginger and combination of ingredients in this unusual dish reflect its Chinese origin. It is a variation of a well-known Chinese dish called spring or autumn rolls, in which the cabbage and fish mixture is served rolled in *crêpes* and fried.

In the month of the lion's sun the eels are fat
It is lucky to catch them on the fifteenth day
Have ready an onion's bronze sphere
Chopped with bacon and fried until
It shines like marble under a pool
Now cook shredded pickled cabbage with the onions
When tender thicken and sprinkle ginger
As a river lays up piebald sand
The cleaned eels must first be boiled
For the same reason house screens are opened after rain
They are next to be fried in the hour of red
The cabbage is added and cooked slowly together
As the Ruler's cavalry wheels and crosses on parade
Eels are presented quite hot
Steaming in their bowl as mist above a mountain lake.

½ **pound meaty bacon, julienned**
1 large onion, finely chopped
1 pound fresh cabbage, finely
   shredded
½ **cup oil or rendered lard**
1 teaspoon flour
½ **cup white wine**

1 teaspoon grated ginger
2 pounds eels, cleaned, heads and
   fins removed, skinned (by
   boiling in salted water for 5
   minutes), and cut in 1½-inch
   pieces
Salt and pepper to taste

In a skillet, on medium heat, sauté the bacon. When it has rendered some fat, add the onion and continue cooking until it is glossy.

Prepare a light brown *roux* with 1 tablespoon of the oil and the flour. Thin the *roux* with wine, whisking constantly until the mixture is smooth and thick. Add to cabbage. Season with ginger and mix well.

Combine eels with the sautéed cabbage and place in a casserole. Season with salt and pepper. Cover and bake in a moderate oven for 30 minutes.

Add the cabbage and sauté, stirring constantly. Cook until cabbage is tender and light golden.

Heat the remaining oil in a skillet and sauté the eels until they are rosy, turning them occasionally.

Saxon Wels in White Wine
(*Tűzdelt Harcsa Szász Módra*)

6 to 8 small wels (1 to 1½ pounds each), cleaned, skinned, and sliced
11 ounces sliced smoked bacon
Salt to taste

2 onions, sliced
1 pound tomatoes, sliced
Pepper to taste
2 cups dry white wine
Finely chopped parsley to taste

Rub the slices of the wels with the bacon. Salt them and let stand.

Line the bottom of a baking dish with the sliced bacon. Arrange the fish, onions, and tomatoes on top of the bacon. Season with pepper and place in a hot oven.

Baste the fish with its drippings and the wine from time to time. When done, place the fish on a platter and sprinkle with parsley. Serve with its own juices.

Transylvanian Fish Soup
(Székely Halleves)

2 onions, coarsely chopped
2 tablespoons rendered lard or oil
1 teaspoon peppercorns
2 tomatoes, cut in half
2 green peppers, coarsely
  chopped
3 parsnips, coarsely chopped
1 celery root, coarsely chopped
2 carrots, coarsely chopped
3 sprigs of basil

4 pounds of various small
  freshwater fishes and fish
  heads, cleaned
Salt to taste
1 teaspoon saffron
2 pounds diced potatoes or 1
  pound noodles (see Note)
2 pounds whole carp or pike,
  filleted
Finely chopped parsley

In a pot brown the onions in fat, then add peppercorns. Dilute with 2 quarts water. Bring to a boil and add the tomatoes, green peppers, parsnips, celery root, carrots, basil, and small fish and fish heads.

Cover, bring to a boil, and simmer for 1 hour without stirring, but rotate and shake the pot often.

Let the soup settle and then strain the liquid into another pot, discarding all solid ingredients. Season it and add the saffron.

Bring soup to a quick boil, then add potatoes or noodles and parsley. Bring to a boil again and cook until half done, then add fish fillets. Simmer until the fish and potatoes or noodles are tender.

NOTE: Noodles may be substituted for the potatoes. If fresh noodles are used, add them at the same time as the fish fillets. The potatoes should be cut into small enough pieces so that they will be ready at the same time as the fish.

In Transylvania, this dish is prepared differently than in Hungary. The major difference is that the Transylvanians do not add paprika—probably the most important spice for the Hungarians.

Sabbatarian Fish Soup with Tarragon
(*Tárkonyos Hallé Szombatos Módra*)

2 pounds fish fillets (see Note)
Finely chopped tarragon and
   thyme to taste
2 quarts boiling vegetable broth
1 cup green peas
1 parsnip, shredded
1 carrot, shredded
1 celery root, shredded

1 onion, finely chopped
½ cup butter
2 tablespoons flour
1 to 1½ cups sour cream
Tarragon vinegar to taste
3 egg yolks
Salt and pepper to taste

Add the fish, tarragon, and thyme to the pot of boiling vegetable broth. Simmer until fish is half done. Add the peas, parsnip, carrot, celery root, and onion.

Prepare a light *roux* with the butter and flour. Add the *roux* to the soup and whisk constantly until it is smooth and thick. Then stir in the sour cream and tarragon vinegar.

Cook until heated through. Remove the pot from heat. Beat the yolks together with a little of the hot soup, then add to the pot of soup. Season to taste and serve.

NOTE: Carp, pike, young sturgeon, or perch may be used. This soup may also be prepared as a one-plate dish with the addition of noodles or dumplings, which could be made of potatoes or matzo meal.

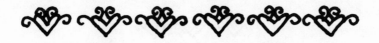

MAIN COURSES

POULTRY DISHES

Rumanian Roast Garlic Chicken
(Pui cu Usturoi or Fokhagymás Csirke)

1 large chicken (about 4 pounds),
   cut into serving pieces
1 tablespoon rendered lard or 2
   tablespoons oil
5 garlic cloves, finely chopped

1 tablespoon flour
Salt to taste
2 tablespoons sour cream
Cornmeal mush (page 30)

Roast the chicken pieces in a moderate oven, in a roasting pan with lard, until tender inside. When done, remove meat from pan and keep warm. Drain the drippings into a saucepan.

Sauté garlic in the chicken drippings until light golden, but do not let the garlic brown. Mix flour with some water until smooth and pour over the garlic. Season with salt, then add the chicken.

Simmer chicken a few minutes, then
sprinkle with sour cream. Let it
simmer again, and serve chicken with
cornmeal mush.

NOTE: Garlic is so popular with the Rumanians in Transylvania that a garlic sauce, called *mujdei,* is offered in restaurants as an accompaniment to roast chicken or fish. However, it is justified to ask whether restaurants should offer that much garlic, or if the consumption of this wonderful and irreplaceable seasoning should remain everyone's private affair . . . To prepare this sauce, crush garlic cloves (to taste) in a wooden mortar, dilute with cold or hot salted water, and let stand for a few hours. If the meat or fish is lean, oil can be added to the sauce.

Chicken with Peas
(*Csirke Zöldborsóval or Pui cu Mazăre Verde*)

2 or 3 tablespoons rendered lard
1 medium chicken (about 3
   pounds), cut into serving
   pieces
1 onion, chopped
2 pounds shelled peas

Salt and pepper to taste
Chopped parsley to taste
1 cup chicken broth
1 tablespoon flour
½ cup milk
2 tablespoons sour cream

Heat the lard in a large frying pan, and sear the chicken pieces on all sides. When done, remove from pan and set them on a plate.

In the same fat, sauté the chopped onion until glossy. Add the peas, then return the chicken to the pan. Season with salt and pepper and sprinkle with chopped parsley.

Add chicken broth, cover, and simmer over medium heat. When meat and peas are nearly done and tender, reduce heat to very low and continue simmering.

In a small bowl, mix flour with milk and 2 spoonfuls of the pan juices. Stir the mixture into the pan juices to thicken them. Continue cooking for 2 to 3 minutes, whisking the sauce constantly to make it smooth. Stir in the sour cream, then serve.

NOTE: Some cooks add a pinch of sugar when cooking the chicken and peas.

Chicken with Kohlrabies
(*Pui cu Gulii or Csirke Karalábéval*)

2 pounds kohlrabies, peeled and
   diced
4 to 5 tablespoons rendered lard
Salt and pepper to taste
10 sprigs of dill, chopped
1 medium chicken (about 3
   pounds), cut into serving
   pieces

1 tablespoon flour
1 teaspoon paprika
½ cup chicken broth
3 or 4 garlic cloves, crushed
2 tablespoons sour cream

Sauté the kohlrabies in 3 tablespoons of lard in a large skillet. When tender, season them and sprinkle with half the chopped dill. Remove them from the skillet and set aside.

Make a golden *roux* with 1 tablespoon of the fat and the flour. Add paprika and chicken broth while whisking constantly, to make a sauce. Add the kohlrabies, chicken, garlic, and salt and pepper.

In the same skillet, brown the chicken pieces in the lard remaining in the pan, adding more if necessary. Drain, and place the chicken on a plate.

Simmer over moderate heat for a short while. Before serving, gently stir in the sour cream and heat through. Sprinkle with the remaining chopped dill.

Sliced Hen with Ginger
(*Tyúkvetrece*)

6 whole chicken breasts, boned
Ground ginger and marjoram to
    taste
½ pound onions, chopped
1½ cups oil

½ pound carrots, peeled and
    sliced
Salt and pepper to taste
1 cup dry white wine
Tarragon vinegar to taste

Rub the chicken breasts with marjoram and ginger, then slice them thinly.

Heat oil in a frying pan, and sauté the onions until glossy. Add the carrots and brown them slightly. Add the sliced chicken and sauté until the pan juices are reduced by half.

Meanwhile, season with salt and
pepper and more ginger. Add white
wine and continue simmering until
chicken is tender. Season with
tarragon vinegar to enhance the
piquant flavor. Serve.

Chicken with Tarragon
(*Tárkonyos Csirke*)

Poor bedraggled taunted bird
in the fowls! pedigree a distant third
Not even addressing or assessing
The princely partridge or courtly quail
Or lordly pheasant of the imperious tail

Happy is the story of that royal seasoning
Tarragon, who rescued from kitchen unreasoning
Chicken from boiling or tasteless broiling
Sweeping into his strong fragrant embrace
The honest farmyard humility of her race

Frying in the fat of that snooty goose
Staunch servant onion, chopped quite loose
Parsnip and pepper diced, carrots sliced
To aid the sautéing of our heroine
"Till her pieces have a skin of brown crinoline"
Socialite sybarite observant white wine

Slowly clothes the bird with a simmering shine
The hero detained now thickly rains
With attendance of his pages pepper and salt
The chicken's softening brings fire to a halt

Into her bath with unctuous benediction
Pure clean sour cream mixes sans friction
Heated and strained, garnish entrained
The birds debuts before a slightly shocked crowd
Filling the room with nuptial perfume
And greeted by perennial lips' smacking loud.

1 tablespoon goose fat
1 onion, grated
1 carrot, sliced
1 parsnip, diced
1 green pepper, diced
1 large chicken, cut into serving
   pieces

½ cup dry white wine
5 fresh sprigs of tarragon,
   chopped, or 1 tablespoon dried
Salt and pepper to taste
½ cup sour cream

Heat the goose fat in a large frying pan and sauté the onion until it turns golden. Add the carrot, parsnip, and pepper.

Before the vegetables are half cooked, add the chicken and continue sautéing.

Add the white wine gradually, then add the tarragon and season with salt and pepper. Simmer, covered, until chicken is tender.

Remove the chicken pieces and mix sour cream slowly into the liquid, stirring constantly. When heated through, strain the sauce over the chicken, saving the vegetables. Garnish the platter with the cooked vegetables.

Poultry with Prunes
(*Mîncare de Pasăre cu Prune or Majorsághús Szilvával*)

40 to 50 pitted prunes
1 cup chicken broth
1 cup butter
1 large chicken, game hen, or
   duck, cut into serving pieces

Salt to taste
1 onion, chopped
1 or 2 tablespoons honey

Soak the prunes in broth for 1 hour to
soften; drain, and reserve the broth.
Sauté the prunes in about ¼ cup of
the butter. Set aside.

In a large frying pan, braise the
chicken pieces over low heat, covered
in ½ cup of the butter. Add salt. When
tender, remove chicken from pan and
place on a plate. Keep warm.

In the same pan, sauté the onion until
glossy in the remaining butter. Pass
the onion through a sieve, along with
the pan juices. Set onion sauce aside.

Return chicken pieces to pan. Add the
prunes and season with salt. Add the
onion sauce and enough broth to
cover. Then simmer over low heat
until it is heated through.

Heat the honey, browning it slightly.
Dilute it with 2 to 3 tablespoons of
water. Stir into sauce before serving.

Menta Piperita by Joseph Domjan

Roast Goose
(*Egész Liba Sütve*)

2½ tablespoons salt
½ tablespoon ground pepper
Pinch of marjoram
1 (8- to 10-pound) goose, washed
and dried

Stuffing (optional)
1 tablespoon rendered lard
(goose lard if possible) or
butter
1 cup boiling water

Mix 1½ tablespoons of the salt, half
the ground pepper, and the marjoram.
Rub the inside cavity of the goose with
these spices.

Stuff the goose with the appropriate
stuffing and sew up the opening.

Rub the goose with remaining salt and
pepper. Tuck the neck skin
underneath the bird and secure it
with a small skewer.

With the goose breast side up, turn
back the wings, place on bottom of
goose, and truss; truss the drumsticks
together. Prick the skin of the goose
all over with a fork and place it on a
rack in a roasting pan.

Spread the lard over the breast, pour
boiling water into the pan, and roast
the goose in a moderate oven,
allowing 20 to 25 minutes cooking
time per pound.

Baste frequently and turn the goose
on a different side from time to time
so that it can become light brown all
over. Remove the string and skewers
and transfer the goose to a large
serving platter.

Stuffed Goose Neck
(*Töltött Libanyak*)

1 pound goose meat, chopped
½ pound pork shoulder, chopped
1 roll, soaked in ½ cup milk and
    drained
6 tablespoons rendered lard
1 garlic clove
Small bunch of parsley, finely
    chopped
1 teaspoon salt
Pinch of ground pepper
Pinch of marjoram
1 raw egg

3 hard-boiled eggs, diced
3 goose necks (about 2½ pounds
    total), rinsed several times in
    cold water
½ cup finely chopped onions
1 carrot, peeled and sliced
1 parsnip, peeled and sliced
½ celery root, peeled and sliced
½ cup wine
3½ ounces tomato purée
1 teaspoon flour

Pass the goose meat, pork, and roll through a grinder twice and place in a large bowl.

In a small frying pan, heat 2 tablespoons lard and sauté the garlic until golden, then remove. Add the parsley. Combine with the ground meat mixture.

Season with salt, pepper, and marjoram. Add the raw egg and mix well. Then mix in the diced hard-boiled eggs.

Fill the 3 necks with this stuffing, then sew the ends with string. Do not stuff them too fully, or the skins will burst while roasting. Season them with salt.

Melt the remaining lard in a large frying pan and add the necks. Fry the necks, turning them over occasionally, until well browned.

Pour the fat from the pan into a baking dish and sauté onions and vegetables. Transfer the browned necks to this dish and cover.

Place dish in moderate oven and let necks stew until soft, occasionally pouring on a small quantity of water. Baste and turn frequently.

When done, lift the necks out of the pan and add the wine. Reduce the pan drippings by half (on top of stove), stir in the tomato purée, and continue heating.

Sprinkle in the flour and cook a minute longer, whisking the gravy constantly to prevent lumps. Pour in enough water to produce a succulent but not too thick gravy, and continue to stir until it is smooth and thick. Boil the gravy well, then strain through a sieve.

Before serving, remove string with which the necks were tied. Slice the necks, pour gravy over them, and serve.

Goose Cracklings
(*Libatöpörtyű*)

Skin and fat of 1 goose
¼ cup milk

1 garlic clove (optional)
Whole peppercorns (optional)

Cut off most of the fat from the skin, keeping some of it on; also leave a little bit of the meat on the inside. Score the inside, without cutting through to the outside, so that the skin remains intact. Cut the skin into 1-inch squares.

Put the fat and skin in a pot and pour in the milk and enough water to barely cover the ingredients. Add the garlic and peppercorns. Begin cooking over a medium heat.

When the water evaporates, increase the heat to render the fat and brown the cracklings. Turn the pieces and do not allow them to burn. They are done when they are golden brown.

Remove the pot from the heat and sprinkle the cracklings with a few drops of cold water. Take out the cracklings; if they are still too greasy, press them lightly with a spoon to remove the excess fat.

Save the rendered goose fat left in the pot for cooking other dishes.

NOTE: Rendered goose fat, the treasure of a Transylvanian household, is made lighter, silkier, and whiter by the addition of milk.

In some regions 1 to 2 garlic cloves and a few whole peppercorns are added for flavoring.

LAMB AND GOAT

Ferenczy's Grilled Lamb Flekken
(Bárányflekken Ferenczy Módra)

Every spring the owner of the well-known Ferenczy restaurant (later called the Fényes Restaurant) at Székelyudvarhely, a marvelously provincial Sekler town, prepared the tasty barbecued lamb medallions called *flekken* in this manner. When he gave up the restaurant, he continued to prepare this dish for his good friends with the old consummate skill. Many Transylvanian-Hungarian writers and artists fondly and enthusiastically recall the delicious tastes and the unforgettable feasts at Ferenczy's, which were accompanied by the best wines the region could offer.

Salt, pepper, and paprika to taste	**1 baby lamb, cleaned, boned,**
Bread	**membranes removed, and meat**
Slab bacon	**cut into 4- or 5-inch square or**
	round pieces

Place a large wooden board or platter in the middle of a set table around which the guests are seated. Have salt, pepper, paprika, and plenty of bread handy.

Heat a cast-iron baking sheet or large skillet on top of the stove until almost glowing hot. Rub the grill with bacon. Place the lamb slices on the skillet and sear them until crisp. When a thin red crust appears, turn slices over.

When the other side is also rosy crisp, remove the *flekken* from the pan, place on the wooden board, and cut into bite-size pieces with a very sharp knife.

Serve hot and allow guests to season the meat according to taste. Do not let the meat cool off, or the lamb will lose its flavor.

NOTE: For seasonings it was also customary to use mustard, ground ginger, or dried, crumbled herbs besides the obligatory salt, paprika, and pepper.

Braised Leg of Lamb
(*Berbécscomb Párolva*)

**1 leg of young lamb, boned and
    membranes removed**
Marjoram to taste
10 sprigs of parsley, chopped
1 tablespoon chopped chives

Coarsely ground pepper to taste
Thyme to taste
½ onion, grated
2 or 3 hard-boiled eggs, chopped

Rub meat with marjoram and place in a pot. Add parsley, chives, pepper, and 1 cup water. Cover and braise in a moderately hot oven 3 to 4 hours, or until meat is tender, adding more water as necessary.

When meat is done, remove from pot. Strain sauce, and mix in thyme, onion, and hard-boiled eggs. Bring to a boil. Return meat to the sauce, and continue to simmer for about 10 more minutes.

Lamb with Eggs
(*Tojásos Bárány*)

2 onions, chopped
4 tablespoons rendered lard
4 pounds lamb's forequarter (front leg, shoulder, and neck), cut into 1- to 2-inch-square pieces

15 sprigs of parsley, chopped
Pepper to taste
8 eggs, beaten
3 sprigs of fresh mint, finely chopped
Salt to taste

In one or two large frying pans, cook the onions in the lard until glossy, but do not brown them. Add meat and sauté, occasionally adding a spoonful of water as the natural juices evaporate.

When the meat is tender, allow some of the juices to evaporate, taking care that a generous amount of fat remains. Sprinkle with chopped parsley and some pepper.

Mix eggs with finely chopped mint. Pour over the meat, stirring constantly, as you do when preparing scrambled eggs. Season with salt and pepper.

VARIATIONS
To make a richer dish, sliced mushrooms may be added. Sauté them lightly in butter and scatter them on top of the meat after scrambling the eggs.

Stuffed Breast of Lamb
(*Töltött Bárány*)

1 lamb's breast, trimmed of fat
Chopped fresh mint or dried mint
   to taste
2½ cups milk
2 rolls
1 lamb's brain, cleaned, soaked,
   blanched, and diced

1 onion, grated
2 tablespoons oil
2 eggs, beaten
Salt and pepper
Chopped parsley to taste
2 or 3 tablespoons rendered lard
1 cup dry white wine or water

Rub the lamb's breast with mint. A few hours before cooking, soak the breast in 2 cups of milk, then drain and pat dry. Lift the upper skin to make room for the stuffing.

In a frying pan, cook onion in oil until wilted, then remove from heat. Add the roll and brain mixture, eggs, salt and pepper, more finely chopped mint, and parsley. Mix well.

Prepare the stuffing: soak the rolls in the remaining milk, squeeze out the excess milk, and crumble them. Add them to the lamb's brain.

Stuff the meat with this mixture and sew up the opening. Place in baking pan with the lard in a moderately hot oven and braise, adding wine or water as needed. Baste frequently with its drippings during roasting. Cook until tender, then increase heat and roast until reddish brown on the outside.

Braised Mutton with Marjoram
(*Birkasült Majorannás Mártással*)

2 pounds mutton (from the leg),
    membranes and suet removed
    and sliced into 2- to 3-inch
    pieces, about 1 inch thick
Salt to taste
1 small onion, finely chopped
1 carrot, peeled and finely diced
1 parsnip, peeled and finely diced
2 tablespoons rendered lard
1 tablespoon flour
¼ cup beef broth or water
Pepper and marjoram to taste
4 or 5 large potatoes, boiled

Pour hot water over the mutton to blanch it. Wash again in cold water several times. Drain, pat dry, and then salt the meat.

Place meat in a pan with the vegetables. Cover and braise in its own fat until tender. Remove meat from pan and strain the pan juices.

Prepare a brown *roux* with the lard, strained pan juices, and flour. Add the broth and cook, whisking constantly, until smooth and thick.

Adjust salt if necessary and season with pepper and marjoram. After 2 or 3 minutes put meat in pan again and cook in the sauce until heated through. Garnish with plain boiled potatoes.

Mutton Stew from Bözödujfalu
(*Bözödujfalusi Birkapörkölt*)

Salt to taste
2 pounds mutton or lamb (from the leg), suet and membranes removed, and chopped into 1-inch pieces
2 onions, finely chopped
2 or 3 tablespoons rendered lard
Pepper to taste

3 tablespoons tomato sauce
1 cup rice
2 cups light lamb or beef broth or water
½ pound mushrooms, sliced
Marjoram to taste
1 cup sour cream

Pour boiling salted water over the meat to blanch it. Drain, and pat dry. Sauté the onions in the lard until golden yellow. Then add pepper, and the mutton.

Cover and simmer, adding a tablespoon of tomato sauce from time to time. When half cooked, add the rice and broth. Steam for 10 minutes, then add mushrooms and marjoram.

Simmer until meat is done. Stir in sour cream and heat it through before serving.

NOTE: Bözödujfalu is a little Sekler village where the inhabitants are known for being stubborn and excessively old-fashioned. They've always favored mutton over spring lamb.

Jamez or Armenian Stuffed Leg of Kid
(*Töltött Gödölye Comb*)

Jamez is one of the best-known and favorite roast meat dishes of the Transylvanian Armenians.

1 kid's liver, washed and dried with a towel, and finely chopped
1 kid's leg, washed and dried with a towel
1 quart milk
4 onions, coarsely chopped

½ pound smoked bacon, diced
Salt, pepper, paprika, marjoram, peppermint, and crushed garlic to taste
3 tablespoons rendered lard, melted

Soak the liver and leg in milk for ½ hour. Drain, and pat dry. Cut an opening in the leg for the stuffing, and separate it when ready to stuff.

Prepare the stuffing: in a large frying pan, sauté onions with bacon until glossy. Add the liver and cook briefly.

Remove pan from heat and season with salt, pepper, paprika, marjoram, peppermint, and garlic. Stir and simmer for a few minutes longer.

Stuff the meat and sew up the opening. Roast it in a very hot oven, turning it over a couple of times. Reduce heat and baste frequently with melted lard. Roast until there is a red and crispy crust on the outside and the meat is tender. Slice and serve.

VARIATIONS

For a smaller number of servings use a kid's shank. Slice it and place some stuffing on each of the slices. Roll and secure with a wooden toothpick.

This dish may also be prepared with young lamb.

Buzsenyica or Smoked Goat's Leg and Pork Ribs
(*Füstölt Kecskesonka és Sertésborda*)

Buzsenyica was a famous Transylvanian-Armenian delicacy. Like *hütyü,* the blood sausage, it was prepared by Armenian women who sold them from tents in the country markets. Armenian families raised their own goats, as they were considered to be a precious staple. Nearly every part of the slaughtered goat was used for some purpose. The marinating of the meat for this dish was done in a birchwood vat or basin, hand-carved by artisans of great skill. István Petelei, a Transylvanian writer and storyteller, erected a literary memorial to the dish, calling it *zsbonyica* in his short story entitled "The Food." This version comes from a very old cookbook. It is recommended that the recipe be followed very closely and done by those who "know cooking."

Herb and Spice Mixture
(for every 10 quarts water)

1 pound salt
1 cup juniper berries
2 tablespoons coriander seeds
1 teaspoon allspice
1 teaspoon basil
1 tablespoon thyme
2 tablespoons chopped watercress
1 cup fine sugar
1 tablespoon saltpeter

Marinade
(for every 10 quarts water)

1 teaspoon peppercorns
1 teaspoon caraway seeds
1 teaspoon marjoram
4 garlic cloves, crushed
3 onions, sliced

1 pair goat legs (from a young but fat goat), cleaned
1 side of pork ribs
1 cup vinegar (for every 10 quarts of marinade)
Fresh or dried juniper berries

Prepare the herb and spice mixture:
Combine all ingredients except the sugar and saltpeter. Rub the meat with half these spices (reserve the other half) and all the sugar and saltpeter.

Prepare the marinade: Combine the peppercorns, caraway seeds, marjoram, garlic, and onions with 10 quarts water in a marinating basin (preferably of birchwood). Immerse the meat in the marinating basin and let soak in a cool place for 5 days. Turn the meat over every day.

At the end of 5 days, remove the meat and pour the marinade into a separate container (reserve it for later). Put the meat into the basin again, and pour in enough water to cover.

Remove meat again, measure the water, and pour it into a large pot. Using the remaining half of the herb and spice mixture, season according to the original formula, proportionate to the quantity of water. (For example, if you need only 5 quarts of water to cover the meat, then add only the remaining amount of the spice mixture. It is not necessary to add any more sugar or saltpeter.)

Add more peppercorns, caraway seeds, marjoram, garlic, and onions according to the quantity of liquid. Boil for 10 minutes.

Put the meat back in the birchwood basin and pour in the marinade. Turn the meat over once a day for 12 days. Then hang it and, using cold smoke, allow it to turn golden brown.

Chill, then mix with the reserved first marinade and add 1 cup vinegar for every 10 quarts liquid.

If possible, use young oak, beech, or blue beech cuttings and sawdust for smoking. Throw a handful of a mixture of dried or fresh juniper berries over the embers every day.

Serdán or Stuffed Goat
(*Töltött Kecske*)

Serdán, stuffed goat's stomach (or bladder), is one of the dishes the Armenians brought with them from their original homeland in the Caucasus; it is still very popular today.

½ pound veal (from the leg), diced
1½ pounds kid (from the legs), diced
½ cup goose cracklings (page 210), cut into small cubes
1 onion, chopped

½ cup rendered lard, melted
Salt, pepper, paprika, crushed garlic, and ground caraway seeds to taste
1 goat's stomach or bladder, washed thoroughly and cleaned.

Mix veal and kid meat with the cracklings. Set aside.

In a frying pan, sauté the chopped onion in half the lard until browned. Season with salt, pepper, paprika, garlic, and caraway seeds. Mix the seasoned onions together with the meats and stuff the goat's stomach or bladder with the mixture.

Sew up the opening to the stomach or skewer it closed. Place in a roasting pan in a hot oven and baste constantly with the remaining melted lard. Add a few spoonfuls of water occasionally, and roast until red. Slice and serve.

NOTE: Boned leg of lamb, suckling lamb, or kid may be stuffed in the same way if a goat's bladder or stomach is not available.

ROASTS AND OTHERS

Grilled Pork Medallions
(*Sertésflekken*)

**2 pounds boneless pork loin,
sliced and pounded about ⅓
inch thick**

**Salt, pepper, and paprika to taste
Juice of 2 grated onions
2 ounces slab bacon or some oil**

Sprinkle the meat slices with salt, pepper, and a little paprika, then lightly brush with the juice of the grated onions.

Flekken or medallions can have an expecially delicious taste if the seasoned slices are first matured or aged in a covered pan in a cool place for several hours. This allows the complementary flavors to penetrate the meat. This process will also make the grilled meat tender and give it the inimitable flavor and aroma.

Rub a hot charcoal grill with bacon or
brush with oil. Grill the meat on both
sides until brown. If the charcoal is
glowing, grilling time should take 4 or
5 minutes or less. During grilling do
not pierce the slices with a fork, or
the most valuable juices will be
wasted.

VARIATION

In Vásárhely and its environs, the meat is not pounded and it is prepared with onions.
Another difference is that the meat is basted with wine during grilling.

NOTES: Flekken, the tastiest Transylvanian grilled-barbecued meat, should be made
from the choice part of the pork. The flank or any other cut of pork may be used if
nothing else is available. These, too, can also be delicious if they are grilled over
charcoal.

Clean the grill thoroughly before grilling the meat; this prevents burned or rancid
material from adhering to the fresh meat. The hot grill should then be brushed with oil
or rubbed with a piece of bacon or bacon rind.

Garnish the meat with any type of salad, depending on the season. If the *flekken* is
not barbecued outdoors, but broiled in the kitchen, garnish it with potatoes.

Pork Shanks Saxon Style
(Kronstädter Schweinkaue)

2 pork shanks, split, washed,
  and dried
5 tablespoons rendered lard
2 medium onions, chopped
Dash of caraway seeds
1 garlic clove, crushed

2 pounds sauerkraut, drained
1 teaspoon paprika
1 tablespoon flour
1½ cups sour cream
1 tablespoon chopped fresh dill
Salt to taste

Preheat oven to moderately high.

Place the meat in an ovenproof skillet. Melt 3 tablespoons of the lard and pour it over the meat. Put the pork in the oven and bake for 20 minutes, until golden brown outside but still raw inside. Remove meat from the skillet.

Add remaining lard to skillet and place on low heat on top of stove. Brown half of the chopped onions in it. Add the caraway seeds, garlic, and 1 cup of water.

Return meat to the skillet and place it in the oven at a reduced (low) temperature. Cover and bake for 40 minutes. Baste the shanks several times with the drippings. When the water evaporates, add more.

Sauté the remaining onions and the paprika with fat taken from the skillet. Meanwhile, cook the sauerkraut in a little water until tender. Add the onions and paprika.

Combine the flour, sour cream, and chopped dill. Stir this mixture into the sauerkraut. Cook over low heat for an additional 5 to 10 minutes.

When the meat is tender, remove it from oven and cut into serving-size pieces. Season with salt.

Arrange the sauerkraut on the bottom of an oval ovenproof serving casserole, and place the sliced meat on top of it.

Cover the casserole and place in a low oven for another 5 minutes (or until it is heated through) before serving. Serve hot.

Stuffed Flank of Pork
(Töltött Sertésdagadó)

2 pounds pork flank, boned

Stuffing
2 rolls
½ cup milk
½ pound pork liver
¼ pound smoked bacon

1 cup rendered lard
1 small onion, chopped
Dash of pepper
Pinch of marjoram
1 teaspoon paprika
2 eggs
Salt to taste

Preheat oven to moderate. With a sharp knife, make a large slit in the center of the side of the flank for the stuffing.

Prepare the stuffing: Soak the rolls in the milk. Press excess milk out and crumble rolls into small pieces. Pass the liver and bacon through the largest holes of a meat grinder, and add the ground mixture to the milk-soaked roll; set aside.

Heat half of the lard in a skillet and brown the chopped onion in it. Add the pepper and marjoram. Remove from heat and add the paprika. Mix well and add the eggs. Stir well until blended. Add the ground liver and bacon mixture and mix again. Season with salt.

Stuff the slit in the meat with this mixture and sew up the opening (or skewer it closed).

Heat the remaining lard. Place the stuffed meat in a skillet or roasting pan and pour the hot lard over it. Sprinkle the top with 2 tablespoons water. Cover the skillet and braise the meat in the preheated oven for 1½ to 2 hours, basting occasionally. If necessary, add more water.

For the last 10 minutes of baking, increase the heat and uncover the skillet to make the outside of the meat crisp. Slice meat before serving.

Variation

For a different stuffing, soak 2 rolls in milk. Press out the excess milk, crumble the rolls, and mix with 2 tablespoons rendered lard, ½ pound sliced sautéed mushrooms, 2 eggs, and finely chopped parsley, salt, and pepper to taste. In addition to this stuffing, place 2 hard-boiled eggs and 2 sausages inside the pocket in the meat. Sew up the opening in the meat (or skewer it closed) and proceed as above.

Rumanian Grilled Sausages
(Mititei)

10 large garlic cloves, finely chopped or crushed in a press

2 teaspoons baking powder

½ teaspoon ground cloves

2 teaspoons well-crumbled dried oregano

2 teaspoons freshly ground black pepper

2 tablespoons kosher salt

3 tablespoons sweet paprika

1 pound ground chuck

1 pound ground lamb

1 pound ground pork

Oil for grilling (optional)

Soak the garlic in ¼ cup lukewarm water. Stir in the baking powder, cloves, oregano, and pepper.

Add the salt and paprika to the ground meats. Pour in the garlic–water mixture, then add 1½ cups more water. Blend mixture so that it is firm but not too stiff. For maximum flavor, cover the meat and leave it in the refrigerator for several hours or overnight.

To shape sausages, wet hands and take a scant ½ cup of the meat mixture. Form it into a sausage about 4 inches long and 1 inch wide. Continue in this manner until all of the mixture is used up. The yield is about 25 sausages.

Cook on a hot grill or in a greased skillet until sausages are dark brown on all sides and no juice oozes out.

NOTE: These fresh sausages are formed by hand rather than stuffed in casings; then they are grilled. The meats need to be ground very well. If you have a meat grinder, put the meats through the grinder three times. If you are using a food processor, chop the meats in batches, using on and off pulses, until the ground meat is very smooth.

Serve the sausages with bread, mustard, and a mug of cold beer. A very popular Rumanian food, these are served as frankfurters here.

Homemade Pork Sausages
(*Házikolbász*)

On a passing, birth, or sudden guest-day
Mother makes a sausage for quick eating.
Chopping fatty pork, then soon she's away
To borrow neighbor's machine for grinding.
Blending in salt, paprika, pepper, cloves
She visits auntie's for missing allspice
On the way looking for garlic she roves,
Crushing it for juice to mix in a trice.
Soaking four rolls for kneading in stuffing
She will run across the street to cajole
Someone to give up their sausage casing;
Our cousins will have a machine to dole
Which stuffs in the casing the finished mix;
We twist the sausages each foot or so,
Tying the ends and hanging them from sticks.
If anyone in town away shall go
Sausage-making becomes a pretty fix.

4 pounds fatty pork shoulder
Salt and ground pepper to taste
1 tablespoon paprika
Pinch of ground cloves
Juice of 2 crushed garlic cloves

4 rolls
1 cup milk
Sausage casings, washed well
   three times

Cut up the pork into small pieces, then put it through the large holes of a meat grinder. Season with salt and pepper, paprika, cloves, and the garlic juice. Soak the rolls in milk, squeeze out the excess milk, and crumble. Add to the mixture and mix well together.

Stuff the sausage casings with this mixture, using a sausage stuffer to push in the mixture. Don't fill casings too tightly.

Twist the sausages every 8 to 12 inches. Tie the ends of the casings twice where twisted and cut the length of sausages in half. Wash the sausages in cold water, hang them in pairs, and dry them on a horizontal bar in a cool place for 1 or 2 days.

NOTE: Since fresh sausages (which are made with bread and milk) cannot be preserved for a long time, they should be prepared just shortly before consumption. Bake them in a moderately hot oven, in a greased pan, with the addition of 2 or 3 tablespoons water. When brown on the bottom, pierce with a fork, turn over, and brown the other side. If possible, the sausages should be baked directly before the meal.

Pork Sausages with Caraway Seeds
(*Köményes Kolbászkák*)

2 rolls
1 cup milk
3 pounds fatty pork flank, finely
   diced or very coarsely ground
Salt and pepper to taste
1 tablespoon paprika

1 teaspoon caraway seeds
1 garlic clove, crushed
Ground ginger to taste
2 onions, finely minced
1 pound pork suet

Soak the rolls in milk. Drain rolls and squeeze out excess milk. Season the pork with salt and pepper, paprika, caraway seeds, garlic, and ginger. Mix it together with the rolls and finely minced onions. Shape mixture into little finger-length sausages and wrap them in suet.

Grease a baking dish and arrange the sausages in it. Let rest for 1½ hours in a cool place.

Bake sausages in a hot oven until crispy, basting frequently with their juices and turning them over at least once. Serve them without gravy.

Ragout from Marosszék
(*Marosszéki Heránytokány*)

5 ounces smoked bacon, diced
1 medium onion, chopped
1 teaspoon paprika
1 pound stewing beef, cut into
**   2-inch-square pieces**
Pinch of caraway seeds
½ teaspoon chopped fresh
**   marjoram**

Salt and pepper to taste
1 cup dry white wine
1 pound lean pork shoulder, cut
**   into 2-inch pieces**
1 tablespoon rendered lard
½ pound mushrooms, sliced
½ cup sour cream
1 tablespoon flour

In a large skillet, render the bacon. Add chopped onion and sauté it over low heat for about 5 minutes, until wilted. Remove from heat.

As it cools, add paprika and ½ cup water. Place over heat again for a few minutes. Add beef, caraway seeds, marjoram, salt and pepper, and half the wine. Cover and cook about 20 minutes over low heat.

Add the pork and remaining wine. Cover and cook over very low heat until meat is nearly tender. If necessary, add a little more wine.

About 10 minutes before the meat is done, melt lard in a separate frying pan. Add the mushrooms, sauté for a few minutes, then add to the stew.

Just before serving, mix sour cream with flour and stir into the ragout. Keep warm over low heat, until everything is blended together and the sauce thickens. Serve hot.

NOTE: This meat dish is probably the joint creation of all the Transylvanian people. Some groups omit paprika and use more pepper; others add sliced pork kidney and heart to the mushrooms.

Roast Tenderloin with Grape Must
(Mustospecsenye)

3 pounds beef tenderloin
½ pound smoked sliced bacon
1 cup rendered lard or oil
1 tablespoon sugar
1 pound mixed soup greens, cleaned and chopped
1 large onion, chopped
¼ cup flour

1 cup tomato purée or 3 whole fresh tomatoes, peeled, seeded, and chopped
1 green pepper, chopped
2 cups fresh grape must
Salt and pepper to taste
Juice of 1 lemon

Bard the beef with the bacon. Grease a roasting pan with the lard or oil. Place the beef in the roasting pan, and roast it in a moderate oven until the outside turns reddish brown but the meat is not yet cooked through. Remove the meat from the pan and pour drippings into a saucepan.

Caramelize the sugar in the drippings until it turns yellow. Add the soup greens and onion. Sprinkle with flour and whisk constantly to prevent lumps.

Add the tomato purée, pepper, and half the must. Reduce the mixture, while whisking constantly, until it becomes a medium-thick sauce.

Place the partially roasted beef in the roasting pan and add the remaining must. Season with salt and pepper and add the lemon juice. Braise the beef in a moderate oven.

When the meat is completely tender, remove it from the pan. Add the drippings to the sauce and simmer until sauce becomes thick. Strain, then serve hot with the meat.

Veal Leg with Goose Liver
(Borjúcomb Vagdalt Libamájjal)

3 rolls
1 cup milk
1 pound veal leg, ground
1 onion, finely chopped
2 tablespoons rendered lard
1 whole egg
1 egg yolk
10 tablespoons butter

Salt and marjoram to taste
10 sprigs of parsley, chopped
2 tablespoons bread crumbs
1 large goose liver, cut in half
Ground pepper to taste
2 cups sour cream
1 pound mushrooms, sliced

Soak the rolls in milk, then squeeze out excess milk. Mince them together with the veal and place in a large bowl.

In a frying pan, sauté the finely chopped onion in the lard until golden yellow; mix it with the meat. Add the whole egg and the yolk and 4 tablespoons of the butter. Season with salt and marjoram and chopped parsley. Mix well by hand.

Sprinkle cutting board with bread crumbs, place the meat mixture on top, and divide into two large patties. Place half a goose liver in the center of each meat patty. Form into an oval shape, and put in a buttered baking pan. Sprinkle it generously with sour cream, pepper to taste, and some of the remaining butter, cut into pats.

Bake in a hot oven until done, about ½ hour, basting frequently with the drippings. In the meantime, sauté the sliced mushrooms in the remaining butter. Combine meat drippings and mushrooms. Serve this gravy separately.

Cholent from Szatmár
(Szatmári Csólent)

Cholent, a hearty dish made of beans, barley, and meat that is simmered for a long time, is traditionally prepared by the Jews for their Sabbath. If poultry is used, it is slaughtered on Thursday and then soaked in salted water. The dish is prepared Friday evening and left in the oven for 24 hours (because no fire can be lit on the Saturday Sabbath). A good oven should keep warm until the following day.

9 ounces small white beans (preferably navy), rinsed
1 pound fatty beef brisket, washed
3½ ounces pearl barley, rinsed

Salt, pepper, and paprika to taste
1 small onion, finely chopped
1 garlic clove, chopped
1 parsnip, sliced
1 carrot, sliced

The night before serving, put the beans, brisket, and barley in an earthenware or enameled casserole. Season with salt, pepper, and paprika, and add the onion, garlic, parsnip, and carrot.

Pour in enough water to cover ingredients. Cover pot and tie cloth through handles and over lid to make it airtight. Leave casserole in a very low oven until noon the next day. Serve warm.

VARIATIONS

Instead of brisket, goose meat or a fat hen may be used.

According to some recipes, a sliced or chopped hard-boiled egg is also added to the beans.

The Sabbatarians' Sholet
(A Szombatosok Sóletje)

The Sabbatarians use the Hungarian spelling and pronunciation for this dish, which they call *sholet;* the Orthodox Jews call it *cholent.*

One hears between friends who argue all day
Sitting with their coffee in a Budapest café:
Remember how in the old town they cook the beans?
It takes half a day, though meanwhile mother cleans;
Yes and all those old hands smell so sweet
Of onions fried in goose fat on low heat;
And then they add flour and a crushed garlic clove.
Well despite all that away we drove
You wait a day, you wait a day
Time to stay, always that way;
They add the beans into that kettle
And top them with water when they settle;
Beans have such flavor, even dazzle
Seasoned with pepper, tarragon, and basil.
No, the taste came from the addition, on top
Of smoked beef and goose legs, back, neck, and crop;
We've always demurred, don't say a word
The beans never stirred, yet flavors get merged.
While they cool for later eating
All that's needed is an hour's heating;
That beans could bake so long in quiet
Shows the honor accorded our diet!
Yes, and shows no thought to modify it;
Ah the village life, the village life
Everyone thinks alike and sleeps all night.

1 onion, finely chopped	**2 goose drumsticks**
2 tablespoons rendered goose fat	**1 goose hindquarter**
1 tablespoon flour	**1 pound smoked short ribs of**
1 garlic clove, crushed	**beef (*flanken*)**
2 pounds large dried white beans	**Salt, pepper, tarragon, and basil to**
1 stuffed goose neck (page 208)	**taste**

In a large ovenproof casserole cook the finely chopped onion in the goose fat until wilted. Reduce heat. Sprinkle with flour, whisk it constantly, and add the crushed garlic.

Mix in the beans and add enough water to cover by 3 inches. Add the stuffed goose neck, drumsticks, hindquarter, and smoked beef. Season with salt, pepper, tarragon, and basil.

Bring to a boil, then cover. Put in the oven and let simmer for 5 to 6 hours on very low heat. Shake the pot occasionally but do not stir the ingredients.

Serve the casserole the following day, but first reheat it in a low oven for 1 hour.

GAME AND GAME BIRDS

Marinated Hare
(Nyúl Borospácban)

Marinade
2 cups dry red wine
2 cups vinegar
Salt and pepper to taste
Peel of 1 lemon
2 bay leaves
1 onion, sliced
1 tablespoon juniper berries
1 carrot

Meat
3 pounds hare meat (saddle and
  two legs), blood drained,
  membranes removed, and
  washed and dried
Salt to taste
6 ounces sliced bacon, cut to thin
  slivers for barding
½ cup sour cream
Dash of dry mustard
1 tablespoon flour
6 lemon slices

Prepare the marinade: In a large
saucepan combine 1 quart water and
the wine, vinegar, salt and pepper,
lemon peel, bay leaves, onion, juniper
berries, and carrot. Bring to a boil.

Pour the hot liquid over the hare in a large pot. Cover and let soak for 2 to 3 days, turning occasionally. Remove the hare from the marinade (reserve the marinade); season with salt.

Bard the legs and saddle with the bacon and place on a rack in a roasting pan. Strain the marinade and pour in half of it. Bake in a moderate oven. Baste frequently with the marinade. When done, remove hare from pan and set aside.

Mix well together 2 tablespoons of sour cream, the mustard, and the flour. Pour mixture into the pan juices, stirring constantly. Bring to a boil on top of the stove and reduce amount by one third. Mix in remaining sour cream.

Decorate hare with lemon slices. Serve sauce separately.

Allium by Joseph Domjan

Saddle of Hare with Juniper
(Borókás Nyúlgerinc)

Thick brush smoke sailing over snowbound fields
Wind-tossed spruces turning up silver shields
Winter's bone-chilling winds brush past
Bringing the sound of a distant hunter's blast
It is not the cook's task to bewail the hare
Taking the saddle, skinned, free of hair
Give him a new coat of mottled brown bacon
And keep him baking when the bacon's done even
Though blizzards approach with cruel dark ice
There are crinkly onions to fry, smoked ham to slice
Bones brew to broth, saved from long-gone veal
To add pepper, garlic, vegetables, the hare's grease
And the dusky blue berries of winter's hard niece
Symbol of all things cold, barren, and wintry
Fruit of that white lady far from the pantry
So infused will the broth now mix with the ham
Reduced with white wine to the thickness of jam
The hare, sliced, arranged to true form
Perfumed with a spirit rising above the white storm
Juniper so piercing, beautiful, forlorn!

3 pounds saddle of hare, blood drained, membranes removed and washed and dried
10 thin slices smoked bacon
1 cup butter, melted
½ pound raw smoked ham, chopped
Butter

1 onion, chopped
1 cup vegetable or veal bone broth
1¾ ounces juniper berries, crushed
1 teaspoon peppercorns
1 cup white wine
Salt and pepper to taste

Rub the saddle with the bacon. Then wrap the saddle with the bacon slices and fasten with string. Bake in a roasting pan in a moderately hot oven, basting frequently.

When the bacon becomes golden yellow and glossy, remove and discard it. Continue to bake the meat, basting it with melted butter and its own drippings, until tender.

Remove from oven. Keep meat warm. Drain and reserve the drippings from the hare.

In a saucepan, sauté smoked ham in butter. Add the onion and continue to cook until onion is soft. Add the broth. Season with juniper berries and peppercorns; then add the drippings from the hare. Reduce the sauce by half. Skim off fat while reducing.

Remove the meat from the bones, slice it, then set it back on the bones again. Transfer the meat to a serving dish, cover, and keep warm.

Add the wine to the sauce. Bring to a boil and reduce the sauce by a third. Season with salt and pepper if necessary. Before serving, strain the sauce and stir in a teaspoon of butter to make it smoother.

NOTE: In Saxon and Rumanian kitchens garlic is also used to flavor the sauce.

Hare's Liver with Lemon
(*Citromos Nyúlmáj*)

2 cups hare's blood
2 teaspoons vinegar
Salt to taste
2 pounds hare's liver, cleaned,
    gallbladder removed, and sliced
Pepper to taste
¼ cup Cognac
1 cup olive oil
½ pound very meaty bacon, diced
1 cup butter

1 large onion, chopped
1 tablespoon flour
1 cup red wine
1 garlic clove
10 sprigs of parsley
1 bay leaf
2 sprigs of thyme
½ pound mushrooms, chopped
Juice of 1 lemon
Croutons made from 3 rolls

In a bowl, mix the hare's blood with vinegar and salt; set aside.

Season the liver with salt and pepper, and marinate in Cognac and olive oil for ½ hour.

Cook the bacon in boiling water for 10 minutes, then chill in cold water. Fry the bacon in half of the butter until it becomes light yellow. Remove from pan.

Sauté the onion in the same fat. Sprinkle the onion with flour. Mix well and continue sautéing.

Remove the liver slices from the marinade and add them to the onion. Reserve the marinade. Pour wine over liver and add enough water so that the liquid almost covers the liver. Add the garlic, parsley, bay leaf, thyme, and the marinade. Cook liver until it loses its red color or is tender. Take out bay leaf.

Meanwhile, in another pan sauté the mushrooms in the remaining butter, and add the fried bacon. When the liver is done, place it on a serving dish (save the pan juices) and top with the mushroom and bacon mixture.

Strain the pan juices from the liver through a fine sieve and into a saucepan. Add the blood and vinegar mixture and cook, stirring constantly, until reduced by half. Flavor with lemon juice to make the sauce more piquant. Pour the sauce over the liver and serve with croutons.

Peppered Roast Saddle of Venison
(*Szarvascímer Borsosan*)

1 onion, chopped
1 tablespoon rendered lard
1 saddle of venison, cleaned
2 carrots, finely chopped
2 parsnips, finely chopped
1 celery root, finely chopped

2 bay leaves
¼ teaspoon ground cloves
Salt and freshly ground pepper to taste
2 cups red wine

Brown onion in lard in a large pot. Add meat and sear it. Add ¼ cup water and the carrots, parsnips, celery root, bay leaves, cloves, and salt.

Then braise the meat (without a cover) over low heat, occasionally adding a little red wine. When meat is nearly tender, remove the bay leaves. Strain the sauce through a sieve, and flavor with pepper.

Pour the sauce and any remaining wine over the venison. Continue to simmer over low heat for another ½ hour.

NOTE: Sauté 10 ounces of shelled chestnuts in butter and season with salt and pepper. Use as a garnish for the venison.

Saxon Boar Leg
(*Wild Schweinschlegel*)

1 small boar leg or shoulder
Salt and pepper to taste
2 cups dry red wine
1 cup beef broth
1 teaspoon sugar
½ teaspoon ground cinnamon

1 cup butter
4 eggs
1 cup bread crumbs
Bread crusts
1 cup plus 2 tablespoons rose hip jam

Season the meat with salt and pepper. Place it in a baking pan and pour in 1 cup of wine and the broth. Cover pan and braise in a hot oven, basting occasionally, until done.

Combine the sugar with the cinnamon. Mix the butter with the eggs. Blend with the sugared cinnamon and the bread crumbs. Set the mixture aside.

When the meat is about ready and tender, pour off half of the pan juices and reserve.

Cover the meat with the butter–egg–bread crumb mixture. Soak the bread crusts in the remaining 1 cup of wine. Then cover the meat with them. Place in hot oven and finish roasting.

Strain the reserved pan juices through a sieve and into a saucepan; skim off the grease. Add the rose hip jam, and reduce until thick. Serve sauce separately from the boar leg.

VARIATION

Some recipes indicate that vegetables (chopped onions, carrots, and parsnips), bay leaves, and juniper berries are to be added to the braising liquid. These give additional flavor to the sauce, but should be discarded when straining the sauce.

NOTE: Saw off the leg above the joint. Skin the meat and wipe it with a wet cloth.

Braised Snipes
(Szalonka Párolva)

4 snipes, cleaned, washed, and
   dried
Salt and pepper to taste
1 apple, sliced
6 prunes, pitted
1 cup white wine
Pinch of ground ginger
Pinch of rosemary

Lemon juice
Flour for dusting
¼ pound sliced bacon
Lemon peel to taste
2 bay leaves
½ cup chicken broth
½ cup sour cream

Season the snipes with salt and pepper. Soak apple and prunes in wine
flavored with ginger and rosemary.
Drain. Stuff the snipes with this
mixture, sew up the cavity, and
sprinkle with a few drops of lemon
juice.

Dust the stuffed birds with flour. Place
them in a pan lined with bacon. Add
lemon peel and bay leaves, cover, and
braise in a moderate oven. During
cooking, pour broth and remaining
wine into the pan. Baste occasionally.

When snipes are tender, remove bay
leaves. Mix in sour cream and cook
for a few more minutes. Remove from
heat, place snipes on serving platter,
and strain sauce over birds.

Charcoal-Grilled Snipes
(*Nyársonsült Szalonka*)

4 snipes, cleaned (entrails and
    liver reserved) and washed and
    dried
Salt and pepper to taste
¼ pound sliced bacon
½ cup butter

1 onion, finely chopped
Chopped parsley to taste
¼ cup juniper berries
¼ cup pine nuts
Croutons made from 2 rolls

Season the birds with salt and pepper.
Cover the breasts with bacon slices
and fasten with toothpicks. Skewer
snipes on the spit. Grill over charcoal
for 10 to 15 minutes.

Meanwhile, chop the entrails and liver. Sauté in butter with onion, parsley, juniper berries, and pine nuts. Season with salt and pepper.

Spread the liver mixture on the croutons. Remove the bacon from the snipes, place them in the middle of a serving dish, and surround with the croutons.

Braised Fieldfares with Blueberries
(*Fenyőmadársült Kökénnyel*)

3 fieldfares, cleaned (entrails, livers, and gizzards reserved)
2 tablespoons butter
¼ cup chopped onion
Salt and pepper to taste
¼ pound sliced bacon

1 ounce Cognac
½ teaspoon juniper berries
2 cups chicken broth
2 tablespoons blueberries
½ cup white wine

Sauté the birds' entrails, livers, and gizzards lightly in a skillet with the butter and onion. Replace the gizzards and livers in the birds' stomach cavities and sew up the opening.

Season the birds with salt and pepper and cover them with bacon slices. Place them in the skillet containing butter and onions. Sauté for 15 minutes. Add Cognac and juniper berries.

Then cover the skillet and braise for
15 to 20 minutes. During cooking,
baste the fieldfares occasionally with
broth and pan juices. Cook sauce until
reduced by half. When done, strain
the sauce.

Cook the blueberries in the white
wine for 5 minutes and add to the
sauce. Serve sauce separately in a
bowl.

Pheasant with Sauerkraut
(*Fácán Savanyú Káposztával*)

3 pheasants, cleaned
½ pound sliced smoked bacon
1 large onion, chopped
1 cup rendered lard
2 pounds sauerkraut

2 cups fruity white wine
1 teaspoon caraway seeds
½ teaspoon ground ginger
Salt and pepper to taste

Wrap the pheasants in bacon and roast
on a spit or under a broiler until half
done, then remove them.

Meanwhile, in a large pot sauté the
onion in lard. Add the sauerkraut and
sauté until both are glossy.

Add wine, and season with caraway seeds and ginger. Cover and simmer until sauerkraut is tender. Add the pheasants and continue to simmer until birds are tender.

When the pheasants are done, remove them from the pot. Cut them up into serving pieces, and at the same time reduce the juices in pot by half. Season with salt and pepper to taste. Place the sauerkraut on a serving dish, arrange the pheasants on top, and serve.

Partridge in Grape Leaves on a Spit
(*Fogoly Nyárson*)

2 or 3 partridges, well cleaned
Salt and pepper to taste
6 sprigs of rosemary

2 to 3 pears, sliced
½ pound sliced smoked bacon
10 to 15 large grape leaves

Season the inside of the birds with salt and pepper. Stuff with rosemary and pear slices and sew up the opening. Wrap partridges with slices of bacon, and cover with large grape leaves; fasten together with skewers or string.

Skewer partridges on a spit and roast them over glowing coals for 20 to 25 minutes. When done, remove the grape leaves and bacon slices and serve.

Wild Duck in Sauce Suprême
(Vadkacsa Finommártással)

1 wild duck, cleaned and washed
   thoroughly
7 tablespoons butter
Salt and pepper to taste
1 cup beef broth
1 cup dry red wine, preferably
   Burgundy
1 tablespoon vinegar
1 whole onion, studded with
   cloves

A few bay leaves and sprigs of
   basil
½ cup bread crumbs
1 teaspoon flour
Dash of dry mustard
1 celery root, thinly sliced
1 turnip, thinly sliced
1 carrot, julienned
1 cup sour cream

Place the duck in a roasting pan with 2 tablespoons of butter. Season with salt and pepper. Sear the duck in a very hot oven. Remove from oven.

Pour the broth and wine over it. Season with vinegar and pepper and add the studded onion, bay leaves, and basil. Cover and simmer on top of stove until duck is tender. Remove the bay leaves and basil.

Melt remaining butter in a frying pan, and brown the bread crumbs and flour in it. Mix in a dash of mustard and add the vegetables. Sauté for a few minutes. Add the sour cream and cook until heated through.

Pour the sauce over the duck. Cook together for a few minutes. Remove the onion. Serve.

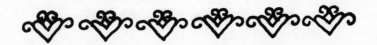

ACCOMPANIMENTS

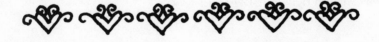

VEGETABLES IN THE OLD-FASHIONED WAY

Sabbatarian Artichokes
(Articsókafőzelék Szombatos módra)

Interestingly, artichokes are not grown in Transylvania, being a Mediterranean plant that needs a warmer climate, without frost. However, I discovered this recipe in the handwritten book by the wife of a Unitarian bishop whose ancestors were the house-keepers of the Count Teleky family of Szék. The Telekys traveled in Europe and brought back a few artichoke plants, which they cultivated in their hothouse. The family cookbook was written between 1840 and 1860.

3 to 4 young artichokes
Salt and tarragon vinegar to taste
1 tablespoon butter
½ teaspoon chopped parsley, or
  to taste

1 cup clear bone or vegetable
  broth
1 tablespoon flour
½ cup white wine
3 to 4 tablespoons sour cream
Pepper to taste

Remove the outer leaves and stem of the artichokes. Cut off the upper half from the artichokes and peel the bottoms. Scoop out the choke. Chop artichokes into small pieces and put in a pot of salted water. Season with tarragon vinegar, then parboil.

Remove artichokes from cooking liquid and drain well. Sauté artichokes in butter with chopped parsley, adding a little broth as needed. When tender, sprinkle with flour and add more broth. Heat the sauce until smooth and thick, stirring constantly.

Mix wine together with sour cream; add to artichokes. Cook gently until hot. Add salt and pepper to taste and serve.

Parsleyed Celery Root
(Zellerfőzelék)

1⅓ pounds celery root, peeled and grated or julienned
3 tablespoons sour cream

2 tablespoons butter
Salt, tarragon, and chopped parsley to taste

Mix the celery root with 2 tablespoons of the sour cream.

In a frying pan, sauté celery root in butter for 5 minutes. Season with salt, tarragon, and chopped parsley.

Top with remaining sour cream and let it heat through before serving.

Cabbage in Tarragon Sauce
(*Káposzta Főzelék Tárkonnyal*)

1¾ pounds cabbage, cored, outer
  leaves removed, and shredded
Salt to taste
2 tablespoons rendered goose fat
1 onion, finely chopped

2 tablespoons flour
Pepper to taste
Chopped tarragon or dill to taste
1 cup sour cream

Put the cabbage in a pot in a small amount of salted water. Cook until tender.

Heat goose fat in a small saucepan, add the finely chopped onion, and sauté only until onion wilts. Add flour to prepare a *roux,* stirring constantly until smooth and thick. Season with salt, if needed, and pepper.

Add ¼ cup of the liquid from the cabbage to the *roux,* whisking it constantly, and then thicken the cabbage with it. Add tarragon and boil for 10 minutes. Blend in sour cream. Let it heat through and serve hot.

Kohlrabi with Egg Barley
(*Karalábé Tarhonyával*)

5 ounces *tarhonya* (egg barley)
  (page 267)
2 tablespoons rendered goose fat
1 cup chicken broth or water
Salt to taste
1 onion, finely chopped

2 tablespoons butter
1 teaspoon chopped parsley
5 or 6 kohlrabies, peeled and
  diced
1½ cups sour cream
1 tablespoon bread crumbs

In a skillet, fry the *tarhonya* in some of the goose fat until it turns light brown. Add chicken broth, season with salt, and cook on low heat until done, adding more liquid if needed. Sauté onion in butter until glossy. Mix sautéed onion with the parsley and add to *tarhonya*. Set aside.

Boil the kohlrabies in a pot of salted water until tender and drain.

Arrange the ingredients in layers in a greased baking dish: first a layer of diced kohlrabies, then *tarhonya,* then sour cream. Repeat layering until all the ingredients are used.

Sprinkle bread crumbs and a little bit of goose fat on top. Bake in a moderate oven until done, or till bread crumbs become browned.

Lettuce in Butter Sauce
(Fejes Saláta Vajmártásban)

2 or 3 heads of lettuce, outer
   leaves removed and quartered
2 cups sour cream
2 tomatoes, sliced

Salt to taste
Pinch of basil
4 tablespoons butter
3 or 4 tablespoons bread crumbs

Blanch lettuce very quickly in boiling water, drain, then dry on a towel.

Generously grease the inside of a baking dish. Put in 4 tablespoons of sour cream and layer the lettuce, sliced tomatoes, and a sprinkling of salt and basil on top. Repeat layers until all ingredients are used.

Top dish with remaining sour cream and the butter, cut into several pats. Sprinkle with bread crumbs and bake in a moderately hot oven until the top is golden brown, but no longer than 10 minutes. Serve warm.

NOTE: It is best to use bibb or tight heads of Boston lettuce, but the heart or middle of romaine lettuce will also do excellently.

The cold sour cream and butter will melt in the oven, but they will keep the lettuce and tomatoes quite fresh.

Lentils with Tarragon Vinegar
(*Lencsefőzelék Tárkonyecettel*)

1 pound lentils
3 or 4 bay leaves
Salt to taste
1 whole onion, peeled
2 tablespoons grated onion

1 tablespoon rendered goose fat
1 teaspoon sugar
Dash of pepper
2 tablespoons flour
Tarragon vinegar to taste

Soak the lentils overnight in water to cover. The next day, drain and rinse them. Then put them in a pot with enough cold water to cover. Add bay leaves, salt, and the whole onion. Cover and simmer until tender. When done, discard the bay leaves and onion.

Sauté the grated onion until wilted in the goose fat with the sugar and a dash of pepper. Add flour and prepare a brown *roux*. Thin the *roux* slightly with some of the liquid from the lentils, whisking constantly.

Add the *roux* to the lentils and let it thicken the mixture. Season with tarragon vinegar, heat, and serve.

NOTE: The taste of this dish is enhanced when smoked goose meat or pork chops are cooked with the lentils.

Sabbatarian Beans
(*Szombatos Paszulyfőzelék*)

3 cups dried white beans
Salt to taste
1 carrot
2 or 3 tablespoons rendered
   goose fat
1½ tablespoons flour

1 onion, finely chopped
1 garlic clove, crushed
1 teaspoon chopped watercress
Tarragon vinegar to taste
1 cup sour cream

Soak the beans overnight in water to cover before cooking. Drain and rinse beans. Place beans in a pot and add enough water to cover them by 3 inches. Salt the water and add the carrot.

Make a golden *roux* with the goose fat and flour. Add the finely chopped onion and crushed garlic. Thin the *roux* with some cold water, whisking constantly, then thicken the beans with it.

Season beans with watercress and tarragon vinegar. Before serving, mix in sour cream and bring to a light boil.

NOTE: Smoked goose meat, when cooked with the beans, will add an exquisite flavor.

Layered Green Beans
(Zöldpaszuly lerakva)

1 pound green beans, cleaned and cut in half
1 small onion
Salt to taste
Butter

4 or 5 tablespoons bread crumbs, sautéed in butter
2½ cups sour cream
2 eggs
1½ ounces hard cheese, grated
Pepper to taste

Cook beans and onion in a pot of lightly salted boiling water. When the beans are tender, remove from heat. Drain, and discard onion.

Butter a baking dish. Mix the beans with the sautéed bread crumbs. Sprinkle beans with 3 tablespoons of the sour cream, mix, and add to baking dish.

In a bowl, whip the eggs together with the remaining sour cream, half the grated cheese, salt, and pepper until creamy.

Pour egg mixture over the beans.
Sprinkle with the remaining grated
cheese and dot with butter. Bake in a
preheated moderate oven until done.

Saxon Sour Beans
(Sauerbohnen or Savanyú Zöldbab Szászosan)

2 pounds green beans, cleaned
Salt to taste
2 slices smoked bacon
3 tablespoons flour

3 tablespoons vinegar
1 or 2 tablespoons sugar
Pepper to taste

Cook green beans in a pot of lightly
salted water. When tender, drain and
reserve 2 cups of the liquid. Fry bacon
until crisp; reserve the bacon
drippings. Crumble bacon and add to
beans; set aside.

Prepare a golden *roux* with the bacon
drippings and flour. Slowly pour in
the reserved cooking liquid from the
beans. Add the vinegar and sugar, and
season with salt and pepper. Stir
continuously until sauce is completely
smooth and thick.

Add the beans to the sauce and bring
to a boil. Reduce heat, simmer for a
few minutes, and serve beans hot.

NOTE: These beans are served as a side dish with roasts.

Green Beans in Mustard Bread Crumbs with Onion Sauce
(Dágádz Fászul or Rántott Zöldpaszuly)

**1 pound green beans, cleaned
  and cut into small pieces**
Salt to taste
2 eggs
2 tablespoons flour
1 tablespoon grated hard cheese
**Pepper and chopped parsley to
  taste**
½ teaspoon dry mustard

½ cup bread crumbs
Oil for frying
1 tablespoon oil or rendered lard
1 onion, finely chopped
Dash of very hot spicy paprika
1 cup tomato purée
Chopped mint to taste
1 tablespoon vinegar
2 teaspoons sugar

Parboil the beans in a pot of boiling salted water and drain them.

Beat the eggs in a bowl. Add 1 tablespoon of the flour and the cheese. Season the eggs with salt, pepper, and chopped parsley. Combine the mustard and bread crumbs in another bowl.

Dip the beans in the egg mixture, then roll in the bread crumbs. Taking a spoonful at a time, fry the beans in a skillet of hot oil. Brown both sides until crisp.

Meanwhile, prepare the onion sauce. Make a light brown *roux* with the oil and remaining flour. Add the onion and paprika. Add tomato purée to sauce. Season with salt, a little pepper, mint, and vinegar.

In another saucepan, heat sugar until
caramelized, add ¼ cup water, and
add to the onion sauce. Bring sauce to
a boil. Garnish beans with the hot
piquant onion sauce.

VARIATION

According to another recipe, sour cream may be mixed in with the beaten egg batter
for the green beans.

Sautéed Onions
(Hagymatokány)

Sautéed onions have always been one of the most popular and wholesome dishes in
the peasant diet—perhaps because they are cheap and plentiful and can be prepared in
a very short time.

2 tablespoons oil
4 large onions, sliced
Salt to taste

Dash of hot or sweet paprika
Pepper and vinegar to taste
2 tablespoons sour cream

Heat oil in a skillet and cook onions
until wilted. Season with salt and
paprika.

To make the onions a little less sweet,
add a little pepper and vinegar. Mix in
sour cream before serving.

If necessary, this excellent dish can be varied by inventive cooks. For example, the onions can be sautéed together with 2 or 3 sliced green peppers and sliced sausage. Eggs, too, may be added. Season the mixture with paprika and pepper. The flavor is enhanced by the addition of a teaspoonful of tomato purée and mustard. The Seklers prepare this dish with bay leaves.

NOTE: The flavor of sautéed onions is appreciated to its full extent when they are served with cornmeal mush.

Casserole of Onions Marinated in Red Wine
(*Vörösborban Pácolt Sülthagyma*)

½ **cup tarragon vinegar**	**Salt and pepper to taste**
2 tablespoons oil	**Pinch of marjoram**
1 cup dry red wine	**2 large onions, thickly sliced**
1 slice of lemon peel	**1 tablespoon butter**

Make a marinade from tarragon vinegar, oil, wine, lemon peel, salt and pepper, and marjoram. Put the onion slices in a bowl and pour the marinade over them so they are completely covered. Place the bowl in a cool spot (or refrigerate) for a couple of hours.

Butter a baking dish and add the onions and their marinade. Bake in a moderate oven until onions are golden brown and tender.

NOTE: Serve as a side dish with poultry or beef.

DUMPLINGS
AND WHATNOT

Potato Croquettes
(Chremzli or Pityókafánk)

**3 medium potatoes, peeled and
shredded**
4 or 5 eggs
**Salt, pepper, and ground nutmeg
to taste**

1 tablespoon flour
2 tablespoons grated hard cheese
Oil for frying

Add the potatoes to a kettle of fully
boiling water. Cook for 1 minute.
Drain the water, then press the
remaining liquid out of the potatoes.

While the potatoes are still warm, stir
in the eggs, salt and pepper, and
nutmeg.

Add the flour and the cheese. Mix
well. Form croquettes with a spoon
and flatten them slightly.

Heat oil in a frying pan, and fry the croquettes. When one side has become brown and crispy, turn over and brown the other side. Drain on paper towel and serve.

Potato Dumplings
(*Knédli or Pityókagombóc*)

Old tales slip from hidden hillsides, vanished hamlets, sealed caves
Like the powers of the white spirit salt, who bade kings and slaves
To battle so women could salt their boiling water;
The potato is a strange god from some world opposing shore
Even boiled, chilled, and grated it speaks a journey's lore
Remade to something of our land in dumpling batter;
Mixed with purifying matzo flour, joyful eggs, farmer's cheese
Blending in this local life, the local Lord, the freshened breeze
Shaped into plump things by a wet hand's patter;
See now the waiting steaming pot as judgment's harsh retort
Forcing those hidden centuries to uncover and report
Though with her power over such matter
The cook scares away the spirits with icy water
And makes the family fatter;
Old tales slip from hidden hillsides, vanished hamlets, sealed caves
Can we still ingest our hist'ry and send the cook our raves?

2 medium potatoes	1 tablespoon sour cream
3 tablespoons matzo cake meal	1 tablespoon cottage cheese
1 tablespoon rendered goose fat or oil	Salt and pepper to taste
2 eggs, beaten	Hot chicken broth

Boil the unpeeled potatoes until tender. Clean the potatoes well, then grate or mash them. Blend in matzo meal, goose fat, eggs, sour cream, and cottage cheese. Mix well and add salt and pepper.

Let stand for 1 hour. If mixture is too hard, add a little hot broth or warm water. Shape dumplings with wet palms or large spoon. Drop into lightly boiling salted water or broth and boil until done.

Let boil over medium flame to allow dumplings to swell properly. Slow down the boiling of the water every so often by adding a little cold water. In Transylvania, this is called "frightening the dumplings."

Remove the dumplings from water and drain. Add to hot chicken broth, cook for a moment, then serve together.

Saxon Speck Dumplings
(*Speck Knödel or Szász Szalonnás-gombóc*)

½ **pound smoked *speck* (bacon), diced**
1 medium onion, minced
2 eggs

2 tablespoons bread crumbs
1 tablespoon milk
Salt and pepper to taste
About 1 cup (or more) flour

Mix *speck,* onion, and eggs together in
a bowl. Soak bread crumbs in milk
until soft, and add to mixture. Season
with salt and pepper. Mix in enough
flour to give the batter substance.

Drop spoonfuls of batter into a pot of
lightly salted water and boil lightly for
about 8 minutes, or until the
dumplings come to the surface of the
boiling water. Yields approximately 25
dumplings.

NOTE: Saxon *speck* dumplings can be served either as a main course or as a garnish for
lean beef or game, covered with melted butter. The dumplings are also excellent when
served in soup. Be sure not to cook them in the soup for longer than 8 minutes.

Cheese Dumplings
(*Sajtos Gombóc*)

4 rolls
1 cup milk
5½ ounces hard cheese, grated
Salt to taste

Pinch of caraway seeds, ground
2 eggs, separated
2 tablespoons softened butter
7 tablespoons melted butter

Soak rolls in milk for a short time until they become soft. Drain, and press
out any excess milk. Chop into small
pieces. Mix rolls with most of the
grated cheese (reserve some for
later), salt, and caraway seeds.

Beat the egg whites until they form
stiff peaks. Fold egg whites, yolks, and
softened butter into the roll mixture.

Shape small dumplings from this mixture and cook them in a pot of lightly boiling salted water. Drain, and roll in melted butter. Arrange on a serving dish and sprinkle with the reserved grated cheese.

Cornmeal Dumplings with Sheep Cheese
(*Juhtúrós Kukoricagombóc*)

1 pound sheep cheese (such as *brînză* or feta)
6 eggs, separated, whites stiffly beaten
Pinch of salt
1 teaspoon caraway seeds, ground

½ medium onion, grated
7 tablespoons butter
3¾ cups cornmeal
Bread crumbs sautéed in butter
2 cups sour cream

Combine the cheese, egg yolks, salt, ground caraway seeds, onion, and butter in a large bowl and beat until foamy.

Mix in the cornmeal and beaten egg whites. Shape mixture into small dumplings, and cook in a pot of lightly boiling salted water until done.

Top with sautéed bread crumbs and sour cream and serve.

NOTE: Farmer cheese can be substituted for the sheep cheese.

Matzo Fritters
(*Übergezogene Maczes* or *Bundás Pászka*)

This side dish is usually prepared for Passover.

3 eggs, separated   **1 cup milk**
2 tablespoons matzo cake meal   **Oil, for frying**
6 matzos

Beat egg whites until stiff peaks appear. Fold in the yolks and the matzo meal.

Break matzos into medium-size pieces and soak in milk for a few minutes, then drain. Place 2 or 3 matzo pieces on top of each other. Brush one side with the egg mixture.

Place in a skillet of hot oil, with the side covered with the egg mixture facing down. Then brush the top with the egg mixture and turn over when the bottom browns. Cook that side until it browns. Serve hot as a garnish for broiled meats.

VARIATIONS

The crisp matzo fritters can be dusted with confectioners' sugar and cinnamon and eaten as a hot dessert.

Egg Barley
(*Tarhonya*)

8 eggs   **1 teaspoon salt**
1 cup milk or water   **8 cups flour**

Mix the eggs with the milk and salt in a large bowl. Gradually add the flour, a little bit at a time.

Mix vigorously, rubbing the dough against the sides of the bowl. Continue rubbing the mixture with your open palms until it breaks or crumbles into small pieces of dough. The consistency of the dough should be very hard and crumbly.

Rub the dough through a large-holed metal sieve, or against the side of the large holes of a grater, in order to break the dough into small pieces (⅛ inch to ¼ inch in size).

If any larger pieces of dough remain, sprinkle these with a little water, knead the dough again, and rub or grate it into small pieces as above.

Spread the egg barley on a floured cloth in a single layer so all the pieces are in contact with air. Let dry for 2 to 3 days.

While drying the *tarhonya,* mix it up several times to make sure that every little piece is exposed to air and is completely dry on all sides.

NOTE: Well-dried *tarhonya,* an important staple in any fine Transylvanian kitchen, will keep in a covered glass jar or well-sealed tin box for many months.

To Cook Tarhonya

½ cup dried egg barley (*tarhonya*)

3 tablespoons rendered chicken fat, goose fat, or lard
1 teaspoon salt
Chicken broth or water

In a large casserole, brown the egg barley in the fat for about 5 minutes. Stir several times. Add salt and chicken broth to cover.

Cover the casserole and put it in a moderate oven. Cook until done. The *tarhonya* is usually cooked by the time the broth or water is absorbed, about 45 to 50 minutes.

VARIATIONS

Tarhonya may be boiled in salted water like any other pasta, but it can often take longer to be properly cooked and usually isn't as tasty.

NOTE: Paprika may be added as a seasoning.

Layered Noodles with Sheep Cheese
(*Rakott Túrós Tészta*)

Noodles

2 cups flour
2 eggs
Pinch of salt and pepper
1 cup lukewarm water (optional)
1 to 2 tablespoons rendered goose fat, melted

Filling

7 ounces sheep cheese (*brînză* or feta)
2 to 3 sprigs of fresh dill, chopped
1 cup sour cream, mixed with 2 to 3 tablespoons rendered goose fat

Prepare the noodles: Mix flour, eggs, salt, and water if necessary (see page 83). Cook noodles in boiling salted water until tender. Drain.

Add goose fat to noodles and mix. Place a layer of noodles in the bottom of a baking dish.

Add the filling: Cover with a layer of sheep cheese. Sprinkle with chopped dill, and lightly spread on a layer of the sour cream and goose fat mixture.

Continue layering until all ingredients are used, ending with a layer of sheep cheese. Bake in a moderate oven until the top is crisp and brown.

SAUCES FROM A SIMPLE KITCHEN

Spicy Onion Sauce
(*Csípős Hagymamártás*)

3 onions, chopped
2 garlic cloves, crushed
¼ cup chopped tarragon
1½ cups beef broth or water

2 teaspoons vinegar
Salt and pepper to taste
2 teaspoons prepared mustard

Put onions, garlic, and tarragon in a saucepan with the broth and cook until onions are tender.

Reduce the liquid by half. Then dilute with ½ cup water and the vinegar. Season with salt and pepper. Bring to a boil, then remove from heat.

Mix in mustard. Strain through a sieve and serve.

NOTE: This sauce is served with boiled meats and roasted pork.

Sorrel Sauce
(*Sóskamártás*)

**1 pound sorrel, cleaned, washed,
  and ground**
2 tablespoons oil
1 to 2 tablespoons flour

A few drops of lemon juice
2 cups chicken or vegetable broth
Pinch of nutmeg
Salt and pepper to taste

In a saucepan, sauté sorrel lightly in
oil. Sprinkle with flour and lemon
juice.

Add the broth to the sorrel. Bring to a
boil and reduce sauce until medium-
thick. Flavor with nutmeg and salt and
pepper.

NOTE: Serve with boiled meats or roast beef, especially if it is larded.

Sage Sauce
(*Zsályamártás*)

1 tablespoon rendered lard or oil
1 tablespoon flour
**1 cup chopped sage leaves or 1
  tablespoon dried sage**

½ cup beef broth
½ teaspoon mustard
4 tablespoons sour cream
Tarragon vinegar and salt to taste

In a saucepan, heat the lard, add flour, and cook, stirring constantly, until mixture is smooth and the flour is completely coated by the lard. Add the sage and broth, stirring constantly with a whisk to prevent lumps until the mixture thickens.

Let sauce boil lightly, then add mustard, reduce heat, and mix in sour cream. Cook until heated through. Add tarragon vinegar to enhance the piquant flavor and season with salt.

NOTE: Serve with roasted young lamb and roast chicken.

Cornel Sauce
(*Sommártás*)

4 cups cornel, cleaned and pitted
A few juniper berries
2 cups red wine

Pepper, honey, lemon juice, and orange juice to taste

In a saucepan, boil the cornel and juniper berries in red wine until soft. Remove from heat. Press mixture through a sieve and discard solids. Return it to the saucepan and flavor with pepper, honey, lemon juice, and orange juice. Bring it to a boil again.

Stir continuously while boiling and reduce until it thickens. Pour into a sauceboat and serve.

NOTE: This sweet and pungent sauce is usually served with game and roast fowl. It may also be eaten as a dip with bread.

Pickled Cucumber Sauce with Tarragon
(*Tárkonyos Uborkamártás*)

4 hard-boiled eggs, minced
½ cup oil
Salt and pepper to taste
2 teaspoons chopped tarragon

1 tablespoon grated onion
5 pickled cucumbers (gherkins),
  finely chopped
½ cup pickle juice (optional)

In a bowl, mix hard-boiled eggs with oil and season with salt and pepper and tarragon.

Add the onion and the pickled cucumber. Mix thoroughly. If desired, add pickle juice to adjust the flavor. Serve cold.

NOTE: Pickled cucumber sauce is usually served with cold salted (corned) beef or cold boiled poultry.

Black Pepper Sauce
(*Borsos Mártás*)

4 medium onions, chopped
1 cup beef broth
6 to 8 mushrooms, sliced
2 apples, peeled and diced

1½ teaspoons coarsely ground
  pepper
Salt and tarragon vinegar to taste
1 egg white, beaten
3 to 4 tablespoons milk

In a saucepan, simmer onions in the broth until tender. Add the mushrooms and apples and cook until tender.

Strain ingredients through a sieve into another saucepan. Season with the ground pepper and salt and tarragon vinegar. Boil sauce until it is reduced to medium thickness.

When desired thickness is reached, fold in beaten egg white, add milk, mix, and serve.

NOTE: This sauce can accompany roast duck or goose.

Mint Sauce
(*Fodormentamártás*)

1 tablespoon sugar
5 teaspoons finely chopped fresh mint

2 tablespoons oil
Juice of 1 to 2 lemons
1 hard-boiled egg, minced

In a bowl, mix together continuously with a whisk the sugar, mint, 4 tablespoons boiling water, and the oil.

Add the lemon juice and stir until sauce becomes thick. Do not cook sauce. Fold in the minced egg, then refrigerate until cold.

NOTE: Serve this cold minty-lemony sauce with hot or cold fish dishes or spring lamb.

Garlic Sauce
(Fokhagymamártás)

3 tablespoons rendered goose fat
3 tablespoons flour
4 garlic cloves

Salt to taste
1½ cups sour cream

In a small saucepan prepare a light *roux* with the goose fat and flour. With the flat of a knife, crush the garlic, and mix it into sauce.

Thin the *roux* immediately with ½ cup cold water, whisking constantly to prevent lumps until it is smooth and thick. Season with salt, mix in sour cream, and let sauce come to a quick boil. Strain through a sieve before serving.

NOTE: Serve this sauce with baked fish or poultry.

Dill by Joseph Domjan

Horseradish Sauce with Almonds
(Mandulás tormamártás)

As August's oven winds drying wheat's yield
Among the stalks spirals dust in the field
So horseradish leaves furl and twist and gyre green
Marking the roots delving—white, thick, and clean
Roots come out in the old woman's hand
And where there's a breeze there she'll stand
To grate the root into a pan
Beetfaced, eyes burning, tears down the cheek ran;
With two cups sour cream and a spoonful of flour
Thrown together with one hand's shower
Of finely chopped blanched almonds, all blended
With the root to quiet its fire,
Quick cook it in meat broth so splendid
Touched with salt and sugar by desire
Gives sauce to make the mouth a pyre
And build the blood so it shan't tire.

2 cups sour cream
1 tablespoon flour
A few drops of lemon juice
1 fresh horseradish root (½ pound), grated

1 cup chopped blanched almonds
1½ cups chicken or vegetable broth
Salt and sugar to taste

Mix the sour cream with the flour in a bowl, preferably a wooden one. Sprinkle a few drops of lemon juice over the grated horseradish and add it to the sour cream. Add the almonds.

Bring the broth to a boil in a saucepan and add sour cream mixture slowly, stirring constantly. Then cook sauce on low heat for 10 to 15 minutes. Season with salt and sugar.

NOTE: Blanched, skinned, and chopped walnuts may be substituted for the almonds in this recipe. This sauce goes well with boiled meats.

Goose Giblets Sauce
(*Libaaprólék mártás*)

4 goose giblets, chopped	**4 tablespoons butter**
1 cup red wine	**1 to 2 tablespoons flour**
1 onion, chopped	**5 to 6 mushrooms, diced**
Tarragon, marjoram, salt, and	**½ cup sour cream**
pepper to taste	**A pinch of paprika**

Put the giblets in a saucepan and add red wine. Season with onion, tarragon, marjoram, salt, and pepper, and cook giblets until tender.

Prepare a golden brown *roux* with the butter and flour. Thin the *roux* with the giblet broth, whisking constantly to prevent lumps until smooth and thick. Add mushrooms and giblets.

Simmer for 10 minutes. Remove from heat and mix in sour cream. Heat it lightly, and sprinkle with paprika before serving.

NOTE: Serve this sauce with goose, duck, or turkey. It can also be made with chicken, duck, or turkey giblets.

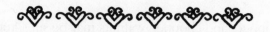

SALADS, PICKLES, AND VINEGARS

Cucumber Salad
(*Uborkasaláta*)

2 or 3 medium cucumbers, peeled and sliced	**Pepper, tarragon, and vinegar to taste**
Salt to taste	**1 tablespoon oil**
1 clove garlic, finely chopped or crushed	**4 tablespoons sour cream**
	1 teaspoon chopped dill

Sprinkle the cucumbers with salt and refrigerate for 1 hour.

Drain, but do not squeeze cucumbers. Mix in garlic. Add ½ cup water, pepper, tarragon, vinegar, and oil.

Refrigerate for another 30 minutes, then douse cucumbers with a mixture of sour cream and dill.

VARIATIONS

This is a Rumanian version; most cooks prefer to omit the garlic from this recipe. Instead, they mix sliced onion into the salad. Young green onions or scallions and chives may also be used. In the Sekler homes cucumber salad is made without garlic, but with onions and often a sprinkling of paprika; also, oil is not used.

Eggplant Salad
(*Padlizsánsaláta or Salată de Vinete*)

2 large eggplants
Salt and pepper to taste
1 cup oil

Lemon juice to taste
1 onion, chopped
Sliced tomato, for garnish

Prick eggplant skin in several places. Grill eggplants over charcoal or broil under a gas burner. Rotate frequently. Cook until skin becomes crisp and the flesh tender.

Dip hands in cold water and peel the eggplants while still warm, holding the stem with one hand or on a fork. Place eggplant on a board and beat to a pulplike mass.

Place pulp in a bowl. Season with salt and pepper and add small drops of oil while stirring constantly (as in the preparation of mayonnaise). The longer it is stirred, the whiter it will become.

Mix in lemon juice, drop by drop, to make it more piquant. When ready, fold in the onion or serve it separately. Decorate with slices of tomatoes.

NOTE: Buy eggplants that are very fresh, dark, shiny, and long (but not too thin). Eggplant salad is usually served with fried peppers.

Beet Salad
(*Céklasaláta*)

3 or 4 medium beets, skins
thoroughly washed
Vinegar and salt to taste

A dash of sugar (optional)
1 teaspoon caraway seeds
1 small horseradish root, grated

Boil the beets in a pot of water, or bake in a moderate oven, until tender. Chill in cold water so that skins can easily be removed. Peel.

Slice beets and pour on a dressing made of vinegar and salt. A dash of sugar can be added to the dressing for those who prefer a sweet taste.

Season with caraway seeds and grated horseradish. Keep in jar for several days, until pickled.

VARIATION

Wise housewives do not cook or bake beets; rather, they peel and grate the fresh raw vegetable. The same dressing and seasoning should be used, and the beets should be pickled for 2 to 3 weeks. During this time, the beet becomes soft, yet it retains its original flavor and complete vitamin content.

NOTE: Beets are tastier when baked in an oven. In many areas of Transylvania, beets were put in a hot oven after the baking of bread had been completed.

Dandelion Green Salad
(Pitypang Saláta or Salată de Păpădie)

First summer's sun kisses the waiting ground
And up shoot the dandelion children round
A maiden picks just their fresh young leaves
Her spurned suitor merely sits and grieves
As she cleans and washes one half pound,
All rinsed with salty water in a bowl
Touched with vinegar's sour sorrowed soul
More salt, and pepper, and then they're oiled
Then lightly pressed by sliced eggs hard boiled
While the boy plucks the yellow blossom's roll
Finely chopped dill skirts the salad fair
Whose piquant lacy leaves are light as air
A dash of tarragon and then it's done
Guess who sits and eats it, guess which one . . .

½ pound young dandelion leaves, cleaned, washed carefully, rinsed with warm salty water, and towel-dried
1 tablespoon oil

2 teaspoons vinegar
Salt and pepper to taste
2 hard-boiled eggs, sliced
1 teaspoon finely chopped dill or tarragon

Put dandelion leaves back in the refrigerator so they will become crisp again. Then arrange them in a salad bowl.

Sprinkle with oil, vinegar, and salt and pepper. Decorate the salad with the sliced hard-boiled eggs. Sprinkle with dill. Toss salad gently so that the leaves are evenly coated with the dressing.

NOTE: Pitted and quartered sour cherries may also be added to the salad, for both taste and decoration.

Honeyed Acacia Flower Salad
(Akácvirág-Saláta)

Wild branches are waving like late summer wands
Girls are running down dappled vine-gowned lanes
To pick from the trees by geese-swollen ponds
Acacia blooms untarnished by late summer rains—
This plant's sweet sighing in work-finished fullness
Garlands the salad with livid lissome crowns
On a bed of shredded layered lettuce
Under honey and sour cream it drowns.
Oh delicious salad, gone by September
Why must you say what we won't remember?
Over green leaves cottage cheese falls like snow
As the lettuce will be buried we know;
Honey balanced by the bite of onion
Frought also with dill, summer's mounting minion
And pale sun in the juice of the lemon,
So gather, eat, laugh; here come more children
It will all be gone in an instant.

6 heads of lettuce (bibb or Boston), washed, dried, and shredded
Salt to taste
1 tablespoon acacia flower honey
½ cup cottage cheese, crumbled apart
Chopped fresh dill to taste

Pepper to taste
Juice of 3 lemons
4 cups acacia flowers, lightly steamed for only 5 seconds
1 cup sour cream and 2 tablespoons light cream, mixed together

Arrange salad in layers in a glass or porcelain salad bowl. Start with 2 heads of the shredded lettuce. Season lightly with salt.

Dissolve honey in ¼ cup warm water. Sprinkle lettuce lightly with some dissolved honey. Then spread over it a thin layer of crumbled cottage cheese, a sprinkling of chopped dill, pepper, and the juice of 1 lemon. Scatter layers lightly with a few acacia flowers (reserve some to garnish salad).

Continue layering until all ingredients are used. Top salad with sour cream mixture and refrigerate for 30 minutes before serving.

Scatter the remaining acacia flowers on top and serve.

NOTE: Serve the salad with grilled steak, smoked pork dishes, or fried fish. Thinly sliced onions are also delicious when mixed into this salad. Squash blossoms, pea flowers, or sweet Japanese chrysanthemum flowers could be substituted for the acacia flowers.

Lamb's Lettuce—A Salad That Rivals Gold
(Galambbegy vagy Arannyal Versengő Saláta)

This is a recipe from Haromszék, the Seklers' main county.

3 or 4 medium potatoes
Salt, pepper, and wine vinegar to
taste
1 garlic clove, finely minced

2 or 3 heads of lamb's lettuce
cleaned and washed
1¼ cups sour cream

Boil potatoes until done in lightly salted water, peel, and slice. Set aside and keep warm.

In a saucepan, bring about 2 cups water to a boil. Add salt, pepper, and wine vinegar. Put garlic in a piece of cheesecloth tied with string and add to pan. Cook for a short time and remove.

Blanch the lamb's lettuce for ten seconds in the liquid in the pan. Drain on paper towel. Mix gently with sliced potatoes. Dab on sour cream and serve warm.

VARIATION

In the winter the dish can be made without using lamb's lettuce. In that case, it is called a warm potato salad, and is prepared with chopped scallions.

NOTE: Lamb's lettuce is similar to sorrel, but the leaves are a bit fuller. Sorrel can be substituted for it, as can arugula.

Blushing Tomatoes in Sour Cherry Vinegar
(Szende Paradicsom Meggyecetben)

Sour cherry leaves, washed
2 or 3 sprigs of thyme
2 or 3 sprigs of dill
2 or 3 sprigs of anise or ½ teaspoon aniseed
2 bay leaves
White peppercorns
2 tablespoons sugar

½ teaspoon salt
4 to 5 sprigs of sour cherry (the young green parts)
6 pounds partially ripe (half reddened) tomatoes, washed
Weak or half-diluted sour cherry vinegar (page 289)

Cover the bottom of a 4-quart (covered) jar, ¼ inch thick, with sour cherry leaves. Sprinkle with all the herbs, peppercorns, sugar, and salt. Put the cherry sprigs in the jar.

Fill the jar with the tomatoes so that they fit tightly against one another up to the neck of the jar. (Leave ½ inch of space at top of jar.)

Pour in weak sour cherry vinegar. Cover with more cherry leaves.

Seal the mouth of the jar with parchment paper and place the jar on a rack in a water bath (the water level should be three fourths the height of the jar). Bring to a boil. Let boil for 10 minutes.

The tomatoes in the jar will reach the temperature of the boiling water—but do not allow the water in the jar to boil.

While still hot, remove the jar from the water bath.

Place the jar in a wooden container lined with pillows (this is the best method for slow cooling). Cover the jar with wool cloths so that the cooling will occur at a slow rate.

When cooled, cover jar and store in a cool dark place.

NOTE: This method of preparation can be used for canning other vegetables as well. The ingredients do not necessarily need to be cooked—but then they keep for only a short time.

Marika's Tomato Peppers for Winter Days
(Marika Alma-Paprikája Téli Napokra)

1 pint strong vinegar
1½ quarts water
½ teaspoon salicylic acid
1 cup sugar
3 teaspoons salt
2 spears fresh horseradish (cut
    from the fresh horseradish
    root), about 4 inches by ¼ inch

½ teaspoon mustard seed
1 bay leaf
A few whole white peppercorns
6 to 8 pounds peppers, washed
    (see Note)

Put all the ingredients except the peppers in a pot. Bring to a boil.

Meanwhile, pierce the peppers in four or five places with a fork to allow the liquid to seep in.

Add the peppers to the boiling mixture and cook them for 1 minute. Remove the peppers from the liquid and set them aside in a large bowl. Cover and let stand for 30 minutes.

Carefully place the peppers in a gallon glass jar. Press them down with a spatula at the neck of the jar to pack them closely.

Discard the bay leaf from the cooking liquid. Put the horseradish spears inside the jar (among the peppers) and pour in the cooking liquid.

When cool, cover the jar tightly with its own lid and store in a cool, dry, and dark place.

One or 2 cloves of garlic or grapevine tendrils may also be used for flavoring the peppers.

NOTE: Choose the peppers carefully. They should be small to medium, full-bodied tomato or apple peppers, not yet in full ripeness.

A Wine Vinegar for Autumn
(Őszre Való Ecetágy Készítése)

**A bunch of green grapevine
   tendrils**
**2 ounces raisins or dried, pitted
   sour cherries or cornel**
1 ear of young corn
2 ounces lentils

3 quarts dry white wine
¼ cup honey
**1 or 2 pieces fresh and ripe fruit
   (any kind), cleaned and
   stemmed**

At the beginning of the summer fill a wide-mouthed glass gallon jar one fourth full with the following ingredients: green grape vine tendrils, raisins (or dried sour cherries or cornel), ear of corn, and lentils. Pour in enough wine to fill jar halfway and stir in half of the honey.

Cover the top of the jar with cheesecloth and tie it down. Place the jar in a sunny spot for 2 weeks. The mixture will first ferment, then turn cloudy before it eventually clears up.

When 2 weeks have elapsed, place the
jar in a cool but not too cold spot. Add
1 or 2 pieces of cleaned, stemmed
ripe fruit of the season to the jar and
let stand.

At the beginning of September add
enough wine to the jar to fill it. Stir in
the remaining 2 tablespoons honey.
Place the jar in a sunny spot again for
1 week (be sure the contents do not
become too warm), then return it to a
cool spot.

Do not move the jar until the first days
of October. By this time the vinegar
will have a layer of sediment on the
bottom, and will be clear on top.

Carefully siphon off a bottleful (1
quart) of the clear, ready-to-use
vinegar and fill the jar again with the
same amount of white wine.

If the vinegar is handled carefully (not
moved or shaken), it will not spoil.
This procedure of draining off the
clear vinegar should be repeated
again from time to time (taste it
occasionally, and siphon it about
every 2 to 4 weeks). Be sure to
replace the removed amount with
fresh wine. It produces a very good
vinegar.

VARIATIONS

Using an existing vinegar base, one can prepare new vinegar from a favorite wine and
some fruit (or other sugar-containing plant) in the following manner:

Fill a 2-quart wide-mouthed jar with wine (or with any kind of fruit soaked in wine).
Cover the mouth of the jar with cheesecloth and tie it down, then put the jar in an
evenly warm place. The top of the wine will develop a skin after a while; stir it back into
the wine by shaking the jar. Continue this process until a ¼- or ½-quart gelatinous wine
skin forms. Transfer this gelatinous wine to a similar size jar. Fill the jar with some

vinegar from the recipe above. Let stand in cool spot. When the contents settle, slowly siphon off the top for use. Replace the removed amount with fresh wine. Be sure to siphon off new vinegar at least once every 4 weeks. Bottle the vinegar and store it in a cool place.

NOTE: If the wine develops a skin on top, be sure to skim it off.

Wine vinegar prepared in such a manner can be used as a base for flavored vinegars as well.

Aunt Kati's Sour Cherry Vinegar with Rose Petals
(*Kati Néni Rózsaszirmos Meggyecete*)

30 pounds sour cherries, washed and pitted
12 pounds sugar
4 whole cloves
Peel of 1 lemon

Rose petals, preferably thick, oily red petals
2 small sprigs of young sour cherry trees
2 cups wine vinegar

Put sour cherries in a 5-gallon enameled pot. Add half the sugar, the cloves, and the lemon peel.

In another large pot, dissolve the remaining sugar in 2 quarts water. Bring to a boil, then add to the sour cherries. Add the sprigs of young sour cherry trees at the same time. Remove from heat.

Cover the pot partially so that the ingredients can still "breathe" but no foreign materials can fall into the pot as it ferments. Place the pot in a sunny spot.

Every day during the next several days, add as many rose petals as the pot can hold. Stir them well into the liquid.

Continue this procedure until the fermenting is well under way; this usually takes about 3 to 5 days. Do not disturb the pot from then on.

It will take about 2 weeks for the ingredients to be completely fermented. At this time, remove the waste and rose petals from the top of the pot and allow the contents to settle again. Leave the pot in a cool place.

When enough clear liquid forms on top, siphon it off very carefully and place it in a smaller (gallon) jar. (Although this vinegar is very weak, it still can be used.) Let the remaining vinegar settle again, and siphon off the clear top liquid as above.

Now add wine vinegar to the cleared liquid. Pour some into bottles and cover. Store in a cool, dark place for 4 weeks before using.

VARIATION

This vinegar may also be prepared from red currants or sweet cherries.

NOTE: This is a very light, brilliantly colored fragrant vinegar that goes very well with salads. It is made in a large quantity here, but the amount can be decreased to half or less, if desired.

Tangy Tarragon Vinegar
(Csipős Tárkonyecet)

**2 bunches of fresh tarragon,
   chopped**
**1 spear or slice of fresh
   horseradish root**

1 teaspoon mustard seeds
6 whole peppercorns
1 clove
1 quart wine vinegar

Combine all ingredients in a sterilized covered bottle or jar. Let them soak in the vinegar for 8 days. Strain the vinegar—pressing out all the liquid—into a saucepan.

Boil the strained liquid well for 10 minutes and let it settle. Refrigerate for 10 minutes, then pour into small sterilized bottles. Cover, and store in a cool dark place.

Blooming Squash by Joseph Domjan

Spicy Herb Essence
(*Fűszeres Herba Esszencia*)

Most eyes are moist as winter falls
When early snows slowly chill our halls
One can't escape the season's blues
By plunging in the market's glowing hues
Brilliant berries, fruit of golden skin
Have long since gone from the wooden bin
Plants that one time burst with green
Hang lifeless dried from a ceiling beam
The freshness of every dish's every taste
Now lies bare below the wintry waste
Yet there are bottles, within whose glass
The smells of summer soon amass
This crystal liquid, top be gone,
Releases the essence of tarragon
This delicate vinegar shaded rose
Unveils that flower to the cold jaded nose
From the cellar thick with lint
Is a vinegar redolent of peppermint
Touched with thyme and lemongrass
The spirit of ginger within its glass
Others have nutmeg, orange, and sage
Aristocratic marjoram is all the rage
So has mother cheated the season
More than any doctor or philosopher's reason.

2 large bunches of tarragon   **6 whole peppercorns**
2 sprigs of thyme   **½ ounce ground ginger**
2 sprigs of mint   **½ ounce ground nutmeg**
2 sprigs of rosemary   **2 sprigs of sage**
2 sprigs of marjoram   **1 teaspoon mustard seeds**
2 sprigs of lemongrass   **2 quarts white vinegar**

Combine all ingredients in a covered
sterilized jar. Let soak for 5 days. Stir
the contents of the jar very well every
day.

Drain the vinegar into a pot and boil it
thoroughly for 15 minutes. Let cool,
then pour into sterilized bottles and
seal with cork or lids. Store in a cool
dry place.

NOTE: If possible, use only fresh herbs. If only dried herbs are available, then use 2
ounces of tarragon and 1 teaspoon each of the other herbs.

This spicy herb essence is used as a concentrated and highly flavored vinegar base.

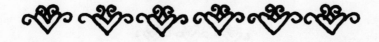

BREADS
AND SWEETS

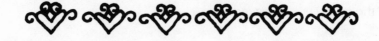

BREAD AND HOMINY

Crusty Saxon Bread
(*Házi Kenyérsütés Szász Módra*)

1½ ounces dry yeast
2 teaspoons sugar
½ cup lukewarm milk
12 cups flour, plus more for
dusting

2 teaspoons salt
¼ cup melted rendered lard, for
brushing top of bread and
greasing pan

Dissolve the yeast and ½ teaspoon of
the sugar in the milk. Let yeast stand
for 1 hour.

Put the flour in a large mixing bowl.
Add salt, remaining sugar, the
dissolved yeast, and 2 cups lukewarm
water. Knead until dough becomes
smooth and elastic.

Shape dough into a round loaf and brush with lard. Line a dough basket (or a simple bowl) with a clean napkin, sprinkle with flour, and place the dough in it. Cover with a cloth. Keep in a warm place (73° to 77°F), and let rise for 1 hour, or until dough is twice its former size. Turn dough over and let rise for another 30 minutes.

Place raised dough on a floured board and shape into a loaf. Score the top of the loaf. Brush a large baking pan or skillet with lard and put the dough in it (the dough should come halfway up the sides of the pan).

Cover with a cloth and leave in a warm place until it rises above the pan. Preheat the oven to a very high temperature and bake bread for 30 minutes, then reduce heat to moderate and continue to bake for another hour.

The baked bread should have an attractive dark brown, crisp, and thick crust. Remove the bread from the oven. With a large kitchen knife, remove the burnt crust. Cool before slicing.

NOTES: Two round loaves can also be baked: cut the dough in half, shape into round loaves, and place on a large baking sheet.

Be careful not to make too soft a dough.

If the bread is covered with a cabbage leaf when it is baked, the crust will be golden brown. Place a cabbage leaf (greased with oil) in the baking pan and the dough on top. Cover the dough with another 2 or 3 cabbage leaves. Make sure that the dough is properly covered with enough cabbage leaves. Let the dough rise, then bake, covered with the cabbage leaves.

Transylvanian Easter Bread
(*Husvéti "Üres" Kalács a Székiek Módján*)

1 package dry yeast
10 cups flour
4 eggs, beaten
2 cups warm milk

5 ounces potatoes, boiled and
**   mashed**
4 tablespoons butter, melted
Pinch of salt
¼ cup sugar

Mix yeast together in a large bowl with 2 cups of the flour, 2 beaten eggs, and enough lukewarm water to form a dough. Knead well and let rise in a warm place.

When the dough has risen to twice its size, add this leaven to the remaining flour.

Mix in milk and 1 cup warm water. Add the mashed potatoes and knead together well.

Continue kneading, then add melted butter, salt, and sugar; mix well. Put dough in a warm place to rise until nearly twice the size. When dough is ready, place it on a floured pastry board and form it into various shapes as desired, such as twists or hearts.

Put the bread in buttered baking pans or on baking sheets, then let rise again for 25 to 30 minutes. Brush the tops of the breads with the remaining 2 beaten eggs, and bake in a moderately hot oven for about 35 or 40 minutes, or until crust turns reddish brown.

Sharecroppers' Wheat and Rye Bread
(*Bérkaszások Fele-fele Kenyere*)

The sharecroppers often got paid in part with fruits of the harvest, and subsequently many of them made bread from a mixture of these different flours, like wheat and rye, or corn, wheat, and potato. During the course of Transylvania's stormy past, tree bark, acorns, and other easily found forest plants were ground and then used as bread "extenders." In small mountain villages corn flour was often substituted for wheat flour.

3 medium potatoes
1 package dry yeast
1 pound rye flour

1 pound whole-wheat or
   unbleached all-purpose flour
1 cup milk
1 teaspoon salt

Boil potatoes in their skins until done. Peel them while still hot, and mash through a sieve or potato ricer. The yield should be about 1½ cups mashed potatoes. Set aside.

Dissolve yeast in ½ cup warm water. Add dissolved yeast to 2 tablespoons rye flour and 2 tablespoons whole-wheat flour in a large bowl and mix well. Place in a warm spot and let rise for 30 to 40 minutes.

Add 1 cup lukewarm water and the milk and salt. Mix well, while gradually adding the remaining flour and the mashed potatoes.

Knead the dough until it separates from your hands and the sides of the mixing bowl. This should take another 10 to 15 minutes.

Put in a warm place and let dough rise to double its original size; this should take about 2 to 4 hours.

Preheat the oven to moderately hot. Place the dough on a floured board, punch it down, and knead it for a few minutes, folding it with your hands. Shape into a loaf, and let rise for about 30 minutes.

Brush the bread with warm water. Score the top, if desired. (See Note.) Bake in a pan or on a baking sheet in the preheated oven for 45 minutes, or until done.

VARIATION

In the larger cities of Transylvania, this bread is made with caraway seeds; add about ½ cup when mixing in the potatoes. For certain holidays, some housewives use only whole-wheat flour and sprinkle the top of the bread with poppy seeds or sesame seeds.

NOTE: If the top of the loaf is first scored, be sure to grease the slits with bacon drippings or butter.

Fried Cabbage Dough Cakes
(*Káposztás Lángos*)

4 cups sifted flour, plus more for
   dusting
1 cup milk
1 teaspoon sugar
1 package dry yeast
1 head of cabbage, cored, outer
   leaves removed, and shredded

3 to 4 tablespoons rendered
   goose fat, plus more for frying
Salt and pepper to taste
1 cup sour cream or garlic-
   flavored rendered goose fat

Set the sifted flour aside in a slightly warm place. In a small bowl, mix ½ cup of the milk with the sugar, yeast, and 3 tablespoons of the flour. Let mixture rest in a warm place until yeast is dissolved.

Meanwhile, sauté cabbage in goose fat until tender or golden brown. Season with salt and pepper. Set aside.

In a large bowl, combine the dissolved yeast with the remaining milk and flour. Knead well to make a medium-soft dough (not unlike pizza dough). Sprinkle with flour and let rise in a warm place for 2 hours.

Mix a few spoonfuls at a time of the sautéed cabbage into the dough until it is all incorporated. Then roll out to ¾ inch thick and cut dough into cup-size circles. Let rise for another 30 minutes, then fry in hot goose fat. Drain on paper towel. Serve with sour cream or sprinkle with garlic-flavored goose fat.

VARIATION

These fried dough cakes are often prepared with sheep cheese, cottage cheese, and chopped dill instead of cabbage.

Mămăligă or Cornmeal Mush
(Puliszka)

1 quart water	**2 cups cornmeal**
1 tablespoon salt	

Boil the water in a pot and add the salt. When the water has reached a rapid boil, pour in the cornmeal slowly, stirring constantly. Cook over low heat for about 20 minutes.

Remove pot from heat, wrap a dish towel around it, and stir vigorously for 3 to 4 minutes.

With a wet spatula, scrape the cornmeal away from the sides of the pot. Continue to cook for another 2 to 3 minutes over low heat. Turn the pot upside down over a wooden board and remove the cornmeal in one piece. It will look like a small, round, and flat bread.

Holding the ends of a piece of thin white string in each hand, cut the cornmeal into slices.

VARIATION

Mămăligă Layered with Sheep Cheese: Grease an ovenproof casserole (preferably with a thick bottom) with 1 tablespoon rendered lard. Then line it with a layer of *mămăligă* as prepared above. Fry 3½ ounces diced bacon until crisp and drain on paper towel. Arrange a layer of bacon and a layer of crumbled young cottage-type sheep cheese (from a total of 11 ounces) on top of the cornmeal. Repeat the layers until the ingredients are used up, making the top layer *mămăligă*. Bake in a preheated moderately hot oven for 10 to 15 minutes.

This cornmeal dish can be served as a meal in itself. In the summer, however, a molded salad goes very well with the dish. Cracklings may be substituted for bacon. In some Transylvanian regions, sour cream is used to cover each layer; a total of 1 cup sour cream should be sufficient.

NOTE: Mămăligă, a favorite Rumanian staple, is a light and healthful dish when served with milk, cottage cheese, stews, or ragouts. Use it to replace bread and other garnishes with meat dishes.

Cornmeal Mush with Pork
(Törökbuza Kásaétel)

**2 cups very coarsely ground
   cornmeal**
1 pound pork, chopped
Rendered lard
**3 medium carrots, peeled and
   chopped**

2 sprigs of parsley, chopped
1 onion, chopped
**½ celery root, peeled and
   chopped**
1 boiled potato, diced (optional)

Soak the cornmeal overnight in water to cover.

In a frying pan, sauté the meat in some lard for only a short time, then add the carrots, parsley, onion, and celery root and continue to cook.

Add the soaked cornmeal and its liquid and cook for about 40 to 45 minutes. Very coarsely ground cornmeal needs nearly twice as much cooking time as rice. Be careful not to allow the mush to become too thick. (If too thick, add more water.) A diced potato may also be added to the dish.

VARIATION

In some of the Sekler counties corn is named "Turkish wheat," because it came to Transylvania through Turkey. "Turkish wheat" is, in fact, the same as regular cornmeal, but the corn is ground very coarsely with a manual grinder or in a wooden mortar. To make plain "Turkish wheat," wash the cornmeal several times, then put it in a pot with cold water and cook over moderate heat, stirring frequently to prevent sticking. When nearly done, salt, and cook until tender. Its finished consistency should be that of boiled rice. If serving it warm, accompany the cornmeal mush with boiled milk—it makes it tastier. Served either warm or cold, it is excellent with yogurt or sour cream.

NOTES: Among the poor peasants, plain cornmeal mush was prepared with pumpkin seed oil or sunflower seed oil, and consumed warm.

Very popular in Transylvania, especially during World War II, this cornmeal mush is used instead of rice in regions where meatless stuffed cabbage or Lenten stuffing is prepared.

Cornmeal Porridge with Buttermilk
(*Bálmos*)

In Kolozsvár before World War II, it was as common a sight to see women selling cornmeal porridge as it was to see the *bütyü* (blood sausage) vendors or the baked-pumpkin sellers.

1 quart buttermilk   **2 cups cornmeal**
Salt to taste   **2 to 3 eggs, beaten**
1 cup sour cream (optional)

Keep the buttermilk for a few days after its expiration date, allowing it to sour. Then pour it into a large pot and season with salt.

Place it on top of the stove and cook over medium heat. Bring to a boil and stir in the sour cream.

Reduce heat and continue to boil. Gradually add the cornmeal, stirring constantly.

When the cornmeal is cooked, add the beaten egs. Stir for 1 or 2 more minutes, then remove from heat and serve hot.

"Swallow It" or Rumanian Cornmeal Cake with Buttermilk
("Taci şi Înghite" or "Kapd Be!")

2 cups milk
2 cups buttermilk or whey
    (or water)
Salt
3 cups cornmeal

1 cup sour cream or ½ cup sheep
    cheese (young cottage-type)
2 tablespoons butter
½ cup sour cream (optional)

Pour the milk and buttermilk into a pot. Add the salt and bring to a boil. Then add the cornmeal and prepare a thin mush. Mix the mush with sour cream.

Pour the mixture into a greased baking dish or casserole (preferably a glass ovenproof one). Bake in a hot oven for 10 to 15 minutes.

Dot the top with butter and serve hot. If the dish was made with sheep cheese, then top it with sour cream.

VARIATION

In some regions, the above recipe takes a slightly different form. Prepare a stiffer corn mush in a pot and stir well. Form it into doughnut shapes with a buttered spoon, 2 for each guest. Before baking in a greased baking dish, place a raw egg and a pat of butter in the center of each doughnut. Bake and serve.

LEAVENED CAKES, SCONES, AND PANCAKES

Pastry Horn of Torda
(Kürtőskalács)

Kürtőskalács is a traditional Transylvanian sweetmeat. In many places it is called "stick doughnut," since it is prepared from a type of dough similar to the kind used for doughnuts. Pastry horns were once also flavored with anise and ginger.

¾ ounce dry yeast
2 tablespoons sugar
¼ cup lukewarm milk
8 cups sifted flour
2 whole eggs
4 egg yolks

1 pound (4 sticks) butter, melted
¼ cup confectioners' sugar, plus
  more for dusting
1 teaspoon salt
2 cups milk

Mix yeast with sugar and milk; let it dissolve. In a large bowl, combine dissolved yeast, flour, whole eggs, egg yolks, 12 tablespoons of the melted butter, confectioners' sugar, salt, and milk.

Knead dough well and let rise. When dough has risen halfway, roll it out and cut it into ½-inch strips. Wind strips in a spiral around buttered metal baking tubes.

Insert a spit through tubes. Rotate them over glowing charcoal. Baste with remaining hot melted butter when browning begins. When horns are crisp, dust them with confectioners' sugar and return them to the fire; the sugar should caramelize and form a glaze. Pull pastry off tubes carefully so that it remains intact.

VARIATIONS

In some regions the hot pastry is rolled in crushed or ground sugared walnuts.

Saxon Pie
(*Hangklich or Szász Pite*)

½ ounce dry yeast	**Pinch of salt**
1 quart lukewarm milk	**7 cups sifted flour, plus more for**
6 eggs	** dusting**
1 cup butter, melted	**Filling (see below)**

Dissolve the yeast in ½ cup of the lukewarm milk and let it ferment for 10 to 15 minutes. Then pour the remaining milk into a large mixing bowl.

Cover a table or board with a clean cloth, dust with flour, and roll out the raised dough to ¼ inch thick.

Place the pastry on the paper. (For this procedure, the assistance of another person will be necessary.) Put the pastry on a baking sheet together with the paper. Bake in a hot oven for 10 minutes, or until golden brown.

Add the eggs, butter, salt, and fermented yeast and then the flour. Knead until dough forms blisters. Dust with flour, cover with a clean linen napkin, and let rise to double its volume.

Fill the pie with any of the fillings listed below. With a hot knife, cut dough into 9- or 10-inch squares. Cut waxed paper squares to the same size.

Fillings for Saxon Pie

Egg Filling
½ cup rendered lard
½ cup melted butter

7 eggs, beaten
Salt to taste

This filling may be prepared the night before.

Heat the lard and butter together, and spoon the beaten eggs into the hot fat. Add salt. Cook until it begins to thicken. Stir until mixture cools and becomes hard and smooth. (It will be similar to a hard omelette.)

Fill the pastry with the filling and bake as above.

Cherry Filling
2 cups sour cream
5 eggs, separated

½ cup sugar
4 cups pitted tart cherries

In a bowl, mix the sour cream, egg yolks, and sugar well. Beat the egg whites in another bowl until they form stiff peaks; fold whites into sour cream mixture.

Cover the pastry evenly with cherries, then pour the creamy filling over it. Bake in a hot oven until golden brown.

NOTE: When making the pastry for this sweet pie, add ½ cup sugar and use less salt than for a savory pie—a dash of salt should do.

Saxon cherry pie is equally delicious made with sweet cherries or sour morello cherries.

Cottage Cheese and Raisin Pie
(*Mazsolás Túrós Lepény*)

1 package dry yeast
¾ cup milk
½ cup sugar
1¼ cups flour, sifted
10 tablespoons butter
6 eggs, separated

7 ounces cottage cheese
¾ cup raisins, soaked in water or
sweet wine overnight, drained
Pinch of salt
1 tablespoon vanilla sugar

In a small bowl, make a flour paste from the yeast, milk, 1 teaspoon of the sugar, and ¼ cup of flour. Set aside.

In a large bowl, beat the butter, egg yolks, and remaining sugar until creamy.

Press the cottage cheese through a sieve. Add cheese to butter and egg mixture.

In another bowl, beat the egg whites until stiff. Blend into cheese mixture with the remaining 1 cup flour.

Add raisins, salt, and yeast mixture. Blend all ingredients well. Pour mixture into a greased and floured baking pan and let rise in a warm place for 1½ hours.

Then put the pie in a slow oven and bake until golden brown. Cut into squares and sprinkle with vanilla sugar before serving.

NOTE: Vanilla sugar, which is sold in boxes (sealed in individual packets), can be found in most food specialty stores, particularly Hungarian ones. It is available at H. Roth & Son, 1577 First Avenue, New York, NY 10028, and Paprikas Weiss, 1546 Second Avenue, New York, NY 10028.

Armenian Midwife's Milk Loaf
(Örmény Bábakalács)

The milk loaf was an obligatory delicacy at Armenian wedding feasts. On such an occasion, not 10, but 40 or 50 loaves were baked! These were made not only for the guests, but also as gifts for friends.

1 quart milk	**4 cups whole eggs**
4 cups sifted flour, plus more if necessary	**2 cups butter, melted**
4 cups powdered sugar	**2 ounces dry yeast, dissolved in a little of the lukewarm milk**
4 cups egg yolks	**Pinch of salt**

Heat the milk in a saucepan. Put flour in a large bowl and scald with the hot milk. Stir constantly until flour becomes smooth. Cool, then mix in the sugar.

Continue stirring and add the egg yolks, then the whole eggs, followed by the melted butter and dissolved yeast. Finally, add the salt.

Mix thoroughly and let rise for 5 hours. If the dough is too soft it may be hardened by adding more flour. (It should be somewhat harder than the ordinary milk loaf dough—or medium-hard.)

Knead dough briefly, let rise until doubled, beat it down and let rise again. Divide the dough into 10 portions and put each in a buttered loaf pan.

Bake the loaves in a moderate oven for 45 minutes.

NOTE: The latest cookbooks recommend serving the milk loaf with coffee.

Honey Cake in the Armenian Manner
(*Kátá or Mézes Béles*)

In Transylvania *Mézes Béles* was a favorite carnival-season dessert; however, the Armenian families, who called it *Kátá,* prepared it at Easter.

As couples dancing spin in swirling
Yeast in water warmed dissolves twirling.
Butter honeyed waiting yeast's troubling
That with whisking soaks in bubbling.
As paper lanterns fall tearing crashed,
Beat in bright egg yolks with ground cloves mashed.
Loud stomping oaths and imprecations
Fall like rye flour rains the rations
Just what dough needs hard'ning in kneading
Waiting rising from yeast cell seeding.
As the music rises for shaking
The dough is rounded and shaped for baking;
Oven brushed with egg all day heating
Night's feasting party seizes eating.

1 ounce dry yeast
2 cups butter, melted
4 cups honey
3 egg yolks, beaten

1 teaspoon cloves, ground
2 pounds rye flour, or as much as is needed

Dissolve the yeast in a little bit of lukewarm water. Whisk the butter in a bowl and mix in the honey, then the dissolved yeast, 2 egg yolks, and ground cloves.

Knead in as much rye flour as needed to make a hard dough (similar to a noodle dough). Let rise in a warm place in a covered bowl. The dough should be left to rise from the evening of Holy Thursday until Saturday morning (in other words, about 1½ days).

Shape dough into a round or oblong form, brush with remaining egg yolk, and bake until done. Since the cake takes a longer time to cook than a milk loaf, it is usually left in a low oven until 6 in the evening.

Sour Cream Doughnuts
(*Tejfölös Fánk*)

8 egg yolks
2 cups sour cream
1½ cups lukewarm milk
¾ ounce dry yeast
5 cups sifted flour

Pinch of salt
2 cups rendered goose fat
1 teaspoon sugar, plus more for
**   dusting**

In a double boiler, over low heat, beat egg yolks together with the sour cream. Let mixture get slightly warm while stirring it constantly.

Meanwhile, prepare a leaven with ½ cup of the lukewarm milk, the yeast, and ½ cup of the flour. Let rise until doubled in size, then mix with remaining flour, salt, sugar, and remaining 1 cup lukewarm milk.

Add sour cream and egg mixture and stir until batter becomes smooth and soft. Let rise in moderately warm place for 1 hour. Spread batter out on a floured board and shape into small dumplings, about 2 inches in size. Cover with a damp cloth and let them rise again half as much.

Heat fat in a deep frying pan. Fry doughnuts in the hot fat. Turn over to brown other side. Since the doughnuts will puff up and float on top of the fat, a light yellow ribbon of dough will remain between the two brown fried sides.

Drain the doughnuts and dust with sugar.

Piped Doughnuts
(Kitoló Fánk)

2 cups hot milk	**1 tablespoon sugar**
2 cups flour, sifted	**6 egg whites, beaten**
14 tablespoons butter	**Oil for frying**
Salt to taste	**Vanilla sugar for dusting**
10 egg yolks	

In a double boiler, cook the hot milk, flour, and butter. Stir constantly until the mixture thickens.

Remove from heat, add salt, and continue to stir. When cool, gradually add the egg yolks, then the sugar and beaten egg whites.

Heat the oil in a deep frying pan. Fit a pastry bag with a 1-inch nozzle and fill it with the batter. Squeeze out 5-inch-long sections of batter into the hot oil and fry until brown. Dust with vanilla sugar before serving. Drain.

Goose Crackling Scones
(Libatöpötyűs Pogácsa)

5 cups flour, sifted	**Salt to taste**
½ cup rendered goose fat	**Pinch of pepper**
1½ cups chopped goose	**¾ ounce dry yeast**
** cracklings (page 210)**	**2 tablespoons fruity white wine**
4 egg yolks, beaten	

In a large bowl, make a dough from
the flour, goose fat, cracklings, 3 egg
yolks, salt, and pepper. Dissolve the
yeast in the wine and add to the
mixture. Knead well. Let dough rest
for ½ hour.

Knead and fold dough over three
times. Roll out dough to 1 inch thick.
Cut into circles with a cookie cutter,
and score the tops with a knife.

Arrange scones on a greased baking
sheet and let rise in a warm place for
1 hour. Brush with remaining beaten
egg yolk and bake in a moderately hot
oven until lightly browned.

VARIATION

Sauté shredded cabbage in lard or goose fat until golden brown, season with salt and
pepper, and mix into the basic dough.

Walnut Scones
(*Diós Pogácsa*)

1½ cups sifted flour
14 tablespoons butter
½ cup confectioners' sugar
2 egg yolks, beaten

2 cups ground walnuts
1 teaspoon cinnamon
Juice of ½ lemon
1 whole egg, beaten

In a large bowl, make a dough from
the flour, butter, sugar, egg yolks,
walnuts, cinnamon, and lemon juice.
Knead it thoroughly.

Roll out dough to ½ inch thick. Cut
out scones with a round cookie cutter
and place on a buttered baking sheet.
Brush with the beaten egg and bake in
a moderate oven until golden brown.

Armenian Honey and Hazelnut Scones from Szamosujvár
(Chátlamá or Szamosujvári Örmény Mézes Pogácsa)

This dessert was not only made for the home. According to Károly Kós, the dean of
Transylvanian folklore writers: "The most famous delicacy at fairs were honey scones
from Szamosujvár . . . at the Páncélcsehi fair, most of the scone vendors came from the
Armenian town of Szamosujvár. . . ."

7 ounces honey
¾ cup plus 2 tablespoons sugar
2 cups flour
2 eggs

1 teaspoon sifted cinnamon
Pinch of saffron
1 teaspoon baking soda
Hazelnuts, almonds, or walnuts

Bring honey and sugar to a boil in a
saucepan. Put flour in a large bowl
and pour honey–sugar mixture over
it. Let cool, then start kneading in the
bowl. Gradually add eggs, cinnamon,
saffron, and baking soda. Knead
thoroughly.

Roll out dough to ½ inch thick. Use a
large cookie cutter to cut out circles.
Place some nuts in the center of each
circle.

Arrange scones on a greased and floured baking sheet. Let stand for 30 minutes, then bake in a hot oven for 15 to 20 minutes, or until golden brown.

Hungarian Crêpes or Pancakes
(Palacsintatészták)

This first recipe is for a thin, flat pancake, similar to a *crêpe;* the one that follows is a thicker, higher pancake made with yeast.

Thin Pancakes
3 eggs
2 cups lukewarm milk
3 cups sifted flour
1 teaspoon salt
1½ to 2 tablespoons sugar
Rendered lard or melted butter

In a large bowl, combine the eggs with half the lukewarm milk. Add flour gradually while stirring constantly. Add the remaining milk and the salt and sugar.

Heat some lard or melted butter in a flat skillet or *crêpe* pan (preferably one not used for preparing anything else). Coat the bottom of the pan with the fat.

Drain off the excess fat, then pour in a small amount of batter (just enough to thinly cover the bottom of the pan), and quickly spread it around the pan.

When one side is browned, flip the pancake over, brown the other side slightly, then remove from pan. If the batter happens to be too sticky, add 1 more egg, mixing it in well.

Continue this process until all the batter is used up. Add 1 teaspoon of melted butter to the pan before frying each pancake and drain off excess.

VARIATIONS

Without a doubt, these thin pancakes or *crêpes* are the most popular dessert in this corner of the world. Every ethnic nationality has its own simple or complicated variation and filling. Pancakes stuffed with *orda* and Armenian pancakes stuffed with meat are some of the recipes that use these *crêpes* (however, without adding sugar to the batter). One popular variation is a *crêpe* filled with apricot preserves and ground walnuts. My favorite *crêpe* is one filled with rose hip jam (some call it wild rose jam), because of its splendid color and delightful, slightly tart taste. It is served with a sauce made with rose hip syrup flavored with kirschwasser.

NOTE: If the pancakes aren't going to be used immediately, put squares of waxed paper between them to avoid sticking.

Thick Pancakes

1 cup lukewarm milk
3 eggs
2 tablespoons sugar
Pinch of salt
1 package dry yeast
3 cups sifted flour
½ cup seltzer or club soda
Melted butter, rendered lard, or
  oil for frying

In a large bowl, combine the milk and eggs. Slowly add the sugar, salt, and yeast. Stir until very smooth while continuing to add flour. Let mixture stand in a warm place for at least 1 hour.

Before frying the pancakes, stir in the seltzer.

Use a well-greased flat skillet or *crêpe* pan. Put 1 tablespoon of butter or oil in the pan; then rotate the pan so that the fat covers the bottom. Drain off the excess fat, then heat the fat in pan well.

Pour a small ladleful of batter into the center of the *crêpe* pan, rotating the pan until the bottom is covered. Do not leave any areas uncovered.

Fry it until the bottom of the pancake is barely golden brown. Turn it over and fry the other side, for about 20 seconds.

Continue to make pancakes until all the batter is used up. Add another teaspoon of fat to the skillet before cooking each *crêpe*.

The pancakes should be about 1/10 inch thick. Adjust the amount of batter you add to the pan after the first two are done.

NOTE: If the pancakes aren't going to be used immediately, put waxed paper between them to keep them from sticking together.

Pancakes prepared with yeast and seltzer become softer and thicker than in the recipe above. They are used with other foods and in the preparation of certain desserts.

Verzár or Armenian Spinach Pancakes
(Örmény spenótos Palacsinta)

The dish *verzár* was not listed by Szongott (a popular Armenian writer at the end of the nineteenth century) among the Armenian dishes because he traces the origin of the word to the Rumanian *verza*. In the Rumanian gastronomy *verza* means a type of stuffed cabbage. However, Transylvanian Armenians were fond of these pancakes, which they named after the only Transylvanian Armenian Catholic bishop, Verzár Oxendius, who—in addition to converting the Greek Orthodox Armenians to the Catholic faith—organized their industry and trade and obtained privileges for them.

1 recipe for thin pancake batter (page 317)
Oil for frying

Cabbage Filling

1¼ pounds fresh cabbage, grated
Salt to taste
1 tablespoon rendered lard
½ onion, minced
Pepper and hot paprika to taste
Sour cream for topping pancakes

Spinach Filling

1¼ pounds spinach, washed and trimmed
3 eggs, separated
1 garlic clove
Salt, pepper, and ground nutmeg to taste

Prepare thin pancakes and fry them lightly in oil on both sides in a greased frying pan. Set pancakes aside while making the filling.

For the cabbage filling: Season cabbage with salt and let stand for a few minutes. Heat lard in a frying pan, add the onion, and sauté until wilted.

Squeeze cabbage to press out juice, and sauté it with the onion. Continue to cook over low heat, while stirring frequently, until cabbage browns slightly and all its juice has evaporated. Season with pepper and paprika. Mix well.

Spread filling over pancakes. They may be rolled up or layered one on top of another. Spread on sour cream. Heat in a low oven before serving.

For the spinach filling: Cook spinach in boiling water until tender. Drain and strain through a sieve. Chop spinach.

Mix spinach with egg yolks, garlic, salt, pepper, and nutmeg. Beat the egg whites until stiff and fold into mixture. Fill pancakes as above. Heat in a low oven before serving.

Variations

The cabbage filling may be prepared without onions; sauté the cabbage in goose fat and add some chopped parsley or dill. Season only with salt and pepper.

PASTRIES, SWEETS, AND TIDBITS

Pastry Rings from Háromszék for a Sekler Wedding
(*Háromszéki Rakott Ág*)

Traditionally, this pastry is prepared by a group of women at country weddings for a great number of guests.

25 eggs	**½ cup vinegar**
1 teaspoon salt	**5½ pounds flour, sifted**
5 cups sugar	**Oil for frying**
½ cup baking soda	**1 cup vanilla sugar**

Beat eggs in a large bowl. Slowly add salt and sugar. Dissolve the baking soda in vinegar and mix with eggs. Then gradually add flour to bowl.

Knead mixture thoroughly until dough holds together. Place dough on a board and continue to knead until firm.

Cut dough into pieces, 1 piece per person, and continue working it. When dough is well kneaded, cover with cloth to prevent it from drying out.

Form dough into small loaves. Roll out each loaf to noodle thickness and leave on a white linen tablecloth to dry. Approximately 18 pastry sheets can be made from this amount.

Allow the sheets to dry a little, not more than ½ hour. Then, beginning at the edge of the pastry sheet and moving in a spiral, cut dough into ribbons. Heat oil over a low flame while preparing dough, then raise heat.

Roll a ribbon loosely around your hand. Then slip it off slowly and carefully from your hand and into the oil so that ribbons don't stick together and keep their rolled shape. Fry pastry in hot oil for a few minutes. When it is golden brown, remove from oil. Drain. Sprinkle with vanilla sugar.

NOTE: Traditionally the finished pastries are tied on to three-pronged wooden branches (stripped of their bark) with string or colored ribbon. Then some of them are displayed in the middle of the buffet tables among the sweets.

Cinnamon Horn
(*Zimmt Krapfen or Fahéjas Tekercs*)

1½ cups butter
6 eggs
1 teaspoon salt
1 teaspoon vinegar
½ cup sugar
1 cup sifted flour
2 egg whites, beaten
Oil for frying

Powdered sugar and cinnamon, mixed together
Sweetened whipped heavy cream or vanilla pastry cream for filling (optional)
Ground walnuts or chopped pistachio nuts for garnish.

Combine 1 cup butter, 1 cup warm water, 4 eggs, salt, vinegar, and sugar in a large bowl and stir until smooth. Add enough flour to make a medium-soft dough. Knead the dough.

Roll out the dough until very thin. Melt the remaining butter and sprinkle some of it on the dough. Fold the dough over into thirds. Then roll it out again in a long shape, sprinkle with additional melted butter, and fold into thirds. Repeat this two more times. Cover the dough with a cloth.

Let dough stand in a cool place overnight. The next morning, roll the dough out thinly, and cut into strips 2 by 7 inches.

Moisten the ends of the strips with beaten egg whites. Then wind them around a cone-shaped metal mold, and brush with the remaining 2 eggs, beaten. Fry in hot oil until golden brown. Drain on paper towel. Let cool, then roll in the mixture of powdered sugar and cinnamon.

The horns may be filled with
sweetened whipped cream or vanilla
pastry cream. Decorate with ground
walnuts or chopped pistachio nuts.

"Pillowcases"
(*Hausen Blasen or Párnahuzatok*)

3 cups flour
1 teaspoon baking powder
2 teaspoons sugar
¼ teaspoon cinnamon
½ cup butter
2 teaspoons honey

1 cup milk
3 eggs
Oil for frying
Powdered sugar and cinnamon to
  taste, mixed together

Sift together the flour, baking powder,
sugar, and cinnamon and put in a
large bowl. Crumble the butter into
the mixture and stir in honey.

Pour in the milk and stir well. Add the
eggs. Knead the dough well until it
loses all its stickiness.

Place the dough on a floured board.
Let it rest for about 15 minutes. Knead
dough, then roll out until as thin as
possible. With a knife, cut the dough
into squares or triangles.

Fry the dough in hot oil. The dough
will puff up like pillows. When golden
brown, remove from pan and drain
on paper towel. Sprinkle with the
powdered sugar and cinnamon
mixture.

Kindli

A dessert offered to guests at Purim, a day of joy.

> *To Esther, gracious Queen, with joy*
> *Send thy daughters bearing oil,*
> *Honey, flour, egg yolks, and wine*
> *Knead these all to a fine alloy*
> *So the dough is hard by toil;*
> *Separate to stand as a sign*
> *Into three loaves, as Mordecai*
> *Waited three days for all to die*
> *Or niece to save from Haman's try.*
> *Roll each loaf to a quite thin sheet*
> *Like dire edicts he sent out;*
> *Brush their tops with melted honey*
> *And oil as the Queen's words sweet*
> *Brought to banquet that evil lout.*
> *Take sugar, walnuts, lemons sunny*
> *Grate their peel, with raisins dried*
> *Mix together, by thirds divide*
> *And on each sheet the mixture slide*
> *Dress again with honey and oil*
> *Roll into a parchment's coil*
> *Brush and place on greased baking foil*
> *Score before once like the King's wrath,*
> *Just on top like a gallows path*
> *Then while baking it give a bath*
> *Of honey in the moderate heat;*
> *When done let rest this kingly treat*
> *Three days shall soften Esther's sweet.*

2 cups flour, sifted	**2 cups sugar**
1 cup oil	**2 cups walnuts, chopped**
3 egg yolks	**1 cup raisins, chopped**
3 tablespoons honey	**Grated peel of 2 lemons**
1 cup sweet white wine	

Mix together flour, ½ cup of the oil, egg yolks, 1 tablespoon of the honey, and wine in a large bowl and knead until dough becomes medium-hard. Separate dough into 3 loaves. Let them rest ½ hour.

Roll each loaf separately into a very thin sheet. Heat remaining oil and honey together until honey is melted. Brush top of sheets of dough with a third of the oil and honey mixture.

Prepare a mixture of sugar, walnuts, raisins, and grated lemon peel. Divide the mixture into thirds. Cover each pastry sheet with a third of the mixture, then sprinkle with some more oil and honey. Roll up sheets tightly and brush them all over with more oil and honey.

Place rolls on a greased baking sheet and score the tops before baking. Baste rolls with oil and honey mixture at least twice more.

Bake in a moderate oven until golden brown. After 3 days the pastry will soften.

VARIATION

Flodni or *fládni,* another dessert for Purim, is a variation of *kindli.* Its pastry is identical to that of *kindli,* but its filling differs; additionally, the pastry of the *flodni* is not rolled but layered. After preparing the pastry according to the first two steps above, lay the first sheet in a greased baking pan. Cover with a thin layer of jam, any kind. Place the next sheet on, and sprinkle with 2 cups chopped walnuts. Cover with the third sheet and top with 2 pounds roughly grated peeled apples; then lay on the fourth sheet. Be sure to sprinkle each sheet of pastry and each layer of filling with the melted oil and honey mixture. Brush the top sheet of pastry with oil and honey and bake in a moderate oven until top is reddish brown.

Strudels
(*Rétesek*)

Strudel Dough
(*Rétestészta*)

1½ cups Canadian Manitoba (high gluten content) flour
¾ cup all-purpose flour, plus more for dusting
2 eggs, beaten

½ teaspoon vinegar
Pinch of salt
½ cup melted butter or melted rendered lard

Sift the two types of flour onto a pastry board. Make a well in the center and pour in the following mixture: 1 cup warm water, 1 egg, vinegar, and salt. Mix together.

Knead well on a floured board for at least 10 minutes, or until it no longer sticks to the board. Then, in a bowl, beat the dough very strongly against the sides of the bowl (in order to break up the cells) for another 15 to 20 minutes, until smooth.

Form 2 round loaves from the dough and put them on the floured board. Brush with a little melted butter and let dough rest for 30 minutes.

Cover a square or rectangular table with a clean white linen cloth and sprinkle it with flour. Carefully roll out a loaf of dough until it hangs off the edges of the table. Stretch it until as thin as possible. (It should be thin enough so that you can read a newspaper through it.)

Lightly sprinkle the rolled-out dough with lukewarm water. Trim the thicker edges that hang from the table and put them aside. Sprinkle the stretched-out dough with the remaining melted butter.

Prepare the filling (recipes follow).

Spread the filling over a third of the strudel dough, or over all of it if desired. Fold over the edges that hang off the table, and spread some filling on these edges also.

Fold over one side of dough and sprinkle the top of it with butter. Then fold over the remaining side and sprinkle the top of it with melted butter. When finished, grasp the edge of the tablecloth, lift it slowly, and roll up the dough. Brush the top of the strudel with the remaining beaten egg to make a crisper crust.

Another method of rolling strudel: This method will produce a good strudel, with a bakery appearance. However, it will lack a certain homemade quality, because the filling is not distributed throughout all the layers of dough and the strudel is not covered with caramelized sugar.

Spread some of the filling over a section of the strudel dough, then fold the remaining dough over it, brushing it with butter to prevent sticking. The strudel may also be sprinkled with sugared bread crumbs.

Cut the rolled-up strudel to the length
of the baking sheet and place on
sheet. Bake the strudel in a preheated
moderately hot oven until done.

NOTE: There are several secrets to making authentic, flaky, paper-thin strudel. Choose
the appropriate flour; it should not be freshly milled. Knead the dough well; there is an
old saying, "Knead the dough until you make even the heavens [or ceiling] cry."

Strudel Fillings
(*Réstestöltelékek*)

There are many varieties of strudel filling. Three very popular and outstanding fillings
for strudel are described here. The recipes may seem time-consuming, but the results
are perfect.

Poppy Seed Filling

1 egg yolk
½ cup butter, melted
1 cup milk
Grated peel of ½ lemon
½ cup vanilla sugar
½ pound ground poppy seeds

¼ cup minced raisins
1 tablespoon Cognac
1 tablespoon dark rum
2 tablespoons honey
1 teaspoon cocoa powder
1 egg white
1 teaspoon sugar

In a saucepan, combine the egg yolk,
half the butter, milk, lemon peel, and
vanilla sugar. Heat this mixture over a
low flame, stirring constantly.

When it is hot and almost boiling, add
the poppy seeds.

When the mixture has reached a full
boil, remove from heat. Let cool
slightly, then add the raisins, Cognac,
rum, honey, and cocoa powder

Whip the egg white along with the
sugar. When it begins to stiffen, gently
fold it into the poppy seed mixture.

Walnut Filling

1 egg yolk
½ cup butter
1 cup milk
Grated peel of ½ orange

½ cup vanilla sugar
10 ounces ground walnuts
½ cup dark rum
1 egg white
1 tablespoon sugar

Prepare filling in the same manner as the poppy seed filling.

Farmer Cheese Filling

1 pound rich farmer cheese, crumbled
4 eggs, separated
1 cup butter
½ cup vanilla sugar

½ cup flour
½ cup sour cream
½ cup raisins (soaked in Cognac)
Grated peel of ½ lemon
Pinch of salt
½ cup sugar

Combine the cheese and egg yolks and mix thoroughly. Beat the egg whites, half the butter, and the vanilla sugar until foamy.

Slowly fold in the flour, sour cream, raisins, lemon peel, and salt. Let stand for 15 to 20 minutes.

Spread the filling over the pastry and roll the strudel up in the usual manner. Cut it to fit the length of the baking sheet.

Cut the remaining butter into pats and place them on top. Sprinkle generously with the sugar.

Bake in a moderately hot oven for approximately 30 to 40 minutes.

Cobbler's Turnover
(*Vargabéles*)

Vargabéles is a specifically Transylvanian dessert. According to gourmets, the best example of it was prepared in the Darvas restaurant, one of the most famous establishments in Kolozsvár. (The name of this family will reappear later in the chapter on the town's 200-year-old hospitality trade.) According to the people of Marosvásárhely, genuine cobbler's turnovers were once also prepared in the Guschat's Tag restaurant. However, some remember an even more mouth-watering version at the sections of town called the Édeslyuk, or Súrlott-garádics. ("Sweet hole" and "worn church steps" are the respective translations of these old names.)

1 recipe for strudel dough (page 328)	**1½ cups sour cream**
1¾ cup sifted flour	**2 pounds cottage cheese, strained**
1 whole egg	**3½ ounces raisins**
14 tablespoons butter	**Vanilla sugar and grated lemon peel to taste**
1½ cups sugar	**Melted rendered lard or butter**
7 eggs, separated	

Prepare the strudel dough according to the standard recipe and roll it out. Let it stand in a cool place for 1 hour.

Meanwhile, prepare a stiff dough from the flour and whole egg. Roll out dough as thinly as possible. Tear into small pieces and cook in boiling lightly salted water until tender. Drain and rinse. Set aside.

In a large bowl, combine butter, sugar, egg yolks, and sour cream. Stir until smooth. Mix in the cottage cheese and raisins. Add as much vanilla sugar and grated lemon peel as desired.

Butter a deep baking pan. Cut strudel dough to dimensions of pan. Line pan with 3 or 4 layers of strudel dough. Sprinkle each layer with melted lard.

Beat the egg whites. Fold the cooked dough and beaten egg whites into cottage cheese mixture. Set filling aside.

Cover pastry evenly with cottage cheese filling and top with another 3 or 4 layers of strudel dough.

Brush top with more lard. Bake in a moderate oven for 25 to 30 minutes, until top becomes crisp and golden brown and the filling is also thoroughly baked.

Armenian Nut Turnovers
(*Páchlává* or *Örmény Diós Béles*)

A traditional Armenian dessert, *páchlává* is usually served at family celebrations such as weddings and birthdays. It is a variation of the ever-popular Near Eastern dessert *baklavá*.

Pastry

2 cups sifted flour, plus more for dusting
4 tablespoons rendered lard, melted
1 tablespoon vinegar
1 cup honey, heated
Melted lard

Filling

1¾ pounds walnuts, chopped
1 pound confectioners' sugar
5 ounces raisins
Grated rind of 2 lemons
4 tablespoons rendered lard

Prepare the pastry: Make a strudel dough (see page 328) from flour, 4 tablespoons lard, vinegar, and as much salted lukewarm water as necessary to make a hard dough.

Divide dough in half. Form each half into a round loaf, brush lightly with melted lard, cover, and let it rest for 30 minutes.

Prepare a square or rectangular table by covering it with a white linen tablecloth, as for the strudel dough. Dust with flour and stretch out both loaves of dough until very thin. The edges of the paper-thin dough should be trimmed and should be added to the next batch.

Sprinkle pastry sheets with melted lard. When pastry has dried and is no longer sticky, cut into pieces to fit into a baking pan. Layer half the pastry sheets in the greased baking pan. Sprinkle each layer with melted lard.

Prepare the filling: Mix chopped walnuts with confectioners' sugar and raisins. Add lemon rind. Cover pastry layers evenly with 1 inch of prepared filling and press filling down by hand.

Cover filling with remaining pastry sheets, sprinkling each layer with melted honey.

Melt 4 tablespoons lard. Dip knife in lard and cut pastry into serving-size pieces. Sprinkle the cuttings with honey. Repeat dipping and cutting a few more times so edges will be a bit soaked by the fat and the pieces of pastry will not stick together.

Place pan in a moderate oven and bake pastry for 2 to 3 hours. Remove pan from oven, and pour hot honey into the incisions made for the serving pieces. When honey hardens, remove squares from pan and serve.

VARIATION

In some places this pastry is flavored with rose hip leaves.

Honey Cake
(*Mézeskalács*)

2 cups honey
2 whole eggs
2 egg yolks
¼ cup sugar
2 cups sifted flour
1 teaspoon baking soda
⅓ ounce cardamon, ground

Dash of cinnamon
½ ounce cloves, ground
1 tablespoon rendered goose fat
Flour for dusting
2½ ounces slivered or julienned almonds

In a large saucepan, warm the honey. Mix in eggs, egg yolks, sugar, flour, baking soda, cardamon, cinnamon, and cloves. Blend thoroughly.

Grease a baking pan with goose fat, dust it with flour, and pour in the mixture. Sprinkle the top with almonds and bake for 30 minutes in a moderate oven.

VARIATION

Although this recipe, which was prepared on All Saints' Day (November 1) and called *Mindszenti Kalács,* is very similar to the preceding one, I felt it could not be left out of the collection.

8 pounds honey
2 pounds sugar syrup
2 ounces anise, finely ground
2 ounces cinnamon
2 ounces coriander, finely ground
2 ounces cloves, finely ground

2 ounces nutmeg, finely ground
2 ounces allspice
5 pounds flour, sifted
5 ounces potash
Melted butter and egg yolks, mixed together
Blanched whole almonds

In a pot, heat the honey together with the sugar syrup until mixture can be formed into thin (not caramelized) strands. (Test it by taking a pinch of the mixture; as you separate your fingers, it should form a thin strand.)

Blend in the spices and flour. Store dough in a cool, dry place for 1 week.

Before baking, stir the potash (which should first be sprinkled with water the night before) into the dough. Knead dough thoroughly and roll it out to ⅓ inch thick. Cut out dough with cookie cutters (preferably wooden) in various forms, and brush pieces lightly with a mixture of melted butter and egg yolks. Decorate with almonds.

Place on greased baking sheets and bake in a moderate oven until golden brown.

Armenian Bride's Scones
(Dákták Hálvá or Örmény Menyasszony Búcsúztató Kalács)

According to Armenian custom, *dákták hálvá* was usually made at the bride's house for the wedding feast. However, the dessert was also a favorite at birthday and name-day parties.

1 cup butter
Flour
2 cups lukewarm honey

7 ounces almonds, blanched and julienned (or slivered)
Confectioners' sugar

Melt the butter in a saucepan, and add as much flour as necessary for desired consistency. To test consistency, place a pinch of the mixture between pieces of paper towel and squeeze with your fingers. If the paper does not become oily, there is enough flour in the mixture.

Brown the buttered flour slightly. Add the lukewarm honey, stirring continuously to prevent lumps from forming.

Add the almonds to the honey mixture. Continue to stir over heat.

Sprinkle a buttered cake pan with confectioners' sugar. Pour in mixture. Using a piece of waxed paper, press down on the mixture to make it stick together. Chill, then turn out onto a serving dish.

Cold Lemon Koch
(*Hideg Citrom Koch*)

6 eggs, separated
1¼ cups powdered sugar
Juice and grated peel of 1 lemon
1 envelope gelatin, dissolved in
warm water

Butter for greasing mold
Fruit preserves (any flavor) for
garnish

In a large bowl, beat the egg yolks and
powdered sugar together. Add the
lemon juice and the grated peel. In
another bowl, whip the egg whites
until stiff, fold into the egg yolks, then
stir in the dissolved gelatin.

Butter a mold (such as a ring mold)
lightly and pour in the mixture. Chill
until well set. Turn the *koch* out of the
mold and onto a platter. Garnish with
fruit preserves.

NOTE: This dish is similar to a cold lemon mousse, or an Italian lemon *semifreddo,* and
was a favorite of fine Saxon households.

Noodles with Almonds
(Mandulás Metélt)

Noodles

2 whole eggs
2 egg yolks
1½ cups ground almonds
1 teaspoon confectioners' sugar
1 teaspoon vanilla sugar
Flour
1 quart milk, heated

Cream

5½ tablespoons butter
½ cup confectioners' sugar
½ cup plus 3 tablespoons flour
6 egg yolks
4 egg whites, beaten
A pinch of salt
Butter for greasing pan

Prepare the noodles: Mix the whole eggs, egg yolks, ground almonds, confectioners' sugar, vanilla sugar, and as much flour as it takes to make a stiff dough (see page 83). Knead thoroughly. Roll out dough until thin and cut into fine noodles. Let noodles dry.

Cook noodles in hot milk. Let come to a boil once, then drain, reserving the milk. Set noodles aside.

Prepare the cream: Add butter, confectioners' sugar, and flour gradually to the reserved pot of milk. Stir continuously over low heat until mixture becomes smooth and thick.

Let cool, then blend in egg yolks, beaten egg whites, salt, and the noodles. Mix well, put in a buttered baking pan, and bake in a moderate oven for about 1 hour, until crisp and golden brown.

NOTE: Almond noodles can be served hot with a rum-caramel sauce.

Dáláuzi

Dáláuzi is a confection, similar to nougat, prepared in celebration of the New Year. According to Zakariás Gábrus, an old Armenian song, "Song about the *Dáláuzi*," commemorates this confection. Recipe books published after World War I do not include this recipe, although it was so famous in the past that according to an article in an 1891 issue of *Magyar Hírlap,* even the fences of the Armenians in Szamosujvár were made of *dáláuzi*.

9 ounces honey
9 ounces whole poppy seeds
9 ounces walnuts, chopped

Grated lemon peel or orange peel
**   to taste**
Sugared almonds for garnish

In a saucepan, brown the honey, stirring constantly to prevent burning. It must brown, or else the *dáláuzi* will not harden.

Dry-roast the poppy seeds for 15 minutes in a moderate oven, stirring them frequently. Add them to the honey, along with the chopped nuts. Mix well. Season with a little grated lemon or orange peel.

Wet a pastry board and distribute *dáláuzi* in small mounds. With wet palms, shape the mounds into round, square, or scone (conical) shapes. Decorate with sugared almonds.

NOTE: The poppy seeds may be omitted from this recipe.

Sweet Matzo Doughnuts for Passover
(Chremzli Más Módon)

Chremzli is a Passover tidbit of the Jews from Máramaros-Sziget.

4 to 5 egg yolks
4 tablespoons sugar
4 tablespoons matzo cake meal
2 walnuts, minced
1 teaspoon raisins

1 teaspoon cocoa
Grated peel of 1 lemon
½ cup lukewarm milk
2 egg whites
Oil for frying

In a large bowl, beat the egg yolks until smooth. Slowly add sugar. Mix in the matzo meal. Stir in walnuts, raisins, cocoa, lemon peel, and lukewarm milk.

In a small bowl, beat the egg whites until they form stiff peaks. Fold whites slowly into the mixture so peaks do not break.

In a deep pan, heat oil until very hot. Drop tablespoonfuls of batter into the oil and fry on both sides until crisp. Drain on paper towel and serve.

THE HERBS AND SPICES
OF TRANSYLVANIA

by Paul Kovi and István Szöcs

Anise (Pimpinella anisum)

Also called fragrant anise or Oriental anise, or sweet fennel. In Hungarian, *ánizs;* in Rumanian, *anason, anison,* or *chimion dulce;* in German, *Anis;* in French, *anis;* and in Russian, *bedrenec anis* or *anis nastoyashchi.*

The seeds are used for an herbal tea, which is sweet and strongly fragrant. They are also primarily used to season liqueurs, pastries, scones, and milk loaves, and are a favorite spice of the sweets sold at fairs.

It originated in the Mediterranean region, but it was already known in Transylvania in the Middle Ages, when it was grown in gardens. It is often mixed with cinnamon or cloves in drinks or cakes.

Basil (Ocimum basilicum)

Also sweet basil. In Hungarian, *bazsalikom;* in Rumanian, *busuioc;* in German, *Basilicom;* in French, *basilic;* in Russian, *bazilik ogorodnij.*

This extremely versatile and fragrant herb is added to meat dishes, sauces, and salads. Originally—in Greek—its name meant the "king of the herbs." It also oppresses odious penetrating smells.

Borage (Borago officinalis)

Also plantain, wine flower, lamb tongue, ox tongue, or garden ox tongue. In Hungarian, *borvirág;* in Rumanian, *limba mielului;* in German, *Buretsch Wohlgemuth;* in French, *bourrache;* in Russian, *ogurechnyik aptyechnij.*

Its leaves are primarily used to prepare pickles, such as gherkins.

Caraway, caraway seeds (Carum carvi)

Also garden caraway. In Hungarian, *köménymag;* in Rumanian, *chimen* or *chimion;* in German, *Kümmel;* in French, *cumin;* in Russian, *tmin obiknovennij.*

In Central Europe caraway seed soup is perhaps the most common soup for children and the elderly, and is also an item on inexpensive menus. This "Cinderella" of our spices is indispensable in preparing roasts, pastries, breads, and vegetables.

Coriander (Coriandrum sativum L.)

Also coriandrum tree. In Hungarian, *koriander, pakilints,* or *temondádfü;* in Rumanian, *coriandru;* in German, *Gemeiner Koriander;* in French, *coriandre;* in Russian, *koriander posevnoj.*

Its seeds are included as one of the spices used in marinades, meat products (particularly sausages), and sauces. Coriander seeds can be used whole or ground, and its leaves are used dried or fresh as a garnish or flavoring.

Dill (Anethum graveolens L.)

In Hungarian, *kapor;* in Rumanian, *mărar;* in German, *Kapper;* in French, *aneth;* in Russian, *ukrop ogorodni.*

A frequently used herb, both fresh and dried. Its fresh leaves are a must in pancakes or tarts with cottage cheese. Dill is also indispensable as a seasoning in preserved gherkins and in salads.

Fennel (Foeniculum vulgare)

Also garden fennel. In Hungarian, *édeskömény;* in Rumanian, *lolura;* in German, *Fenchel;* in French, *fenouil;* in Russian, *fennel obiknovennij.*

Some people confuse it with anise, and there is a definite similarity in their flavors. It is used to season bread, scones, milk loaves, and liqueurs.

Juniper (Juniperus communis L.)

Also pepper pine or dwarf pine. Its seed is often called "pine seed." In Hungarian, *boróka;* in Rumanian, *ienupăr;* in German, *Gereiner Wacholder;* in French, *geniévre;* in Russian, *mozhelnyik.*

In addition to it being an herb and a liquor flavoring, its berries are used to flavor gin, which is called "pine water" by the Seklers. A refreshing nonalcoholic drink can also be made from the fresh juniper berry, and the dried berry is an important additive in marinades made for wild game, bacon, ham, and various other meat products.

Lovage (Levisticum officinale)

In Hungarian, *leostyán, lescsihán, lostya,* and *löböstök;* in Rumanian, *leuştean;* in German, *Liebstock;* in French, *liveche;* and in Russian, *lyubestock.*

This herb is more commonly known in Hungarian cuisine as a spice for drinks and vinegar, but the Rumanians season their soups, sauces, and vegetables with lovage leaves.

Marjoram (Majorana hortensis)

In Hungarian, *majoranna;* in Rumanian, *mágheran;* in German, *Dolst* or *Garten Majoran;* in French, *marjolaine;* in Russian, *majoran sadovij.*

Marjoram is used in meat dishes, and particularly in white and black sausages. Sometimes it is even added to wine.

Nigella (Nigella sativa)

Also devil-in-the bush, gith, or bishop's wort. In Hungarian, *fekete kömény;* in Rumanian, *negrilică;* in German, *Schwarzkümmel;* in French, *nigelle;* and in Russian, *chernoushka.*

In the past, special pretzels were made with nigella seeds. Nowadays the Rumanians add it to their *telemea* curd cheese.

Paprika

This spice is generally called *paprika* in most languages.

Without any doubt the most popular spice in Transylvania. It is the powder made from the ripe, reddened, and ground flour of dried pepper. This certain species of pepper, cultivated primarily in Hungary, Spain, and Argentina, is left out to ripen till bright red. Then it is harvested, air-dried, and ground.

Pimpinella (Pimpinella saxifrage)

In Hungarian, *Csaba írja, baba-íre, érfű, földi töményfű,* or *rákfark;* in Rumanian, *pătrunjel de cimp;* in German, *Biberlein;* in French, *bibernelle;* in Russian, *bedrence kamnelomkovij.*

Used to season sweets. It is effective in curing hoarseness and coughing.

Savory (Satureia hortensis)

Also pepper herb or garden hyssop herb. In Hungarian, *borsfű* or *csombor;* in Rumanian, *cimbru;* in German, *Bohnenkraut;* in French, *sarriette;* in Russian, *chabyor sadovi.*

It complements various dishes, and definitely cannot be omitted—together with dill—from "slushy" cabbage. It can be used either fresh or dried.

Tarragon (Artemisia drancunculus)

In Hungarian, *tárkony* or *tárkonyürömi;* in Rumanian, *tarhon;* in German, *Dragun;* in French, *estragon;* in Russian, *polinestragon.*

Particularly enjoyable in dishes made of smoked meat, lamb chitterlings, and soups made of lamb or calf's head, but it is also useful in white bean soup, salads, and pickles. An excellent additive in flavoring vinegar. Its leaves are used fresh or dried, or are preserved in vinegar.

Thyme (Thymus serpyllum)

Also wild thyme or balsam herb. In Hungarian, *kakukkfű* or *balzsamfű;* in Ruma-

nian, *cimbrişor;* in German, *Feldthymian;* in French, *serpolet;* in Russian, *timjan.*
Used in salad dressings and for seasoning liqueurs and desserts.

Naturally, one does not need to mention the obligatory onion, garlic, and greens, such as parsley and celery, which play a leading role in Transylvanian cuisine, both as vegetables and as spices and herbs.

EXOTIC OR "FOREIGN" SPICES

Black Pepper (*Piper nigrum*) is the most generally used and known tropical spice, which overpowers almost all the other spices in Transylvania's everyday cuisine. Although exaggeration should be avoided, it is safe to say that no meat dish or soup is complete without it. On the popularity list, pepper is followed by bay leaf (*Laurus nobilis*), the main spice of sour soups, potato dishes, and tomato sauce. Cinnamon (*Cinnamomum zeylkanicum*) is essential in desserts, spicy-hot boiled wine, semolina pudding, milk loaf, and compotes. Cloves (*Syzygium aromaticum*), allspice (*Pimenta officinalis*), and, naturally, vanilla (*Vanilla planifolia*) are also used in quantity.

One of the basic spices of old Transylvanian and Hungarian cuisine in general, which recently reappeared and shows an upswing in its use, is ginger (*Zingiber officinale*). It is called *gyömbér* in Hungarian, *ghimber* in Rumanian, *Ingwer* in German, *gingembre* in French, and *imbiri* in Russian. Ginger is of Chinese origin and it spread from there throughout the world. In India, and in Southeast Asia, 250 kinds of ginger are grown. Its long, knobby root is either ground or grated, but despite its popularity, it should be used in moderation; if used excessively, ginger tastes of turpentine. Its name can be traced back to the Sanskrit *zhingevera,* supposedly meaning a horn-shaped formation; this was changed to *zengebil* in Arabic, *singiberis* in Greek, *zingiber* in Latin, *zenzero* in Italian, and *ginger* in English. It was appreciated as early as the Middle Ages in Transylvania. Ginger is recommended when the meat itself has a strong flavor—for example, fresh pork, goose, or turkey. Moderation is strongly recommended, for a large dose not only predominates over all other flavors, but has a stimulating effect.

Ginger should not be confused with the homegrown wood avens or ginger race (*Geum urbanum*), also called wood clove, violet clove, clove herb, or St. Benedictine herb, which is an officinal herb and can be used only in sweet liqueurs, if at all.

THE WINES OF TRANSYLVANIA:

A Guide for Imbibers

by György Csávossy

Wine is a regular decoration on the laden table of Transylvanian families. Its sparkling gold or glittering ruby hue whets the appetite at first glance, and its delicious flavor completes a tasty feast.

According to historians, Transylvanian viticulture has a past that spans six thousand years. The most common native grape varieties of Transylvania are Leányka (or Little Maiden), the Kövér, and the Járdovány, whose bubbles look like crystals when made into champagne. They deservedly acquired the appreciation of experts at numerous international competitions. There are indications that the basic grape of the Tokaj and Cotnari wines, in fact, originated in Transylvania.

The value of the Transylvanian wines is primarily credited to their body, well-balanced acidity, rich bouquet, and aroma; in other words, they are long-tasting wines with a lasting finish.

An old song correctly says, "good wine brings good health." Wine relaxes the body and stimulates all vital functions. It is a genuine medicine.

The word *pharmacy* originated from the Greek *apoteka,* which means wine shop. For centuries, wine was used as the main remedy for most ailments. In her handwritten cookery book, the wife of Prince Apafi (Anna Bornemisza) in 1668 included a large number of glosses on the cellar master, which were then copied by some and passed along to others as a "rare and dear treat." This book includes extremely interesting and historically valuable viticultural instructions, as well as recipes for several tonic wines and their medical indications.

János Nadányi, translator of *Garden Matters* (1669), contributed to it an appendix on the medical use of wines, while the highly important *Pax Corporis* by Ferenc Pápai-Pariz, which was published earlier, also lists the tonic wines. Accordingly, various mental and physical maladies were treated in the seventeenth and eighteenth centuries in Transylvania with tonic wines containing artemisia, sage, rosemary, or chamomile and other herbs.

Moderation should be the universal golden rule of wine drinking. The beauty and aesthetic value of wine make it easier to adhere to this rule. With its wonderful richness of aroma, wine should not be poured down by the bucket, but sipped and carefully savored. Those who discover the key to the noble pleasure provided by the slow sipping of wine will never gulp it down, and consider watering down a noble wine a sacrilege.

Wine making is an art. Wine itself is an aesthetic creation; its tasting and evaluation are true artistic activities. This is not an exaggeration. Wine provides an aesthetic experience, not through only one sensory organ, as with music or painting, but through all our senses.

The chimes of the bursting champagne bubbles can be heard, the amber color of an old wine can be visually appreciated, its flowery fragrance can be inhaled, its fruity treasures can be tasted, and while our tongue bathes in it, we feel its silky or velvety caress.

Until we reach the highest standard of wine enjoyment, we must make a long journey through this titillating sphere called viticulture—just as the novice gallery visitor lacks the knowledge of fine art necessary to enjoy its full value until he becomes informed of its nuances. To more fully appreciate the value of wine, I have provided a few useful hints for our reader.

It is the most elementary task of the taster to recognize the type he is drinking. Naturally, this is only the first step. To critically and correctly evaluate them, much more knowledge is necessary.

The tasting of wine is a subjective process because the personal faculties of the taster decisively influence the result. The degree of sensitivity of each of our sensory organs is quite different: our sight may be sharp while the olfactory organ for smelling may be weak and remain so. However, our taste buds can be considerably trained and educated.

Wine is rich in aromas. It is a great pity that we do not possess the keen smelling ability of wild game, for then we could discern wine's wonderful nuances from the sea of scents. If we examined the wine's volatile components—ethers, esters, terpenes, aldehydes, and acetals—they would reveal the origin, type, age, and mode of maturation.

We can solve all the secrets of wine with our tongue; it helps us to know its essence, fire, value, and soul—with all its virtues, beauties, and, eventually, its shortcomings. Physiology distinguishes four basic flavors: sweet, sour, salty, and bitter. The tip of our tongue senses sweet, the sides taste salty, the front sides sour, and the stem the bitter taste. While the tip is quickest to taste, the sensation there is not durable. The stem is slower but preserves the flavor for a longer period. The finish and the aftertaste are equally important. We are most sensitive to bitter sensations, followed by sweet, salty, and sour, in that order. An unpleasant aftertaste in wine may be traced to mold (on the grapes or in the cask), excess sulfur, hydrogen, cork, bacteriological contamination, or the presence of unwanted metals.

Some flavors dampen each other: for example, in a sweet wine a higher acidity is hardly noticed but it makes the taste of the wine livelier. When tasting, we also respond to temperature and texture. In the case of wine, the sensation of heat can indicate the alcohol content and the quality of the wine. The roughness, smoothness, velvetiness, body, thickness, oiliness, or metallic "feel" of the wine affects the sense of touch or sensation of texture.

The sense of taste is an individual faculty; for the full effect, sensitive and healthy organs are necessary. With practice, with comparative tasting and appropriate training, it can be enhanced. It is imperative that every sip should represent conscious tasting: we have to analyze our impressions, categorize them according to our theoretical knowledge, and retain them in our memory. The more types of wine of different origin and character one can taste, the better one can remember their qualities, and develop a higher sense of taste. Those who only know the wines of a single region will be one-sided and biased in their judgment. If we frequently drink inferior wine, we will be less able to recognize faults.

Other variables affect wine. The provision of favorable circumstances also requires a certain expertise. For example, storing and serving wine at the proper temperature is of great importance. If a wine is served too warm it seems drier and heady (higher in alcohol). In this case, the kind of fermentation and the taste of cork and mold can be easily recognized. Therefore, wine has to be cooled or warmed to the most favorable consumption temperature. It has to be done slowly and gradually. Some red wines should be uncorked one or two hours before consumption, while white wines of a fine bouquet should be opened only immediately before tasting. Older bottled red wines should usually be decanted. The wine has to be poured, slowly, in a thin stream into an empty bottle or decanter, so that the approximately inch-high sediment will remain in the original bottle.

Particular attention has to be paid when serving wine. Do not forget that the beauty of a debutante is emphasized by an appropriate evening gown. Similarly, one can admire and appropriately evaluate a wine only if it is served in a fitting glass. Wine should be drunk from transparent, clear, thin, stemmed glasses, bulging at the bottom and narrowing toward the top. Wine might be more attractive in cut glass, but most purists believe such glasses should not be provided at meals because they can distort the wine's appearance. Unfortunately, impossibly shaped, overly ornamental glasses have come into fashion recently and pander to bad taste. Champagne or sparkling wine should be served in high, so-called flute-shaped glasses, because in tall glasses the Champagne is always more attractive and the V-shaped bottom ensures pretty and even bubbles.

Wine bottles should be carefully opened. The top seal should be cut off with a knife. The cork should be removed with a very sharp corkscrew, possibly with a special gadget, which helps the gradual uncorking of the bottle. Newly bought bottles should be placed on coasters—a practice indispensable in the case of red wine. Old dusty bottles should not be wiped, but placed in a basket held by the handle. After the wine is poured, the bottle should be half turned, so that the last drops do not drip onto the tablecloth. If the bottles are kept in an ice bucket they should be wiped with a napkin before pouring. Champagne bottles should be wrapped in a napkin before opening; after the wire basket is removed, the cork should be slowly turned and held with a finger so that it opens with the least amount of pop, without the wine gushing all over.

After we have created the most favorable conditions necessary for the tasting of the wine, the ceremony can begin.

Wine tasting is a complex activity in which the order of the details is as important as in the process of opening a safe. Like love, our ritual also starts with the pleasure of the eyes. When pouring the wine, we observe its agility and density. Heavy-bodied wines are slower and flow in a more oily manner. When pouring the wine, we also observe the color, the extent of its foam, and its brilliance. Shiny foam indicates acidic wine; wines with a higher alcohol content have a quickly disappearing foam, while the foam of weak or cold wine lasts longer. We expect lasting and tiny bubbles in sparkling wines. The colored foam of red wines indicates a rich content of coloring material.

The color of wines is varied. A young, bright, white wine is often greenish white or greenish yellow. Older white wines have deeper shades—corn gold, straw yellow, or amber—while the oxidative type of wines is tea- or rum-colored. Young rosé wines are bright red; older ones are creamy rose. New red wines have a purple shade, older red wines are ruby or pomegranate red, and even more mature wines are reddish brown. Aged red wines are brick- or onion-skin-colored. Champagnes should be bright, lively, shiny, and light in color.

The sparkling clearness of wines is an aesthetic requirement, and at the same time the diploma of the wine. Without this, even the best wine resembles an uncut gem. Champagnes and younger white wines should be brilliant, but full-bodied red or white matured wines should also be crystal clear.

We now lift the glass to our nose and inhale the scent with tiny sniffs. Do not forget, Camembert has a smell, but wine has a scent or fragrance! We can distinguish the primary or fruit scent, called aroma, from the fermentation and aging, or maturing, scent, which is called the bouquet. Bottled wines have a particularly valuable "bottle bouquet," which, in contrast to the maturity fragrance, is produced as a result not of oxidization, but of the process of reduction. Fine bottle bouquet belongs among the great experiences of wine connoisseurs. The bouquet of the wine is composed of various factors, and is almost unparalleled in its fine complexity. It can be compared to the fragrant symphony of a field in bloom or to a spicy or matured fruit perfume. The finer and richer the scent, the more noble the wine. Rough and aggressive scents are not pleasant, even if they are otherwise strong and winelike. Some wines have a characteristic bouquet. For example, the young Cabernet Sauvignon has an unpleasant smell, while a mature one smells of black currant or strawberry. A well-aged Cabernet resembles the scent of black currant with a certain dustiness added. The Kadarka hints of cloves. A good Traminer has a spicy-rose scent, and the Rhine Riesling smells of violet or elderberry blossom.

After tasting, the sensory organ, the mouth, should be rinsed, then dried somewhat to liberate the taste buds and prevent the wine from being diluted in the mouth. Take a big sip, slightly tilt your head, keeping the wine in the front cavity, and bathe the tip of your tongue in the wine. Then lift your head, shifting the wine to the rear of the cavity, and disperse it over the entire palate. Press the wine to the palate with your tongue and move your jaw as if you were chewing the wine. Professional wine tasters then breathe in some air with their mouths slightly open, which ensures a strong sensation of aroma and scent. Around the dinner table (which is best covered with a white cloth) this ritual would be against etiquette, so it should be avoided. After swallowing the wine, experience the aftertaste; this new sensation will be either brief (from an immature wine) or long-lasting (from a mature one), sometimes referred to as a "lingering farewell."

One reason wine provides the greatest pleasure is because of the complexity and richness of its aromas. When tasting, we judge the alcohol content, the acidity, the sweetness, the dryness, the body, the harmony of the aromas, the flavor, the age, the type and origin of the wine. Older vintage red wine has the taste of bread crust; Aszu wines of locust seed or sultanas. The spicy aroma of the muscatels conveys a slight lemony and anise character. The Traminer tastes like rose preserves, the Neuburger of baked apple, and the Grey Friar of chocolate.

Transylvanian wines were always characterized by a richness and beauty of aromas, because they abound in flavors and fragrance.

The quality of the soil also decisively influences the quality of the wine. According to Ferenc Entz, an outstanding viticulturist of the past century, the soil of the Transylvanian wine regions is identical to that along the Rhine region; it has the same amount of dew and precipitation. Additionally, there is at least twice as much land for grape growing in this favorable location, and because it is situated in a mountainous region, malicious frosts cannot reach the grapes. Thus, it is one of the ideal wine-growing areas of Europe. While grape types growing to the west of the Carpathians produce more sugar, Transylvanian grapes produce more acid, thus giving a better bouquet and freshness to the wine. And because they grow in the mountain slopes of volcanic origin, which are surrounded by cooler dewy forests and protected from the wind, the volatiles produced by the grapes do not burn, as in wine regions that have shorter and drier summers. The special climate and soil produce wines with characteristic aromas almost without rival. Among the vintage wines, considerable emphasis should be placed on a local variety of Rhine Riesling, Leányka, because of its fine aroma and pleasant acid content.

Here is a fairly complete listing of Transylvania's white wines:

Leányka (Little Maiden)

This is the local grape type and the pride of Transylvania. During the success of the Rhine Riesling in the past century, the Leányka was considered even tastier than the Rhine wine. The Leányka befits the table of kings, being light, refined, and aromatic; it excels even in weaker vintages. Its sugar content is quite high, though the acid content is not; thus, the wine is fiery and full-bodied. The famous foreign types are better only during the excellent vintages, but under adverse conditions they lag far behind. It is usually a soft wine, so it particularly excels in cooler hilly regions, primarily in the village of Lekence, along the Küküllő River, and around the town of Beszterce, where the high sugar content further enhances its quality.

Kövér

Another native of Transylvania, the grape is subject to "noble rot," an infection by a fungus that softens the skin of grapes. This allows some juice to evaporate, thus concentrating the sugar and producing wonderful wine. Kövér is also excellent when it is crossed with other varieties. In the past it was crossed with the Leányka, the Királyszőlő, and the Járdovány. Today, together with the Furmint, it is still the basic white wine of the Plébános, an interesting blend of wines that is characteristically Transylvanian.

Szürkebarát or Grey Friar

The prince of quality white wines, even if the Traminer, the Sauvignon Blanc, and the muscatels surpass it in fragrance and aroma, none of them has higher internal values than the Grey Friar. Notwithstanding a few fiery, dry Grey Friars, in Transylvania they are usually semidry, semisweet, or sweet wines.

Traminer

The reddish grape produces one of Transylvania's most prized and popular semi-fragrant white wines. It counts as a star among the quality wines, as indicated by the awards it has received at numerous international competitions.

Sauvignon Blanc

This other outstanding fragrant local wine is grown at Enyed, along the Küküllő River, and at Lekence. It is so aromatic that its abundance and pungency overtake that of the Traminer and occasionally overshadow the Ottonel muscatel.

Furmint

Furmint is one of the most fiery wines of Transylvania. Its high sugar and acid content ensure a rich and refreshing aroma. It matures well in barrels, and when pressed from the overripe grapes it is a worthy companion to the Tokaj wine. Most probably it is a native grape variety. It grows only as a pure type of grape in the area of Erdély-Hegyalja, near the village of Csombord, and it is a basic type of the Plébános wine.

Plébános or Reverend

A blend, the Plébános is a mixture of Furmint, Kövér, a bit of Ottonel muscatel, and a little Riesling, Leányka, and Traminer. These grape types are jointly cultivated and harvested so that the wine is the result of the vintage and not of post-marriage. The Plébános is a semisweet or sweet dessert wine. It is greenish yellow or gold in color; its fragrance is attractive and durable, occasionally recalling the scent of summer apples. The wine is fiery and refreshing, but always very harmonious, extremely rich, oily to the touch, and with a lingering aftertaste.

Olasz Riesling or Welschriesling

This grape, the "jack-of-all-trades" among the Transylvanian wines, is used to produce all types of wines, ranging from first-class table wines to noble rot liqueurlike wine, depending on the soil and vintage.

Királyleányka

This grape produces quality table or mass white wine, and also a rare, natural semisweet wine. The best quality is produced around the town of Zsidve, but the Királyleányka in the county of Szilágyság is also a tasty, attractive wine. In other regions it is used for making a Champagne type of wine, or for crossing. As a dry table wine it is greenish white or greenish yellow, with an indifferent but developed bouquet. It is a light, refreshing or hard wine with medium body, and with slightly herbal-tasting dry aroma. The semisweet wines are satisfactorily harmonious, with a much nicer flavor than the dry wines.

Járdovány

The most significant Transylvanian representative of the mass wines is the basis of the best local Champagne types. It is a native grape, grown mostly in the vineyards of Nagy-Apold, Kálnok, and Szász-Sebes, and is particularly popular in these Saxon regions because of its considerable yield.

Küküllő Gyöngye

The "pearl of the Küküllő River" is a mixture of Királyleányka, Olasz Riesling, and Ottonel muscatel. It is a fragrant full-bodied semidry wine, with moderate alcohol content—a clean-cut representative of the Küküllő wines.

Ottonel Muscat

With its conspicuous fine qualities, dense fragrance, and sweetness, this wine is like light music. It can be enjoyed even without viticultural knowledge. It is golden yellow, with the scent of a lemon flower; a soft, sweetish or explicitly sweet, somewhat thin wine, whose flavor can be compared to nectar seasoned with sage and lemon rind extract. Its scent is so rich that the thinner wines are occasionally one-sided and maliciously described as "hair tonic." A successful dessert wine is always made from overripe grapes, and temperance is recommended in its tasting, for it is like a lover who is beautiful, blond, and perfumed, but deceptive.

We now come to Transylvania's more important red wines.

Cabernet Sauvignon

The king of red wines, because it satisfies every requirement for a quality wine and aging, adding to it its indispensable dark color.

Blauburgundi

This fine red, a variety of Pinot Noir, is somewhat lighter-colored than the Cabernet Sauvignon, which is purple or ruby. Full-bodied, fiery, and very velvety, it is softer than the Cabernet Sauvignon, but similarly invigorating.

Merlot

Merlot is characterized by its full body, softness, velvety quality, and rich deep red color. Its individual character is outstanding.

Kadarka

One of the most famous wines in the Arad-Hegyalja area and and in the village of Rékás is Kadarka. It is pomegranate or bright red, but its coloring may occasionally seem poor. It is a light wine with moderate alcohol content, proportionate body, refreshing quality, and aromatic taste reminiscent of cloves.

Ménesi

This most outstanding representative of the domestic red wines resulted from the crossing of various grapes.

To emphasize the flavors in gastronomic masterpieces, special efforts should be made to ensure a harmony of taste between food and wine, so that the outstanding qualities of each may be enjoyed. Cultured wine consumption requires extensive knowledge and refined tasting abilities. Just as we wouldn't put on a striped shirt with plaid pants, we must not make mistakes in coupling foods with drinks.

First it should be clarified what goes with what.

The French gourmets—who still lead the world in this field—composed their own Ten Commandments of wine drinking. In general, red wines dominate French cuisine, which is not always the case in Transylvania. In the main, the grapes that produce white wine found a home in Transylvania. Thus, we have to consume white wine with some dishes, a practice that would be considered unacceptable by an orthodox French imbiber. The consumers' requirements influence the types of grapes grown, and our consumers' traditions cannot be compared to those of France. The original rules, however, were conceived in good taste and therefore serve as a guide.

We must not think that a certain dish can be accompanied only by white or red wine. It has to be reiterated that a large number of exceptions strengthen our conviction that only rules but not dogmas exist in art. Thus:

Usually, wine should not be served with soups, and particularly not with fruit soups.

Wine is compulsory with fish. A dry, lightly aromatic white wine is best, but a dry *(sec)* or light, full, aromatic rosé is also acceptable. Poached fish is most tasty with Italian or Rhine Riesling, and with Leányka or Királyleányka. Fried or grilled fish is complemented by aromatic quality wines: Sauvignon Blanc or Sylvaner; and if the fish is fatty, a rosé can be offered. If the fish is served with a sauce, then accompany it with a glass of wine from Enyed. A dry, refreshing wine is recommended with trout—Leányka, Riesling, or Furmint, particularly from a young bright vintage. It must be noted that a younger and lighter wine should accompany grilled fish or meat. If the fish is prepared with a wine sauce, the type of wine used in the sauce should be served. A Transylvanian fish soup may be accompanied by a light rosé or a young red wine, like Kadarka.

Roast game, baked ham, and smoked tongue should be served with a red wine, particularly with a Merlot. Roast veal requires a light, high-quality red wine such as a Blauburgundi. *Wiener Schnitzl* made with veal goes best with an aromatic, elegant, harmonious wine, like Sauvignon Blanc.

Boiled beef can be served with not-too-fiery red wines from hilly regions. However, rare meat really requires a more heavy-bodied wine, such as Cabernet Sauvignon or Black Leányka. Beefsteak is most palatable with a heavier red wine, while a scallop of veal or pork is enhanced with a glass of fine-quality white wine, such as Leányka or Italian Riesling. Mixed grills served on a wooden platter are particularly tasty with red wines. Stuffed cabbage should be served with heavy-bodied strong white wines.

Light red wines should be chosen for stew, *gulyás,* and paprika dishes. A Kadarka sipped with veal goulash adds to its flavor, while somewhat heavier and drier wines should be selected for beef *gulyás,* and, finally, heavy red wine should be served with pork *gulyás.*

Roast poultry or fowl should be accompanied by red wines. If the chef did not spare any sour cream from the chicken *paprikás,* then a fine semidry white wine like Leányka or Riesling should be served. Roast duck should be accompanied by a dry, full-bodied red wine from a hilly region.

Wild fowl and game dishes prepared in the hunters' manner require strong red wines. The flavor of boar becomes more decisive when accompanied by a heavy red wine; venison goes with the elegant and lively red wine from the town of Ménes, such as Merlot; while larded pheasant and partridge can be mated very nicely with a younger red wine of fine bouquet. A rich, aromatic red wine goes with the "singed" hare, or *pörkölt,* while an explicitly vintage red wine befits the wild duck. Usually, feathered game should be served with the lighter and thinner red wines; furred game with more fiery and fuller-bodied red wines.

Sweet wines or sweet sparkling wines should be served with dessert. Ottonel muscat, late-harvest Sauvignon Blanc or Grey Friar, Kövér, and sweet Champagne types are ideal with all kinds of desserts and sweets. If you serve oranges or creams as dessert, offer only ice water, even though the medieval poet emphasized:

> *Water is a horrible curse,*
> *Never taste it with your lips,*
> *It will make your spleen ill.*

If cheese is served at the end of the meal, soft and full-bodied wines should be chosen for the dry cheeses and heavier, drier white or red wines go well with piquant, matured cheeses.

Cognac or brandy can be served after the meal.

A few ceremonies connected with wine drinking are also very important at meals. The bottle should be uncorked by the host and then he should serve the guests. However, he should pour the first few drops into his own glass to ensure that he gets any particles of cork. Unknown wines or those that have not been drunk for a long time should be tasted by the host in front of his guests, and only then served. It was mentioned earlier that certain old and big red wines should be uncorked and decanted a few hours prior to the meal.

Quality wines should not be mixed with water, or soda or mineral water, as recounted in François Villon's curse:

> *The citizen should be thrown into*
> *the cellar of Hell,*
> *Who pours water into wine.*

Soda water should be consumed separately, after the wine. However, if a guest requests it, light table wine can be mixed with soda, because it somehow survives the sacrilege. A guest who mixes quality wine with water deserves only the water. Do not misunderstand this, for there are undoubtedly cases when a long cool wine and soda water drink is welcome, but for this purpose dry wine in bulk will do, or the guest should switch to beer. Drinking vintage wine with soda water is like putting the *Mona Lisa* on your bathroom wall.

Wine should be served only in stemmed glasses, which are properly held with three fingers on their stem, without touching the goblet or cup part. The host has the right and duty to propose the first toast, regardless of the high status of the guest. Serving and eating should be stopped during toasts.

How many types of wine should be served? The ideal solution is: a wine for every course. However, this cannot always be adhered to, and naturally it is also a question of your finances. Obviously, if you offer one course, one type of wine will be sufficient. A friendly simple dinner can be solved with two wines: a white and a red. With three wines (two reds and one white, or vice versa) we already have a feast, while four or five wines, at a major event, offer outstanding gastronomic adventures.

When calculating the amount of wine required, take into consideration that one male guest will drink one bottle, but there should always be an extra one, because nothing is more embarrassing than when the guest wants another drink and the bottle is empty. In honor of good vintage wines, candles should be lit on the table. Transylvanian wine is the gem of the table; food is gold, and wine is the diamond attached to it.

In

REVERENCE

of

FOODS

INVITATION TO DINNER: A WELL-LAID TABLE

by Andor Bajor

If one can believe the ancient book of Christian culture that believers call the Holy Gospel, the history of humanity began with eating. Our ancestors ate the forbidden fruit, and ever since, man has earned his bread, living quarters, weapons, and freedom with the sweat of his brow. Some readers maintain that the fatal fruit that caused the downfall of Adam and Eve was the apple, while some botanists believe that our ancestors incurred the wrath of God by harvesting a peach.

I consider the primitive eating habits in the Garden of Eden to be typical of insolent humans. After all, what a way for Adam and Eve to behave, picking the fruit and eating it on an empty stomach, without even washing it or taking time to arrange it aesthetically. If the temptation can be blamed on the snake, the guilt for the rape of the fruit clearly falls on our ancestors. Thus the sin, crowned by the violation of good manners, produced severe consequences: the expulsion from Paradise and the stern command to work.

I consider the advice, curse, and exhortation to earn bread to be the first food for thought. Although "earning one's bread" was metaphorically ordered, this staple became the symbol for all food, despite the fact that a large part of the world's population eats rice, not bread. Moreover, even in countries where bread is the staple, doctors raise objections to its excessive consumption because it is fattening and is not nutritionally complete. Naturally, this does not weaken the heavenly commandment, since, for one thing, it includes the exhortation to work; for another, doctors are wont to proscribe all kinds of food.

The fact remains that man has always earned his "bread," while he ate meat, drank milk, took part in hunting feasts, and for centuries searched the earth for the edible, ranging from a mammoth to algae.

The true heroes of the culinary art were those who ate the first mushroom, black-berry, and raspberry and made soup from beans, lentils, and dried peas. Furthermore, people who ventured to eat the deadly nightshade, experimented with cooking poi-sonous mushrooms, and tasted deadly tubers and roots were the nameless culinary champions. But only those with good experiences survived; the poisoned cooks were quickly forgotten, and no statues were raised in honor of the unknown and daring soldiers of cooking.

Yet it required great courage and originality to make the first fried chicken with a coating of flour and eggs or to fill the first sausage with the pig's insides. But no one has even the slightest idea of who fried the first doughnut and who dared sprinkle tarragon and ginger in soup. Though our history begins with eating, we know virtually nothing about the great chefs who discovered everything from fried frog's legs to spice cake.

Most of those whose experiments presented humanity with various tastes died un-known, and only a few sayings commemorate their creations. For example, if someone expresses himself vividly, we call him a flavorful speaker. If, however, an act or saying is stupid and violates our sense of propriety, we describe it as being in bad taste. Taste has gone beyond the boundaries of cooking; when we speak of good and bad taste now, we often address concepts remote from the kitchen. There are delicious stuffed cabbage dishes and unappetizing novels. While it is difficult to draw a parallel between them, these adjectives show a certain kind of relationship; the preparation of stuffed cabbage is a creative act, while behind the bad novel lurks something repulsive. Some people are called noodles, and yet there are noodles that are well-made and a joy to eat; they aren't silly or foolish in the least.

I do not find it surprising that there is much talk of the art of cooking, though this art is among the most ephemeral; it takes less time to consume it than to prepare it. The proof of a masterpiece in this genre is its disappearance from the plate. But even a speech comes to conclusion, a play ends, and the orchestra fades away when the last note has been sounded. Like a musical score, the only lasting creation in the art of cooking is the cookbook. I usually read cookbooks with skepticism—not out of profes-sional arrogance, or because recipes make laborious reading, but because, to my mind, strict recipes lack spontaneity. Whether it's due to thrift or faintheartedness, they omit the best spices and the challenge that cooking must be done with heart and inspiration.

The best way to write about food is with enthusiasm and cheerfulness. The words must convince the reader that eating is neither a mere fulfillment of a biological need nor a medical prescription, but a rightful and honorable part of the fullness of life. At the same time, it is a spiritual act through which the soul unites with tastes and aromas. When I read about the banquet of Trimalchio, I can practically smell the aroma of meat roasting on Apollo's fire and sense that Bacchus himself is filling my glass with wine.

I don't think it is by accident that Plato developed his supreme ideas on love at the dining table. The ritual of eating has a symbiotic relationship to sublime philosophy, inasmuch as raw dough is related to an oven or a jug of milk to a saucer.

In the literature of the past, writers have tempted humanity with their innumerable examples of tables laden with rich food. From time to time we also find references to long-forgotten food. Not even the most meticulous scholars inquire into why they died out. Was it a change in taste, thrift, or the hustle and bustle of modern life?

Nowadays we are deeply concerned with saving the green plover, the egret, and the whale from extinction. But who is going to preserve the pastry shell or the cream puff for posterity? Nobody would dream of smuggling these gastronomical rarities into today's Noah's ark!

When I read the novels of today or watch new movies, I cannot help noticing that people no longer eat anymore. They rob, murder, make love, and nervously and hurriedly fill themselves with alcohol. Most probably, they are propelled by gasoline inhaled from their car's tank.

Although I am no expert at the interpretation of this art, I believe I can discover some revealing trace, a kind of corpus delicti here: namely, that modern man has ceased to consider eating as a cultural act. Where there is need, there is no choice; where there is abundance, there is no time to eat in a civilized manner. Thus, food merely becomes fuel to keep the engines running. To preserve a semblance of flavors, the modern food industry has tried to undertake the impossible. It prepares a general seasoning that is uniformly added to chicken soup, green beans, and, alas, even *crêpes*. Finally, everything ends up tasting the same: a little spicy, a little pasty, and mostly nondescript. If we continue this trend, an overly thick gravy may be mistaken for a thin pudding. Ultimately we shall have nothing else but a universal food. It is our duty to defend the uniqueness of everything, since only by doing so can we defend our own individuality.

Nonetheless, we are in big trouble. There are four and a half billion people living on this earth who have a right to something to eat; but they also have a right to heavenly tastes and flavors. People spend less time cooking, and modern women are less inclined to restrict themselves to the kitchen as their primary domain. People are constantly in a hurry so that they can attain leisure, or rather the appearance of leisure, watching television every day, or taking nerve-wracking trips that contain innumerable unpleasant adventures. During their travels they do eat unfamiliar foods, but these are not the genuine flavors of foreign cities but mere culinary conglomerations prepared for tourists.

A good many years ago, a delegation from an African country came to Kolozsvár. The leaders of the city wanted to surprise them by serving African food. An outstanding chef from one of the best restaurants there had been asked to prepare some of the specialties from an African cookbook. The cook pored over the collection of the native recipes, then began cooking something, he himself did not know what. Since the exotic dishes did not have Hungarian names, no one could determine the menu from the descriptions. When the dishes were served, the members of the delegation tried to eat out of courtesy. Finally, their leader, profusely apologetic, informed the interpreter that Transylvanian cuisine was so strange to their taste that it would require a superhuman effort to eat it. Afterward the chef swore that the recipes he had prepared were really from the country of their guests. But there were probably slipups in the details, the portions, and the spices. This is how African cuisine came a cropper in Transylvania.

Once I had a similar experience when I ordered *gulyás* (goulash) in Berlin. I felt safe, knowing that *gulyás* enjoyed an international reputation. The waiter brought out a metal bowl and poured its contents into my dish. Upon seeing food I rarely fall into despair, but at that instant it happened. Pieces of salami were floating in a kind of yellowish oily liquid around a pocked species of boiled potato, which emerged from the swirling soup like Ararat in the flood. I suspected a disastrous mistake or the workings of capricious fate when I examined this gastronomical absurdity. It took a while until I could express my suspicion to the waiter that the dish had been prepared from kerosene and walrus hide in the manner of the emergency cuisine of the Alaskan gold diggers. At last he said, politely but with the firmness of the Supreme Court, that what was in my plate was *gulyás,* period! Bitterly, I began to spoon the completely unfamiliar dishwater, no longer to appease my hunger but to annihilate it.

It seems that when foods cross borders, they take on a completely new image and flavor. Perhaps there is a secret gastronomical customs house at the point of crossing that confiscates the original flavors and converts them by some mysterious currency exchange. This is how food phantoms and chefs with delusions of grandeur come into being for the sake of tourists.

Elaborate descriptions of food, generally of the finished dish, make one forget the sinews and splinters of life. The well-laid table—which, according to the folk tales, sets itself—is supposed to raise those sitting around it above the hustle, fatigue, and lurking dangers of everyday life. At such occasions, one realizes that eating is not just necessary, but indeed enjoyable. After a good dinner, thoughts become calmer, more cheerful, and gain entrance to the Nirvana of pure souls. It feels as if transcendent beings— perhaps angels—were sending a message through the delicacies and the diaphanous spices.

No one knows who discovered the special relationship of meat, pepper, and ginger; perhaps Prometheus, when he stole fire from Mount Olympus, also brought a bag of spices with him. These leaves, berries, and powders, inedible by themselves, elevate food into heavenly spheres.

According to an old tale, a king asked his three daughters (to test them) how much they loved him. The first one said, "I love you as I love gold." The second one said, "I love you as I love diamonds." And the third said, "I love you as I love salt." The king flew into a rage and banished the youngest daughter from his court for her disloyalty and her foolish answer. But time passed and the royal pantry ran out of salt. From then on, even the best food no longer had any taste; meat was no longer meat, soup no longer soup. In vain, they sprinkled it with gold dust or diamonds; the food still had no taste. At last the king understood that it was his youngest daughter who loved him best.

One needs only a small, almost imperceptible amount of spice, for that is what imparts character to food. Similarly, as one needs spices for food, one needs love for cooking, or the flavors may vanish without a trace. This last "ingredient" is somewhat imponderable, because one cannot know where love can be obtained and how many pinches of it are needed. And here is where this book comes in to offer some guidance. It must be read with interest and commitment, for it preserves both old traditions and new tastes: the long-kept secrets of Rumanian, Hungarian, Saxon, Armenian, and Jewish cuisines at long last unfold on these pages.

Furthermore, by revealing the mysteries of the art of this gastronomy, this volume will foster a rich spirit, brotherly coexistence, and the preservation of values. Perhaps the community and spirit of the manifold Transylvanian cuisines will help to develop a universal recipe for the future that will sound like this: take the globe, cautiously tie together its five continents, generously sprinkle its deserts, and avoid poisoning its rivers or air as you warm countries and peoples. While carefully breaking up all the weapons, leave room even for the smallest at the well-laid table of this marvelous world.

A MEASURE OF BUTTER

by András Sütő

Let me tell you about what happened when my parents went to church on New Year's Eve and placed the butter in trust of my grandpa. That was because they were afraid we would eat it, since we were always hungry. The butter in the crock was only an inch thick and was to be used for cooking our New Year's Day meal.

My parents said: "Bop him on the head, Father, if any one of them tries to touch it!"

"Leave it to me! I am their guardian," replied the old man, and then he counted us, and right away gave out the orders: "All four of you here, listen! Off you go to bed. Right now! If anyone dares touch the butter, I will break his leg as if it were a chicken's."

This chance was given to all four of us. Then the individual lessons followed. Grandpa took Moses Gaál's novel right out of my hand and slammed it on top of the basin. The mere sight of a book made him furious, since he could not read and felt that a secret enemy lurked behind every printed page.

He reprimanded me, "You only pretend to be reading, I know. You think I'll fall asleep and then you can work on that butter. Right, Mr. Know-It-All? Oh no, you elf! I may not know how to read, but I sure know what you're thinking. Off you go to bed!"

Then came my brother's lesson.

"Don't look at me like that with your innocent blue eyes! You rascal! *You* were the one who ate the butter yesterday! You should be tied to the bed, you're worse than a field mouse! Into bed!"

My other two brothers were already asleep. Grandpa roused them too.

After all this we couldn't but think of the butter.

But still, we all slipped under the blanket. Grandpa cursed in Rumanian; he didn't want to offend his own Hungarian God, since he had received Holy Communion at Christmas. He called us bandits and pagans, and when he turned the flame of the lamp down low, he again mentioned that if anyone was bad he would give us a hard spanking!

So we lay silently in the dim light, and I thought, my Lord, how the little red crock of butter is always in hiding. That is because the holiday meal will be cooked with it tomorrow—otherwise we start the New Year with a lean meal. We had had a glimpse of the butter in the basin earlier in the week, so when my little brother discovered the crock, he spread a thick layer of butter on his slice of bread. My mother then hid it behind the cupboard, but we found it there too. To save it, it was placed in the bottom drawer of the cupboard; from there it was taken to the attic, and then back downstairs (on account of the cat), and thereafter, who knows where.

Grandpa pulled his worn velvet-trimmed leather cap down on his head and, as usual, fell asleep in seconds, facing the wall. All through his life he tried to get a good night's sleep, and couldn't. This night was no exception. Grandpa snored so rhythmically that it made all of us sleepy. Even I could doze off at the sound of it. I would have fallen asleep if the dog outside hadn't started howling bitterly.

"Oh, n-n-no," Grandpa mumbled.

He was such a light sleeper that he heard everything that happened around him.

Now he awakened, wriggled out of bed in his nightgown, knitted his bushy brow, and pondered his next step. Of course! We had forgotten to untie the dog.

"S-s-so. Are you sleeping?" he inquired. "Just let me hear a single stir while I let the dog loose. I'll give you butter over my dead body!"

None of us dared utter a word, and Grandpa, feeling reassured, threw his coat on his back and went outside.

"Shall I bring the crock?" whispered my little brother, who was only pretending to be asleep under the holey blanket. "It's in our parents' room under the straw mattress."

Determined for action, he sprang right out of bed; and my third brother would have followed suit if only Grandpa hadn't stepped in the doorway at the crucial moment. He spryly stormed in, barefoot, as if he had been chased.

"Where do you think you're going? Come here! Let me see your nightshirt. Where did you hide the butter?"

And he want on searching him to see if the crock was there under his little shabby gown.

My brother tore himself from Grandpa's strong clutches and jumped out to the veranda.

"Can't a person even be left alone around here anymore?"

"You're lying, you rascal! Come here or else I'll get you. You don't have anything to do but sneak away for the butter, right? Get in here, you hear?"

Grandpa put his moccasins on. Thinking that the crock might be in the attic, he scurried out after the child.

"Come here, you, and don't make me curse, because I received Holy Communion."

I crept to the window to watch Grandpa chase my little brother around the house twice. I heard his moccasins flapping on the icy lumps of the earth. When finally they came in, his normally neatly combed mustache was pointing in a thousand directions.

He was breathing heavily; his blue eyes were on fire. With frightening anger, he shouted at me.

"You're not asleep yet either? You want to steal too, you pagan? Where's the knife?"

The knife with the black handle lay there silently on the table. Grandpa grabbed it and ran out with it so he could cut the cord from the howling dog's neck. In the morning my father, in his absentmindedness, had tied the cord in a knot again so it was impossible to untie.

We debated very quickly about whether to seize the opportunity. Grandpa would probably fiddle with the knotted cord for a while, rather than cut it; he took the knife along only because his nails couldn't do the job alone.

Then my little brother scurried into our parents' room. He pulled out the crock from under the straw mattress.

By this time, Grandpa had cut the cord anyway. And when he stepped in and saw the crock in my brother's hand, he couldn't even scream; he only hissed. He didn't threaten to hit us; he didn't even call us rascals or pagans; he just slammed down the knife and swatted me on the neck so hard that I hit the basin.

"You're the eldest one. Why did you let it happen?"

Then he started tapping on my brother's head with his bony knuckles. In the meantime, Grandpa's voice returned. He said it was not the butter he felt angry about, but the fact that the Holy Communion he had received at Christmas was ruined by all his cursing.

I grabbed the crock from my brother's hands and hid behind the table. I won't let him do this, I thought. After all, he shoved me against the basin.

Grandpa came after me. My brother was freed, at least for the time being. "I didn't eat any of it!" he screamed, crying. "Because of that, I will break the crock."

"You!" Grandpa bellowed so loud that perhaps even the priest could hear him all the way from the church.

And then, like the loser in a fight, he fell hopelessly on the bed, threw his moccasins off his feet, and slipped under the covers, mumbling.

He almost cried: "I can't get anywhere with you! Do what you want. Eat the butter. Eat it. Break everything in sight. You can even smash my head while you're at it!"

We were all moved by that remark. So then I told my brother to take the butter back, because my mother was right; we must eat tomorrow, too, and who could tell if we'd have guests drop by. We couldn't be put to shame again.

But then Grandpa got out of bed, and with great determination began trying to retrieve the butter. All at once he grew supple from his intense wrath, so much so that in his haste he knocked over the kitchen chair, along with the full water pail that was sitting on top of it, and the dirt floor became all muddy.

"Give it to me!" he shouted.

My brother quickly made his way under the bed with the crock and shouted from there that his head was covered with bumps from Grandpa's knuckles. Grandpa got on his hands and knees and tried to get at him with the broomstick.

"Come out, you rascal! Come on out! I'm going to wring your neck!"

He continued to reach after him angrily, and if my brother hadn't started screaming, "Oh! Grandpa you knocked my eye out!", who knows in what condition he would have crawled out from under there.

"Liar. See, you're lying even now, because there is nothing wrong with your eye!" After the child crawled out, Grandpa began swatting him; then he hit his head with the leather cap.

To save my brother, I grabbed the back of Grandpa's nightshirt and kept pulling on it, but only so he would turn around and look at me. Then I thought I'd escape to the veranda and from there to the attic, among the rags (where I wouldn't catch a cold).

Then our struggle took an unexpected turn.

The third grandchild, Grandpa's blue-eyed pet, who resembled him most, jumped up from the bed and sprung right onto Grandpa's back.

"Don't hit him! Don't hit him!" he yelled. "He didn't eat the butter."

Suddenly, Grandpa's muscles became lax—not unusual for a man who had worked long and hard for his seventy years. He lost his balance and slipped on the muddy ground; and just before he caught the cord of the clothesline, he fell and hit his head on the edge of the stove.

"Oh! What will happen to our dear grandpa now?" we said.

He was sitting on the ground in a daze, holding his hand on his forehead. We didn't even have the courage to pick him up, lay him on the bed, and beg him to forgive us.

In the bewildering silence we heard the fierce wind outside. I figured that by now our priest must have reached the end of the psalm. I was terrified at the thought that my parents would be just bowing their heads in the oakwood pews of the church, to ask for the Lord's mercy, and soon would be on their way home . . .

"Grandpa, dear Grandpa . . ." I whispered.

Grandpa took his hand from his forehead and looked up at me, perplexed and dizzy. That was when we noticed the blood trickling down his face onto his mustache. I jumped up and hugged him, gluing my face to his wound. My little brother hugged him too, and the two others put their arms around him, trying to appease our grandpa. We promised him that from now on we would collect ten times more cigar butts from around the tavern and the mill. And also that when we grew up we'd be able to afford to slaughter two pigs every single winter; we'd have so much fat that his mustache could be waxed and shiny forever from it.

Grandpa sat on the bed and wiped his forehead with the sleeves of his nightshirt. We almost felt guilty that he wasn't even scolding us.

"Where's the butter?" he asked at last.

Gergely climbed under the bed to get the crock and gave it to him.

"Have some! Eat it all, Grandpa."

Grandpa took the crock, sealed the opening with a piece of newspaper, hid it under his pillow, and laid his head on it.

"It'll be in a good safe place here." And guard it he did, as if the last moments of his life had been locked up in that little red crock.

Outside, the strong wind had drowned out the notes emanating from the church organ. The only sounds to be heard were dogs barking, and the distant clapping of feet on the icy earth as people walked home from midnight mass.

Later, I saw that Grandpa, sitting up in his bed, was dunking a crust of bread in the butter. The flame of the lamp, though low, was still flickering. I studied his snow-white mustache, and I watched his trembling old hands, knotty from his eternal work as a servant. And it seemed to me that while he was eating he was addressing an imaginary judge, delivering a silent speech of defense.

After all, he had the will to save the butter. He would have done it, too, but his grandchildren started to break his rules—so what could he do . . .

Our dearest grandpa, I would have loved to have made you a big, big red crock, so big that even the sky could fit in it, and I would have filled it with the finest foods; I would have bought you a peace pipe and stuffed it with good-smelling tobacco; and I would have had a sheepskin coat made for you; and on New Year's Eve we would have ridden through the village in a sleigh with many tinkling bells, so I could have somehow soothed your heart . . .

A SIEGE OF CORN PORRIDGE

by Gyula Szabó

Since I found out that I had to write something culinary for this book, my head has been in a whirl. However, nothing pops into it but thoughts of a cauldron full of corn porridge. No matter what memories I try to recall, the corn porridge keeps returning to fill the void of other lost memories. So there is nothing to do but pray for the help of heaven before consuming my memories of corn porridge. Yet, with a delicious corn porridge, there's no need for a prayer. Rather, you must have enough ingenuity, even on an empty stomach, to find the word to express the proper appreciation for such corn porridge.

I remember one occasion in particular when a potful of corn porridge left an indelible impression. At that time, both my brother and I were laborers. We worked alongside an old deaf and dumb man (whom we considered our "uncle"), who didn't get much pleasure out of life other than hard physical work and an occasional good meal. From the early morning until the dew of dusk, our bodies sweated as we wielded scythes, pitchforks, and rakes. Late one day, my brother headed for the walnut tree to hang the cauldron full of water over the fire. He took a poll on how much porridge he should make. We voted unanimously to fill the cauldron to as much as the branch could stand. The old man, "Pop," expressed his view with a gesture that spoke louder than words, as if he were caressing a woman's beautiful, large, and round bottom. For make no mistake, it was a gigantic pot of porridge. I can't even imagine how three men could possibly have finished it. But finish it we did, though you might say it nearly finished us. Near the end, it was more a desperate siege than a repast in the civilized sense. Or if it wasn't a siege, it was hard work.

While it's difficult for me to comprehend, I know people who do not like corn porridge. But if I describe that night in detail, that supper, that feast of corn porridge, I think everybody would become a corn porridge convert. The enticing aroma alone would have recruited new corn porridge enthusiasts. First came the scent of the corn flour fiercely bubbling in the cauldron; then the sizzling bacon in the pan, crackling in the intense heat; next the sound of the whipped eggs being poured over the sizzling-hot bacon fat; all this to be accompanied by fresh milk (which had been cooling in the cold forest brook) and sheep's milk curd cheese, fragrant from being melted under the hot, baking sun. After inhaling all these heavenly aromas, even the most obdurate of porridge resisters would have succumbed to the temptation. When the round golden porridge was ready, it was worthy of taking its heavenly place next to the sun and Venus, if it weren't needed to fill a larger space—in our stomachs. We started in with such devotion that we were virtually oblivious to the outside world.

Actually, the old man wasn't really very old. Everyone called him Pop because he could neither hear nor speak. It was suspected that his lifelong handicap stemmed from the time when as a child he fell from a flour barrel headfirst into a cauldron boiling with water for corn porridge. This story was probably true, because he was always so worried about his head. Whenever he got up in the morning, the first thing he would put on was his cap; it also was the last thing he took off before going to bed. But this anxiety was also precipitated by the fact that we always used the old man's worn cap to cover the cauldron to keep the steam from rising.

When the corn porridge was ready, Pop did not consume himself with childhood reminiscences; rather, he filled his stomach with the grain. He pushed that porridge down incredibly fast. If he could have spoken, he would have addressed the porridge with words of appreciation. Despite his afflictions, his personality came through— sometimes reminding me of my taciturn father. He stubbornly struggled with his own means of expression, particularly when we didn't understand something. He improvised feverishly, searching for new expressions, expanding his "vocabulary." He kneeled on the ground, cleared it of weeds and twigs, and on the clear dirt tablet drew pictures. There was endless joy and triumph on his face when he saw the spark of understanding light up our eyes. He nodded and caressed us, or tapped our shoulders in appreciation because we understood. But now he was entranced with only the corn porridge.

After the milk and scrambled eggs, we could only pick at the curd cheese and the corn porridge, and our appetites began to diminish. We glanced at each other in alarm and at the large portion of corn porridge remaining. (When you put the porridge up to cook, your eyes are always bigger than your stomach, but when you get down to eating it, there always is too much.) The rest was hard work—a desperate siege, not pleasurable eating. Pop was the first to clamber up; he strolled to the stream for a drink of water to help wash the porridge down, and then came back. Well, it did help him swallow the corn porridge. This showed us the way out. First my brother, then I, then Pop again, went back and forth, beating a path from the cauldron to the stream. Such heroic perseverance and determination I had witnessed only among the ducks and geese when I once put too much corn flour in their feed. They had demonstrated the same thirst we now had. Their bellies were filled to bursting, they quacked, and their eyes rolled around, but they continued to eat the mix; when they reached the saturation point they waddled to the basin full of water, then returned just as quickly to the trough, dizzy and dazed—intoxicated on food. We too could only waddle, tipping over on our noses, our bellies dragging on the ground.

We were so full and consumed with corn porridge that even the reflection of the golden moon looked like porridge to us. But we could not surrender to mere corn porridge. Once we started we had to finish. And finish it we did. But before the last swallow of porridge, we looked at each other almost in despair. Someone had to make one more trip to the stream, but who should go? Finally Pop took the plunge. Somehow he knew, as did my brother and I, that it was his honored duty to do so because on all other occasions he took the last bite of porridge. Ironically, while he still fearfully recalled becoming deaf and dumb because of the boiling porridge water, he was more afraid of going hungry than of eating the porridge. The poor man kneeled down in prayer next to the water basin, and, almost as though in atonement for these fears, dipped his mustached face in; after washing down the corn porridge, he wiped off his mouth as though it were some bathing ritual.

Afterward we loosened our belts and sprawled around the fire, our bellies really hurting. All we could do was pant (and hiccup) in a stupor. Nevertheless, I recall the event as one of the most glorious and most memorable moments of my life.

It wasn't so long, yet it seems as though all this happened at a time when neither microphone, nor radio, nor appetite-inducing pills, nor illnesses diagnosed as psycho-somatic existed; when stomachs weren't so colic-stricken and over-X-rayed, and people weren't obsessed with their waistlines. It was a quieter world, before earsplitting noises bombarded the eardrums, because there were no trains, planes, or rockets and the air belonged to the birds. It was a world where we could beat a path to a stream to save us from defeat by a common corn porridge.

MEMENTOS OF THE RESTAURANTS AND INNS OF KOLOZSVÁR:

From the White Horse Inn to the Weeping Monkey Tavern

by Tibor Bálint

I stroll through the old streets of Kolozs-vár alone. Everything is of stone, iron, and mementos. I look for the old cafés to chronicle the hundred-year history of the town's inns and taverns. Murky light trickles onto the sidewalk through the glass door of a restaurant. It would be pleasant to have a glass of wine there and recall, with a reminiscent smile, memories, but I hurry along, leaving behind the muffled shouting, and whooping and musicians' tunes. A minute later I look back and wonder why my twentieth-century inhibitions prevented me from imbibing. While the spirits might relax, I'd emerge tired, in smelly clothes, with a stale taste in my mouth, peevish from the company, the waiter, the barman, and the atmosphere.

However, I cannot, as a native, shrug my shoulders and turn indifferently away from my original temptation. I want to believe that the wine of the vineyards of Enyed, called the "Little Maiden" or the Leányka, does not encourage revelry and boisterousness. I believe that the aroma of coffee will act as a good spirit, here in King Matthias's birthplace. In this belief, I stop in front of the ruined site of the old Weeping Monkey Tavern. I search for the habitués of the Little Pipe Inn, and I sit under the shade of the Old Nut Tree Restaurant, and I stare at the worn trade signs. Peering through the window of the former New York Hotel and Café, I imagine the warmth, its community spirit, conversations, meetings, and dancing, which took place in this café one hundred years ago. How these scenes must have ignited the writers' imaginations. For here is where Hungarians, Rumanians, Saxons, Jews, and Armenians came to understand each other with the flow of time. In explaining the metamorphosis of these towns, one comes to know that the tastiest tidbits and aroma of coffee are, in essence, the food for thought of this chronicle.

The White Horse Inn

We start with the golden fork that, more than five hundred years ago, glittered in the hand of the Hungarian Renaissance king, Matthias. He, the most famous son of Kolozsvár, delighted scientists and sages with his fork. This culinary baton brought Transylvania nearer to humanism and linked it with the more distant stars of European culture. Indeed, Matthias's animated conversation and sparkling spirit are as noteworthy and remembered as his magic eating utensil.

But we needn't go back that far. Let us search through these scattered pages of the chronicle and beneath the faded blanket of memories for the history of the White Horse Inn on Monostori Street. It was known originally as the Vigadó Café House when it was erected in the nineteenth century. The building was later turned into a meeting place for Parliament. When a fire burned down the Council House, governmental meetings were held elsewhere. Meanwhile, the building was rebuilt and named the White Horse Inn.

By that time, there were several more inns in the town. Clever traders opened up their gates alongside the Outer Torda road. Here, tired travelers and their horses could be cared for. The wafting smell of a roast and the heady perfume from a goblet of wine flowed from inns like The Stag, The Huszár, and many others. It should also be mentioned that the Jews had a separate inn, under the name of the Three Lilies.

The Temperance Union

The flourishing Reform Age in the nineteenth century not only brought about fairy-tale-like palaces, enchanting buildings, and bridges over rivers, it also reawakened the spirit of Bacchus. So naturally there was growth in the production of spirits. In 1808, half of the poultry vendors also sold spirits and cut tobacco.

But there was scant opportunity for other kinds of amusement, although Kolozsvár had two daily newspapers, half a dozen weekly papers and picture magazines, two bookshops, a conservatory, and a theater. During the winter months, however, relaxation, entertainment, and merriment for the young and elder men, and for the blossoming ladies (as well as the riper ones), was solely confined to masquerade parties and balls. There was little else to captivate the imagination, and consequently the liquor flowed freely. It was not surprising that the voice of sobriety was raised.

On August 20, 1844, Ferenc Nagy, the mayor, sent printed circulars to the senior officials of the counties asking them what amount of spirits was distilled and consumed in their districts, and what effect the alcoholic drinks had on the morals of the people and on the increase in crime. Two years later, he set up the Central Temperance Union of Kolozsvár. Members signed the following pledge:

"As of today, we shall not drink any kind of spirituous liqueur, rosolio, punch, rum, or arrack, except if it is prescribed by the doctor for medical reasons until the ailment is cured. We shall strive to persuade others to refrain from liquor."

There was justified suspicion that this persuasion may have taken place in the company of a glass of rosolio, punch, or rum. Needless to say, there were understanding and cooperative doctors. At the time, an eminent writer, Sándor Bölöni-Farkas, returned from North America. He saw the issue of sobriety in a different light. His travelogue was regarded by his contempories as the Bible of freedom, and the inspiration for outstanding deeds.

Biasini's Magic Steeds

Bölöni-Farkas knew, from his trips throughout Europe and America, that it was practical to build modern hotels. Travelers came and went, but there was still no tastefully (and comfortably) furnished accommodation for them in Kolozsvár—only old-fashioned taverns and hostelries. Bölöni-Farkas complained about this to his friend, the famous Italian fencing coach Kajetán Biasini. He urged Biasini to open a hotel, similar to those he had seen in his travels. He suggested that Biasini provide hackney coaches for elegant transportation and organize balls for amusement of the Kolozsvár community. He also spoke of encouraging a classless approach to foster an appearance of equality for the clientele.

The brave Italian possessed a flair for business. As a result, he set up these everyday institutions of bourgeois civilization and culture one after the other. He introduced hackney cabs for local public transport and express coaches for long-distance transport on the Koloszvár–Budapest and Kolozsvár–Szeben–Brassó–Bucharest routes. In 1836, Biasini's coach for ten traveled from Kolozsvár to Nagyvárad, about 120 miles, in eighteen hours, instead of the usual three days.

Biasini felt that transportation of passengers should be done for profit, and after organizing this service, he started another business. He purchased the Szacsvai Inn on Outer Torda Street. In addition, he bought a twelve-yard strip in front of it and planted trees, surrounded by a screen, and installed painted seats. He explained that his aim, when building the hotel, was to ensure that the travelers, regardless of social position, should be completely satisfied, and that the prestige and reputation of the town be enhanced. Four years after starting the rapid-coach service, he opened the city's first attractive and comfortable hotel. The *Erdélyi Hiradó* (*Transylvanian Herald*) immediately, and proudly, announced that the hotel received many distinguished guests. On October 21, Petőfi, Hungary's greatest poet, arrived in Kolozsvár as a newlywed. He wrote:

When I arrived in the suburb of Kolozsvár, I suddenly felt as if I had reached Debrecen; there were tiny peasant houses, and infinite mud on the road. When we drove through the Hungarian Gate into the town the world changed and I let out a great breath of happiness. . . . There I was in small, but busy and jovially colorful Kolozsvár, whose streets I pleasurably admired from the window of Biasini's Inn. . . .

This Italian, who did so much for Kolozsvár, was raised to noble rank upon the recommendation of the 1843 National Assembly.

The Legendary Headwaiter "Prímás"

After 1850, café and restaurant life was replaced by associations and "clubs." There was the National Casinó, set up by Sándor Bölöni-Farkas, and the Tivoli, where gentlemen occasionally went to play tarot or exchange anecdotes. One could become a member of the Gentlemen's Casinó for a reasonable yearly fee. Biasini's hotel and restaurant became busier, and only the National Hotel and Restaurant rivaled it with regard to illustrious guests.

On September 12, 1879, the daily *Kelet (Orient)* reported that the public of Kolozsvár would hear the king of the violin, Joachim, and the European piano virtuoso and gifted composer Johannes Brahms in concert. This was truly a once-in-a-lifetime experience that could be equaled only by the visit of Franz Liszt.

Following this most successful concert, Brahms and Joachim, accompanied by some hospitable notables and local musical eminences, went to supper in the National, where the "primas" or first violinist, János Salamon, led the Gypsy band. Brahms may have had rich experiences with Gypsy music, but to Joachim the violinist, hearing the Gypsy's strings "rejoice with tears" meant even more. János Salamon did not disgrace himself. In fact, he played so well that Joachim called to him after the fourth number, shook hands, and toasted him. But this was only one of the memorable things, for what followed was rather rare in the world. After supper, the two eminent guests started toward their rooms at about ten, and, upon ascending the stairs, they clearly heard somebody superbly playing the Bach chaconne for solo violin. They looked at each other: who could this be? Perhaps there was another concert in Kolozsvár? They asked the porter and were astonished when told that it must be the headwaiter of the hotel, Gábor Nagy.

The legendary headwaiter was one of Kolozsvár's best amateur violinists, and his string quartet regularly played at charity concerts.

Transylvania—The Land of Coffee

In Vienna in 1683, a burgher named George Koltschitzky acquired a café license after developing an unexpected fondness for Viennese coffee-drinking following the unsuccessful Turkish siege, at which time the Viennese acquired a large quantity of coffee. Hungarians, being closer to the Turks, had developed a taste for coffee-drinking much earlier. There were already cafés in Buda during the Turkish occupation of the sixteenth century.

In a cookbook from 1668 there are references to "coffee soup" and "black soup." But a more important fact is included in an earlier report from Mihály Toldalagi, an emissary to his master, Gábor Bethlen, the Prince of Transylvania. On December 1, 1628, Toldalagi wrote from Constantinople that he bought 200 *okkas* of coffee that year. One *okka* was 2.82 pounds, so the amount was 564 pounds.

The café house, together with an appreciation of coffee drinking, was a phenomenon adopted from the Orient. London's first café house was opened in 1652, and Paris followed suit in 1670. Its most perfect form was attained in Vienna and Budapest. The "Viennese-type" café flourished in Transylvania at the beginning of the twentieth century and between the world wars. Here, in addition to what was mentioned earlier, one could read all kinds of newspapers, make telephone calls, and play chess, billiards, and cards. An extraordinary example is the Kolozsvár café of János Taffauer. This confectioner and café owner advertised his premises by offering the honorable clientele three billiard tables and forty-eight popular Hungarian, German, French, and Rumanian papers! The café with music was a Parisian invention, but Gypsy music (at that time) belonged solely to our cafés.

The Knight of the Sun

Sándor Bródy, the fascinaing writer and exponent of "new thought" from Paris, came to Kolozsvár eleven years before the turn of the twentieth century, to review its theaters. He was a discoverer and admirer of life's minor pleasures—sensuality, romance, and exquisite food. One evening after his arrival, he fell in love with the beautiful prima donna Margit Hunyadi. This knight of the sun (as he was aptly called), who favored beauty and gentleness beyond all, was for two years captivated by his pretty Circe. In the meantime, he could not resist taking the opportunity to launch a newspaper entitled *Kolozsvár Life*. This is important in our history of restaurants, for Bródy, newspaper editor, winked his eye at everyone inclined to follow him. He was the Lucifer of flavors and aromas—a rambler on the path of tempting fragrances. He reported on every major event that occurred behind the restaurants' curtains, even within their kitchens, and he was delighted that during his unexpected romance, the Transylvanian kitchen managed to conquer him.

The New York Hotel and Café

Sometime after the turn of the century, the single-story old building of the National Hotel was demolished, and Lajos Pákéy, the eminent architect, was entrusted to design a grandiose and comfortable metropolitan hotel. This is how the New York Hotel and Café, the largest and most eye-catching at that time, was built. It was planned in an eclectic style, but with baroque influences, and it remained one of the most respectable buildings in the inner city. The era of the skyscraper had begun, which, in turn, opened the doors to new restaurants, cafés, nightclubs, casinos, clubs, and societies. The mere expression *fin de siècle* changed into a worldwide mood marking the end of an epoch, which finally and painfully faded away. The bourgeoisie craved the latest news and gossip, opined about the evolution of the world, and considered every new café as a sanctum for meeting and intellectual exchanges. In addition, its importance as a place to strike up business deals (for commercial travelers, landowners, and middlemen) could not be overlooked.

In perusing the guest book of the New York Hotel and Café, the caliber and social status of its clientele is evident. Counts, knights, barons, landowners, and international travelers are only some of the elite who frequented the establishment. For this reason, the simple burghers of the town thought the New York to be inaccessibly luxurious, and immediately after its opening, an instructive anecdote was spread. As the story goes, a nobleman traveling incognito wanted information about public conditions. He entered the posh café and asked for a cup of coffee. The waiter, who evaluated him in his modest outfit, refused to seat him without tails and patent leather shoes. The mysterious guest left and in an hour's time returned dressed like a gentleman and asked for a bucket of coffee. When he was served, he took off his gala cloak and pushed it into the bucket, saying, "Here you are, coat, drink the coffee. It was brought for you and not for me!"

The Charm of the Cafés

The *Kolozsvár Guide* was published in 1902 by the well-known Transylvanian historian Lajos Kelemen. Like the hosts of a large city, their book guided strangers and advertised a one- or two-horse carriage to travel from the railway station into town. From there, transportation to the concert hall or theater was available. In the New York and in the Central, with first-class kitchens and cafés, the price of the rooms varied greatly. The most luxurious café was the new Kikaker, replete with art nouveau paintings.

Kolozsvár was a lively center of culture; while its population remained relatively stable, the number of cafés burgeoned. Advertisements in the period newspapers indicate the quest for success and competition. Some café owners had to beg for public support and patronage. For example, the owner of the Jókai Café kept his establishment open until the early morning. He promised freshly made cabbage soup during the carnival period (for all guests), whether they got drunk on his premises or arrived there already tipsy.

The legendary headwaiter of the former National Hotel and Restaurant, Gábor Nagy, had become owner of the Central Café and Restaurant. The café, located in a courtyard, had a charming garden. Artists arriving from all over the world stayed not in the New York but at the Central, because they enjoyed the company of this intellectual and musically talented man. Nagy was also a genuine innovator in the catering industry: he was the first to propose that a special school be opened at Kolozsvár for training waiters and cooks, and that the curriculum include etiquette, table service, culinary art, viticulture and wine storage, business, and foreign languages. He was such an outstanding personality in the town that when he died a fellow restaurant and café owner said at his funeral, "The garland has fallen from our head!"

This Is the World War, With Respect . . .

In the early 1900s there was hardly a season of the year without one or two new pubs opening in Kolozsvár. Despite the fact that the impact of the economic crisis was already being felt and that the world was full of sinister expectations, one could not foretell the imminent tragedy about to befall Sarajevo. This ominous voice was soon stifled by the booming of guns. A literary café owner wrote a poem about the great drama:

> *This is the World War, with respect,*
> *Its embers set every corner of the earth ablaze.*

After the war, Kolozsvár and Transylvania, which had been influenced by one thousand years of Hungarian life, became occupied by Rumania.

"I Don't Want to See Any More Soldiers!"

Some people reacted to the postwar chaos with timid patience, while others made a profit out of it; but many small, formerly busy restaurants, nightclubs, and dives had to close down. Among these, on the corner of Jókai Street, was the Transylvania Café, whose high-class name appeared on a modest sign. Between 1904 and the end of World War I, it had various owners, but after the war it belonged to Aunt Giza. Everyone who spent at least one postwar night out knew her. It was almost impossible not to stop there for at least one drink. The café had a female orchestra, whose members preferred to sit with the young officers and bailiffs instead of playing. Because of this feminine familiarity, Aunt Giza had considerable trouble with the police and with moralizing reporters. This ten-member orchestra refused to tolerate the interference of the police. A reporter nostalgically said that Aunt Giza had arrived when the war began and left when War Minister Linder declared: "I don't want to see any more soldiers!" It is unclear whether there was any connection between Linder's comment and Aunt Giza's departure, but she did, in fact, dismiss the girls and sell the café.

However, the most elegant and most discreet nightclub of the town flourished on Wheat Market Street at the foot of the castle wall. This is where the notables of Kolozsvár, mostly officers and married men, amused themselves. It was an attractively furbished, usually very busy place with mirrors and palms and parties of gentlemen sitting in the corner tables. A bottle of champagne cost 60 to 100 crowns (for most people this was more than a month's salary), and frequently the bill was exorbitant.

The Melancholic Roast Beef King

József Rapolit, the popular roast beef king (because his restaurant served the best roast beef), became a tenant of the Kolozsvár asylum in the summer of 1922. The recession had ruined him. He constantly complained to his colleagues that his restaurant was failing and, in turn, this made him depressed. Suddenly, he went mad and had to be institutionalized.

To better understand Rapolit's crisis, one should know that the High Commissioner of Taxes had increased the music tax on restaurants and cafés by between 200 and 400 percent to support the Rumanian Opera, which also was on the brink of bankruptcy. A delegation of 100 restaurateurs and hoteliers lodged their protest and threatened a strike, but nothing happened. The recession and unusually heavy taxes not only made Rapolit insane but signaled the decline of the lively and prosperous life of Kolozsvár's hotels, cafés, and restaurants.

Vanilla Curd Cake by Air and 18-Karat Bouillon

By the 1930s the café had at last become the place for which it was destined: the source of fresh information, the exchange mart of opinions, a forum for discussion, a rest place for jaded nerves, a news agency, inspiration for ideas, a bank providing tiny loans with low interest, a free university, the second home for single people, and a stage where exhibitionism and vanity had an outlet. Dezső Szabó, although a tightfisted man, always handed out large tips to the busboys to ensure that they later came to his table and said with a deep bow, "Mr. Dezső Szabó, the writer, is wanted on the telephone." This occurred in the New York, but a grand café on Union Street, the Helikon, was also the venue of peculiar everyday happenings, for its tables were attended by the famous and powerful. The table that was the conversational corner, called the "Chat Post," became a household word in its time primarily because of the arguments and opinions espoused by Gábor Gaál, the drama critic and philosopher. To verbally duel with him, or just to listen to him, was so tempting that several habitués of the Helikon and Camp Fire cafés moved their headquarters to the New York.

The world's best soup, with "18-karat shiny gold dots," was cooked at the Little Pipe in the old part of town. Mrs. Borbáth inspired not only this wonderful meat soup, but also wonderful, savory roasts and braised meats. Thus her cuisine acquired a lifetime of followers and when, after the war, she closed her attractive, cosy restaurant, she continued on occasion to set the table in her home for four or five of her admirers and devotees.

Károly Szita, the famous conductor and music teacher, was living in Kolozsvár in those times. Despite his slight physique, he always had a good appetite and never seemed to get enough of those tasty dishes. However, when the Bootmaker's Arms on Holy Church Street was taken over by the stout, 240-pound Uncle Orosz, the owner's wife regarded this little conductor as a culinary challenge for her kitchen. Orosz invited him to lunch, partly out of compassion and partly because of ambition. Károly Szita ate for a quite a long time and tasted many courses. He suddenly blushed, got up from the table to leave, and expressed his thanks for everything. Uncle Orosz asked him in a hurt voice: "What is the hurry?" Szita looked slightly embarrassed and replied, "Well, I have to have lunch somewhere else . . ."

Perhaps he was so excited by the many delicacies, he could not satisfy himself. Probably the real reason was the tricolored stuffed cabbage dish, which was the specialty of the Bootmaker's Arms Inn. It was a very simple dish. A minced meat mixture was prepared and divided into three parts. Pickled and sweet cabbage leaves were filled with one part of the meat mixture, green peppers with another, and hollowed tomatoes with the remainder. The ingredients were arranged in a circular shape in a pot, starting with the stuffed cabbage, then a ring of the stuffed peppers, and a ring of tomatoes in the middle. It was seasoned, simmered over a low flame until done, then topped with thick sour cream before serving.

The fame of the Darvas restaurant rivaled that of the Little Pipe and the Bootmaker's Arms in the gastronomic history of Transylvania. The most magnificent and still inimitable delicacy of the Darvas restaurant was the *vargabéles*—the vanilla-flavored curd cake with raisins. Those who tasted it and tried to prepare it later, or tasted it in any other deluxe kitchen, never felt the same pleasure. This is no exaggeration, for even during the Second World War, the freshly baked *vargabéles* was transported by air to Pest, where, after all, there were some gastronomic experts . . .

What was the secret of Mama Darvas? It has been said that once, when she could not buy the sweet curd called *orda* at the market, she bought sour milk, because she had several orders that she could not cancel. She processed the milk herself, and discovered that the curd and the *vargabéles* had become so pleasantly and uniquely sweet-and-sour that from that time on she continued the process. In addition, she made the pastry as thin as a feather; in fact, she "plucked" it, so that it became loose, light, and silky in the baking pan. Mama Darvas left each of her three children a handwritten cookery book containing 100 of her original recipes.

How Do I Cry, You Scoundrel!

The building of the Weeping Monkey no longer exists, but its romance has endured. We stopped by the now-ruined site, and reminisced about Androvics, who had opened his inn around the 1930s in the neighborhood of the County Hall, just a few minutes' walk from the Summer Theater. He was a deeply democratic, emancipated man, who had turned the little inn into a warm nest and attractive home for young teachers, clerks, and always hungry and thirsty actors, writers, and journalists.

He never interfered in their discussions nor censured their liberal ideas. In fact, he provided a haven for every freethinker, always the vigilant ear listening toward the street, and if he heard something suspicious he gave a sign to the table. The "conspirators," taking their wineglasses, entered his apartment, which was separated from the restaurant only by a curtain. In the meantime, Mrs. Androvics, dear Mamuka, who partook in this mission, diligently carried large dishes of gently trembling boiled beef for these witty and gifted poor young men, as if they were her sons. She was on a first-name basis with most of them, saying, "Have a bite, don't starve, like at home." In fact, it is this romanticism of the Weeping Monkey, and not any specific delicacy, that made it a special treat.

The Weeping Monkey . . . Who could have been the eponym? Hektor, the busboy, is said to have played a major role in its creation. It is alleged that when the soda water supplier begged for the payment due to him, Hektor said that the boss was bankrupt, presently drunk, and weeping over the billiard table "like a monkey." Mr. Androvics heard this and slapped the boy for speaking out of turn. However, jokingly, he chose it to be the name of the restaurant.

Profane Churches

I stroll through the old streets of Kolozsvár alone. It took me months of work to merely sample the world of the obsolete inns, taverns, and cafés of my town. How many people, how many faces behind the noise, behind kitchen aromas and clinking glasses, were grateful for a tasty tidbit, an original opinion, or a warm glance? These souls of the inns and cheap cafés found enough pennies' worth of illusion to nourish their diminishing belief, hope, optimism, and humanism. These many little eating houses and cafés were their profane churches—a view echoed by the customers sitting at their tin-topped bars.

Under the stares of an audience of companions they could alternately, for an hour or so, be orators and philosophers. With their pint of wine and soda in hand, or raising a fragrant cup of coffee, they could be somebody whose opinion affected the further development of the world. The compulsory courtesy of the waiter belied complete agreement and concurring nods. This was their only outlet—their own forum to expound an opinion about life or their redeeming ideals. Thus, they were indebted to these places, which consecrated them with wine, pear spirits, and the scent of Oriental coffee for their survival.

The technology of the last decades brought many changes throughout the world, and here too. But where are those tiny corners where two men could exchange opinions in peace, tranquility, and an intimate atmosphere? The crisp fragrance of freshly ironed tablecloths wafts only in my memory now. I wish we could rest our elbows on them again and politely listen with keen devotion to each other's point of view.

THE ETERNAL MESSENGER:

A Gastronomic Essay of a Rumanian Poet

by Romulus Goga

Ibelieve the first acts of early man were the acquisition of food, rest, and the discovery of fire and shelter. Throughout history, man has been searching for the imprints of his ancestors—he drew their images or carved them in stone or wood. He prayed to them, or placed them in his home against mysterious forces and against the power of chance. Some inquisitive souls have diligently searched for the origins of ancient civilization among the ruins and under the completely crumbling walls of castles that resisted devastating blows of time and survived as shrines of the spirit. There, in the ashes of ancient fireplaces they discovered fragments of dishes in which spices and scented herbs were once brewed into elixirs that brought unknown dreams, tranquility, spiritual consolation, human warmth and hope. What power drives us toward these first men—our common ancestors?

Most probably the first book inherited by every people from their ancestors included a recipe. This message that was forwarded from generation to generation preserved their traditions and customs. Our very first ancestors adored the bright sky and the sun. Their yellow wafting samp (cornmeal mush) could have been an earthly symbol that represented the sun. The green juice of the grape might have symbolized a sacrifice to the ancient god of cultivation.

If we sit down with a glass of hot milk and a soft milk loaf at a table, our spirit will immediately be surrounded by our ancestors. It was passed down through the ages that the leaves of the nettle, a simple plant, can strengthen our body and remedy our soul and that apricots and grapes can slumber through the seasons by preservation in a bottle. Now *we* are the ones who transmit these messages to the future. I believe that the oldest record of humanity is contained in its dishes, and the oldest and finest shrine is the kitchen. Everything originates from them—gentleness and consolation, love and strength. Sardonic philosophers have alleged that the path to the love of a man is through his stomach, and some contemporary sociologists foretell that the future place of man is in the kitchen.

It is our duty to preserve our culinary customs and traditions, for they contain our individuality and ancestral strength, which every nation contributes to the world's great banquet. We would like to enjoy each other's company at this abundant table—this feast, at which we continue to search for world peace and understanding. Have a glass of wine with us and drink to the health of the future, and look with hope to the laden table, and the crisp piglet with the famous first apple in its mouth; let us fill our hearts with joy, because every day the world starts again and we are the creators.

Every morning I remember our ancestors, each of whom struggled for happiness on his then-alien planet. And I feel the warmth of man's first fire, which has since been inextinguishably burning in my soul.

TRANSYLVANIAN "SUNDAY" SOUP

by Tibor Bálint

I recall the sweet, clanging ring of the noontime luncheon bell that foretold of the "Sunday" soup with its golden dumplings. Although my memory of that fragrant meat soup is fading, just thinking about it arouses joy and hope in me about the future of the world. This soup wasn't merely food, it was a symbol—a solemn ceremony, an appeasing sacrifice, in the mist of steaming frankincense, myrrh, and other scented spices. Its aroma seeped out to the courtyard, and from there to the garden, and from the garden farther into the *world,* proclaiming that a large but modest family had sanctified the seventh day as its deserved day of rest according to the law.

Sundays seemed more dazzling in those days, maybe because we could sleep longer, and by the time we opened our eyes the room was full of light. This light was given a rainbow look by the balmy, simmering consommé, which, like a quiet psalm, praised existence and human initiative. I must confess that I still feel the weekday cooking of this soup to be profane, for me it needs a fitting occasion, a holiday.

Only in a state of tranquility, and some sort of expectant devotion and reverence, does it smell so heavenly; only in authentic surroundings, among people who are convinced that tastes and smells lead us to a higher knowledge and appreciation of our existence, and nurture humanity and good intentions. After all, it's unthinkable that someone joyfully spooning up Transylvanian meat soup should not wish similar gourmet delights for the whole world.

Even the meat brought home from the butcher has a special effect on us: beautiful pieces of rump steak, spare ribs, topside and shin with the porous bones, and the freshly plucked yellow-skinned hen. You look at this still life with a primeval instinct and an artist's excitement in searching for edibles, in things of beauty. You have to keep greed at bay, while noticing the shape of the meat, its color and alluring texture, and luxuriating in the cross-bone with gristle that glistens like a pearl.

At first only the serious and promising fragrance of the various meats wafts from the kitchen; a kind of basic broth that as yet is unaware of the cunning collusion from the imminent addition of spices and vegetables that preserve the tasty salts, secret minerals, and flavors of the earth.

After the vegetables have been added, however, when the meat is almost soft and a steaming vapor permeates all ingredients, an uplifting process begins: the symphony of aromas. I could never resist the temptation of stealing a peek into the kettle of secrets: of marveling at the pieces of meat bathing in shimmering melted gold, with brilliant reddish carrots and sticks of silvery parsnip embraced in it like giant jewels. I watched as the peppercorns—like tiny heads of black-haired children—popped up and bobbed down again, and the lovely meat flowed like a veil; a delicacy for gourmets. In the pinkish bay of mushrooms new flavors dissolved and set out on the sea of savors: the green pepper glimmered beside a piece of savoy cabbage and a blood-red tomato, and the hen had scattered glittering 18-karat coins around itself (the fat). As the steamy atomized flavors escaped from under the raised lid it felt as if a fleeting spring shower had crossed some exotic forest—the magic of Mother Nature had captured me.

Oh, "Sunday" soup, let the sweet and clanging ring of the semolina dumplings—the never-silenced voice of my homeland—lull us for ever and ever!

MY MOTHER'S
STARTER DOUGH

by Paul Kovi

Remembrance of things past—the very essence of sentimental nostalgia—is represented best by the memory of one's favorite foods. For many, I suppose, the thought of flaky strudels and sugar-frosted cakes summons forth the sweetest memories of all. I, for one, vividly remember my mother's bread as if I could taste, smell, and touch it even now. Bread—the staff of life—played a crucial, almost sacred, role not only in our lives, but also in that of our neighbors in the small town where I grew up. The very idea of bread was expressed symbolically in our daily language, embellished in poetry, or used in prayers. No other food deserved to be extolled as life-giving, God-given, or blessed. Bread literally was and still remains the gift of life.

The assigned chores on bread-baking days played an especially important part in my childhood memories. The dough for our bread was homemade, but the baking of it was entrusted to a master baker in the part of town where we lived. For over half a century this marvelous old artisan produced the perfect loaves in his charcoal-heated brick oven for our entire neighborhood. On baking days I could hardly wait for the sound of the midday bells and immediately would dash to the little bakery on the corner to pick up our freshly baked breads. Running home with my precious load, I would indulge in its fragrant, mouth-watering, and tempting aroma. How I longed to break off and taste a hunk of the crunchy, still-hot bread, but this would mean betraying a sacred trust.

My mother was the only person in our house privileged to cut our bread first. In my home, bread was never simply broken—it was a family ritual. Before we could eat, Mother made the sign of the cross over the bread and blessed it. Symbolically touched by the sign of eternal life and hope, the bread was declared ready to be tasted. We would vie for the crusty end pieces. No bread ever tasted better than those warm, crunchy brown morsels.

Even now, when I recall the process of bread making, I am overcome with awe. Bread making was a century-old tradition in our family, repeated ceremoniously generation after generation. This ritual engendered the miraculous. Since my family is of strict old Lutheran stock, the word *holy* was not trifled with; it was applied only to God. The process of bread making, however, was held in the greatest reverence, a hairbreadth from holiness. Everything that constituted part of the bread-making process belonged to this beatified, privileged category.

How well I remember the special baskets, a large oval and smaller round one, in which I carried the dough to our baker. They were always kept separate from other utensils on the shelf, and were never used for any other purpose—they were indeed sacrosanct. The smaller one I have taken with me in my peregrination as a constant reminder of home. Four fine white linen napkins lined these baskets. These linens were also used only on bread-making days and only felt the soft touch of my mother's hands. They were permeated with the wonderful scent of good fresh flour.

But the single most important thing in this marvelous ritual was the starter yeast dough. Every family had its own little yeast reserve; for whatever reason, it was shameful to borrow some. A woman was not thought highly of if she did not respect the starter dough and keep it clean, or if she ("heaven help her") would squander it.

The starter dough was surely passed down to my mother from her mother when she got married and began her own household. And, of course, my grandmother had gotten it from her mother, and so forth and so on. Hence, this starter dough was passed along from generation to generation through the centuries. The little starter dough represented not only our family's past and history, but also its present and future. And principally, it meant, for all of us, the connection with our native land, for we lived off the land, as did my forebears. What we had produced and grown gave us the sustenance of our daily life.

During the bread making, my mother always pinched off about a one-pound piece from the bread dough (the starter dough for the next loaf), flattened it, and put it aside in a safe place to "dry and crack." The two baskets and the four nicely folded little cloths were placed next to it. Our little piece of starter dough waited there patiently, until it would be used for the next bread making. It was during this time that the yeast bread's eternally important role really began. Inside it the yeast fungi slowly but surely multiplied and the little starter dough came alive, continuously letting loose its tiny, aromatic yeast particles into the house's air, which we inhaled and absorbed into our bodies. This process was reciprocal, as our house was filled with the very essence of ourselves.

We also filled the air with the minute particles of our basic chemical makeup and the tiny atoms of our hopeful dreams, tired sweat, and love scent. The little yeast dough absorbed all these substances from the air, transforming and multiplying itself in its own selfishly decided way; thus creating, in this manner, our little house's bacteriologi-cal balance and chemical setup—a unique microcosmos. Our starter dough was unlike all others, for it was a composite of us.

And thus, every house in that little town had its own specific chemical-bacteriological makeup, a historical and spiritual microcosmos that differed from its neighbors'.

Our home was a tiny self-defined unit in the immense universe, and in this specified unit, my mother's little starter-dough represented the dominating center. The little yeast bread was the repository of our family's, and of our individual, human character; the key to tradition, continuity, beauty, and love.

How I pity people today who don't have a tiny little starter dough of their own, as a statement of their own individuality that they could pass down to their daughters and sons. Oh, how I pity all those who simply go to the supermarket, and take home some sort of mass-produced bread; although it might be nice and taste good—since the little machine-made loaf tries to accomplish the eternal duties prescribed to it—but this poor bread has no soul of its own.

IN PRAISE OF THE ONION

by Tibor Bálint

O*Allium cepa,* you quietly drop your golden cloak to provokingly offer your white and hard body to the never-ebbing appetite, that you yourself whet with the thousand variations of your flavor and aroma.

O *cepa,* you kind, red, touchingly flirtatious, and coquettish member of the noble Liliaceae family, you are a world-conquering princess and omnipresent God wherever those who long for fine bites convene. In contrast to your gently, sweetly, and lullingly fragrant sisters, the lilies, *Lilium bulbiferum* and *Lilium auratum,* you do not fascinate humanity with complimentary whisper or trembling sigh, but with the spray of your oil, which immediately brings tears to the eyes and also conjures up delicacy-laden tables even to those who lack imagination.

Of course, you are most fragrant and most tempting in your fresh green spring dress, or when your slender, white, glazed neck is on a bed of bacon, or on a fresh cheese-pillow—only to be greedily and noisily chewed by many hungry teeth!

O *Allium cepa!* When, centuries ago, your lily sisters were lured into cloister gardens in the belief that their virginal scents had a remedial effect, you had already helped cure both painful spasms of the body and convulsions of infants. You brought a cure and also spiritual and physical nourishment to those who, after being freed from slavery, wandered for forty days in the desert. And no wonder you are called "Jewish bacon" or "Moses' roast"!

O *cepa!* During the vicissitudes of time, you provided consolation and relief to the peasant hoeing under fierce sunshine; and, mating with a slice of dry bread, you raised it to the realm of the best roasts.

O *Allium cepa!* You participated at the famous feasts of Trimalchio, sat at ease at the table of the pharaohs, saw Ramses, Tuthankamen, and Cleopatra, and still remain the most common homegrown condiment in Egypt. Your popularity reigns from Mako to Jerusalem, and also to Siberia, where *Fistulosum* (scallion), one of your kind—another of the Liliaceae—blooms and seasons food for multitudes.

Behold, O *cepa,* your name is linked with irreplaceable and beautifully elevated concepts, because you are at once the body and the spirit. When your bosom flashes up from under your tight blouse, it dazzles the watcher, and recalling this mirage, we throw ourselves in front of the well-laden tables, in craving anticipation.

Oh, my dear little *Allium cepa,* in whom the metempsychosis of aromas and flavors occurs in front of our eyes and nose, always moving nearer to perfection on bread or in drippings, sprinkled with red paprika in the stew à la seven chefs, in the miraculous Szeged fish soup or in the capon stuffed with oysters! Existence would be poorer, less colorful, and tasteless without you!

Thus, stay with us, you sweet, piquant, stubborn, hard-bosomed, dear onion! Don't ever leave us, neither today nor tomorrow. And forgive me that while undressing you, fondling your provoking bosoms, I have to cry . . . loudly.

THE MYSTERIES OF
STRUDEL MAKING

by Paul Kovi

I have always loved poppy seed strudel. During the tender years of my youth I was wont to say that if there was a maiden anywhere in the world, even in Egypt, who could make the most delicious poppy seed strudel, I would make the pilgrimage there on foot, to taste it for myself. And if the rumor proved true, I would marry her at once. To reach my destination on foot meant crossing chains of snowy mountains, and hills through strange countries, and even sailing across stormy seas, walking on the billows like a new Jesus Christ. Then I would arrive, never failing, and I would go to all lengths to win her favor. But this was only a dream.

Time passed and I became a university student at Kolozsvár. There my purse grew flat quickly following the frolicky revelings that marked the initiation of freshmen into college life. Through the year, I had money only at the beginning of each month, since my allowance usually lasted for a few days. During the ensuing meager weeks only my mother's tenderly prepared food parcels assured my sustenance. The postal receipts are still preserved by my mother and affectionately remembered as eternal proof of her love. And every one of these weekly parcels contained several feet of poppy seed strudel, the sole request on my part.

My demands for the same delicacy made my poor mother feel ashamed after a while: she kept saying that my friends might think that she was incapable of baking anything else. But so far as I was concerned, her poppy seed strudel guaranteed the perfect continuity of my ties to home and showed the only imaginable sign of a mother's concern for a hungry child.

Even years after that, whenever I returned home to spend my vacations or to celebrate some holiday, my arrival automatically gave me an excuse to ask Mother to prepare the inevitable poppy seed strudel. This tradition did not seem to disturb any of my friends who happened to accompany me; they devoured the delicious pastry with ravenous enthusiasm. Thus, my joy was doubled in being able to share in this pleasure with others.

In 1947 I left home for good and started globe-trotting, which eventually ended with my settling in America. Only in 1968 was I able to return home again; at that time in the company of my fourteen-year-old son. Up until that first encounter I had never understood the almost primordial, unique relationship that exists between grandparents and grandchildren. What was the secret of that unfathomable, harmonious love chain that tied them together with such perfection? To solve this puzzle, I decided to take advantage of our visit and observe how this relationship between the twice-removed generations developed.

My son spoke Hungarian fairly well, and I think he was searching for his past, his heritage, his roots. At first Mother only looked at him, silently examining his features, his eyes, his gestures. Then, serenely and with not just a little pride in her voice, she declared: "He is our kind!" With this pronouncement their forever-lasting blood pact was sealed. After this, only one more test remained. "Well, my grandson," she asked, "what would you like to eat? What should I make for you?" My son's curt but all-encompassing reply poured forth immediately: "Strudel!" The next morning, when the lanky lad woke up at seven, the freshly made strudel awaited him. But not just one kind, as in my childhood, but four.

Those strudels that awaited him were masterpieces! Mother has been famous in the region for her strudels. Even now—she is approaching eighty-five—there is never a wedding in the county to which Mother is not invited. Every ardent bride is eager to have her demonstrate her legendary art.

I can think of nothing that would equal in magnificence the all-enveloping harmony of taste and scent of freshly baked strudel. On this occasion, the first strudel I admired, of course, was the enthralling, mouth-watering, glorious poppy seed strudel, which combines all the secrets of the mysterious East. Next came the dizzying aroma of the walnut strudel, which penetrated into my gastronomical psyche. As Mother made it, with a touch of cinnamon and aromatic rum, it suggested the ambience of a luscious tropical paradise. Its heavy, intoxicating smell intermingled with the cherry strudel's refreshing fruity delicacy: like the juxtaposition of an epic and lyric poem. And finally, the cottage cheese strudel studded with raisins and laced with vanilla . . . I still remember how, as a child, I used to gaze at this supreme creation while it was baking. The sugar oozing through the dough's pores slowly formed a fancy glaze, a golden crown of caramel, on the top and sides of this royal masterpiece.

All my life I have been watching strudel making, trying to memorize the process step by step, stealing the innermost "secret" of this global art through its minute components. Because verily I say: strudel making *is* a mysterious procedure comprising scores of well-concealed secrets. As a matter of fact, it is impossible either to describe or learn this ritual. One must pilfer the formula, breathe it in through the pores of the skin; then one has to shape it, mold it, develop it as a fine sculptor manipulates his clay in nonending devotion.

I often noticed Mother examining the quality of the two different kinds of flours she used, caressing the substance while sifting it through her fingers. When she was making strudel she closed every window and door; no one could enter or leave the kitchen in those sacred moments because, as she was wont to say: "the draft makes holes in the dough." Gradually I have become convinced that preparing strudel is like eating it: replete with complicated rituals and intrinsic mysteries.

On those lucky occasions when I was privy to the entire process, I observed her sifting the mixed flour through a fine sieve onto a board. In the center of the heap she formed a well. An elixir had been prepared earlier from a cup of water, one egg, a touch of salt, and a dash of vinegar. This concoction was poured into the hole, and, working from the middle outward, she stirred and kneaded it forcefully, meticulously, for about fifteen minutes, until the dough was a smooth, adherent mass.

After shaping it into small loaves, she placed them on a generously floured board and spread melted butter or fat on their tops with a tiny brush made out of goose feathers. The dough was covered and rested undisturbed for thirty minutes.

The next step was the delicate stretching. To get ready for this maneuver, she covered our big, rectangular kitchen table with a clean, white, oversized tablecloth, which she again floured with abandon. Then she began rolling and pulling the dough carefully, stretching it until it was hanging off the four corners. Circling the table innumerable times, with her hand under the thinning dough, endlessly manipulating, she never made a hole in the process. I stood there mesmerized by the incredible dexterity of her magic hand, admiring the technique as her wrist rapidly continued its spiral movements in stretching the dough layer farther and yet thinner. Her arms moved like a rotating machine. In the end the dough was so light and translucent that one could blow it off the table or even read a newspaper placed under it. When the desired thinness had been achieved, she tore off the uneven ends and put them aside. Later she would knead these into another loaf.

After the paper-thin dough was sprinkled with melted butter or fat, she placed the prepared stuffing on one third of the sheet or spread it on the whole surface. Holding the two corners of the tablecloth in both hands, she slowly lifted it up and rolled up the filled dough; then it was cut into specific lengths to fit the baking pans. The top was once more anointed with butter; then it went into the preheated oven to bake until it was ready.

In my youth I was quite surprised by her use of vinegar, which always seemed such an unlikely ingredient. But I know now that vinegar helps start its bonding process, just as a touch of salt gives "life" to the precious dough.

Small wonder my friends from Transylvania are often called "crafty highlanders." In one of the Székely counties, in Haromszék, people must be extremely cautious of every move made and every word uttered. Short of that, one may lose one's shirt. Each gesture has its own meaning; every sentence hides a secret double entendre and every word a playful pun. There, even the consumption of poppy seed strudel has its own trick: one must eat a lot of it very fast, because this pastry is such a heavenly delight that if one turns his head for a moment, there will not be so much as a morsel left.

As I was studying and experiencing the art of cooking, a special feeling developed within me that can be summed up only as follows: "Honor and appreciate food!" This motto has sustained me during the lengthy peregrinations until now, when at last I have the opportunity to put it into writing.

FOLK POETRY OF THE WEDDING FEAST

by István Szőcs

The wedding feast is about the only festivity today in Transylvania where most of the folk traditions are still preserved and the customary dishes are authentically prepared. In addition to the gastronomical and cultural legacy, during this ritual a unique poetic tradition also developed over the centuries, and a few fragments of this rich ancient literary repertoire have survived the vicissitudes of time. It is my pleasure to present to you a handful of the existing quaint and charming invitational songs and rhymes.

After several preliminary rites, such as the gathering of guests, the bridegroom's request for relinquishing the bride from her parents, and the bachelors' farewell to the bridegroom, the performers finally appear and begin chanting rhyming couplets. The first is a formal announcement signaling the beginning of the wedding feast:

> *Gentlemen and gentlewomen, come and take your seat,*
> *The tables are laid and everything's complete.*
> *Out in the kitchen the cooks are worrying,*
> *Scolding the wenches to finish scurrying.*
> *For if we delay too long,*
> *The recipe may turn out wrong.*
> *And the serving lads will be downcast,*
> *Unless they can swiftly serve the sumptuous repast.*
> *Their dancing feet are eager still more,*
> *To flirt and twirl pretty wenches 'cross the floor.*
> *Please come hither now with haste and trust,*
> *Eating and drinking a lot you must!*
> *It's high time now to take the first bite,*
> *I wish you dear guest, a supreme appetite!*

Some invitational songs are more romantic and exhibit the fairy tale qualities of local folklore:

> *I came to be the best man, from far-off Persia land,*
> *An ambassador was sent to fetch me, across the burning sand.*
> *Camels followed after him in a long, long line,*
> *Laden with exquisite food and enticing wine.*

After the guests are seated, each course is heralded by descriptive stanzas aiming to whet the celebrants appetite. Some of these are charmingly naive, some border the level of amusing doggerels.

THE SOUP

> *Here is the first course, look at the fancy tray,*
> *Not to drop it, he had to be careful and pray.*
> *I had the cook spice it without fault:*
> *Ginger and pepper and a good pinch of salt.*
> *When the bowls are empty, I'll be happier still,*
> *With guests who have supped and savored their fill.*
> *The tasty meat soup given now here,*
> *Make us delight in food and good cheer.*
> *Come, Gypsy, start the band so we can hear it,*
> *In the name of the Lord, His Son, and the Holy Spirit.*

THE ROAST

> *Now the time has arrived for sharpening your knives,*
> *To cut the fine roasts as different as all your wives.*
> *Ho! I say to thee he who eats like a glutton,*
> *Will grow fat and round as a mutton.*
> *But heed not my words for the roast is sublime,*
> *It even goes faster when washed down with wine.*

THE CABBAGE

> *Straight from Paradise I came,*
> *When I grew cabbage of all sizes, and gave them each a name.*
> *The finest pieces are in the pots asteaming,*
> *The savory taste and aroma have the cooks beaming.*
> *For the heavenly brew tricks were undertaken*
> *By garnishing it with twelve slices of bacon.*
> *Lo and behold, mixing the pig's back and front never fails,*
> *So help us all find some ears and some tails.*

In some regions the last couplet is addressed to the bride: she is challenged to search for the tails—vestiges of the innuendoes of ancient orgies that followed the wedding.

When the many dozens of different pastry trays arrive at the scene, the rhymes become increasingly sweet and noticeably briefer:

THE DESSERTS

Big piles of pastry, delicious and sweet,
Contain no mustard, garlic, or caraway seed.
They're baked until they are perfection,
For this is heaven's own confection.
But eat too much and you will shout,
I think I'm suffering from the gout!
Light and flaky, in sugar they're richly rolled,
Like delicate china dolls with powdered skirts and lacey fold.
Seize up your fork and count your blessings now,
For these exquisite treats the chef deserves a bow.
This toothsome dessert is made from fine flour,
Sugar, eggs, spices and all things not sour.
Chocolate, raisins, poppy seeds, and rum,
If you hesitate, my friend, you won't get a crumb!

Similar rhymes are recited along with the assorted and generous drinks:

THE BRANDIES

Dear guests, be quiet and at ease,
Then I can do my work as I please.
I'll only serve those with true pleasure,
Who enjoy themselves in orderly measure.
The bottle of fine brandy is right in my hand,
I know you'll savor it because it's truly grand.
Made sweet with the honey of sugar beets,
Spiced with almond root to balance the sweets.
Have a sip at a time, which I think you'll favor,
For gulping it greedily is a poor behavior.

The master of ceremony sometimes assumes the role of a good adviser and warns against heavy drinking of spirits:

If on my theme I rightly think,
Every brandy is a bewitching drink.
In summer too much makes one feel sad,
In winter, it numbs you and often makes you a cad.

When the toastmaster chants about wine, however, his commentary sounds ambiguous:

THE WINE

Wine is not of barley, clove, or rye,
Yet often you feel you can fly across the sky.
Even Noah knew the feeling, for he danced with apes,
What could e'ver so effect him but the magic of grapes.

In the midst of toasting and gleeful drinking, additional dishes are served accompanied by rhyme recitation. As people get full, the songs get shorter and funnier:

THE GOOSE DISH

It liked to swim in water, this silly little goose,
It now slides gaily in nectars of wine's rich juice.
With green salad and pickles in vinegar dressing,
Please enjoy it now with the Lord's blessing.

THE CHICKEN DISH

No meat in the world is better or truer,
Fried, crisp, golden brown, or broiled on a skewer.
Or as ragout, early in the day or late,
I highly recommend it as both delicious and great.

THE PORK DISH

All his life the pig grunts his noisy best,
No wonder the poor beast could not be a guest.
Now he's savory food—here, take a sample,
Don't worry, enjoy, he's delicious and ample.

During the feast people remember that this joyous occasion serves another purpose: at the same time it is also a communal festivity, an event that should not be forgotten. In making the fete memorable, a great deal of credit is owed to the indefatigable cooks. The last set of songs is a tribute to them and a final greeting to the newlyweds and the entire wedding party:

Our toiling and hard work were not a bit in vain,
We shall all depart with treasures and gain.
Receive thus our treat as a noble token
Of love, respect, and friendship unbroken.

May God bless the bride and groom!
Long live our cooks and all of whom
Fortune has kissed with so much glee,
And all of us now have to flee.

But not before chanting a happier rhyme,
And felicitations worth more than a dime.
May pink rosebuds line their bridal beds,
And titian cloaks smoothly hide their happy heads.
Let them softly rest on velvety pillows,
And may their bodies entwine in smooth golden billows.

May the Lord bestow on them many a son,
And some pretty maidens equal to none.
May our lives be joyous, serene, and without care,
Farewell, good people; a good-bye we now share!

We too wish the same to all the kind readers of this book, in the hope that it may help you cherish life a little more.

OF SPICES
AND CONDIMENTS

by Tibor Bálint

It is no coincidence that I link spices with scents; vanilla, for example, belongs to the orchid species. Most spices are wonderful, precisely because they not only stimulate our body to more easily consume worldly pleasures, but raise our soul to new heights: to the realm of happy (and mostly unconscious) associations. For example, rosemary acts as a benefactor to the Transylvanian tomato soup or heightens the flavor of roast game and poultry, but it holds our heart in its tiny palm and lulls it.

After summer showers, as the droplets drip from the leaves, shining with all the colors of the rainbow, our lungs and brain expand as we are suddenly struck by the sweet muscatellike aroma of the basil plant—it's as joyous as blissful news. The scent recalls my childhood, when we climbed up to the vineyard of my grandfather, the path lit by the moon and our progress accompanied by an orchestra of chirping crickets, as we delivered his dinner in an earthenware dish. The clay path was dry and warm—like the bottom of the oven during the night after bread baking—and as we inhaled the tantalizing aroma of basil we felt like swinging between the grapevines and the moon. I found out only later that it was not actually basil but the Little Maiden grape that emitted the unique scent of this herb. Without a spoonful of basil, the roast cooked in grape juice would not taste the same, nor would the *pâtés* nor the aromatic chicken with ham.

Another aromatic herb is marjoram. According to a folk song, marjoram should grow in the garden of melancholy people in the company of the pink cloves and lark's heel to act as a remedy to sadness. In fact, if it is mixed with aniseed, fennel, angelica, and mint and then brewed, it is known to ease many pains. But this ancient and popular spice also gives pleasure when it is added to sour soups, and Transylvanian wild duck or *pâté*. And it elevates the senses when it is dried and crushed, and sprinkled inside a duck or broiler chicken.

When our olfactory organ longs for exotic and Oriental spices, the tiny leaves of the modest thyme bush start trembling with self-respect on the dry, grassy plots beside steep mountain paths or on hillocks. It represents the most extensive camp of antisnobs and seems to ask us in a quiet but special scent voice: why do you keep snatching at every exotic type of spice, when thyme grows wild and it rivals many imported herbs? The French appreciate thyme; it is omnipresent in the kitchen of even the simplest people, in the company of peppers, marjoram, basil, and dried tarragon. This herb is the soul of piquant dishes, lung ragouts, and liver mixtures, and the godfather of the Transylvanian ragout, leg of mutton, and game dishes. It is as indispensable as marjoram, rosemary, bay leaf and nutmeg for seasoning *pâtés*.

Savory is the magic wand that seasons the maturing aromatic barrel cabbage or sauerkraut. When I catch sight of this foliaged two-span high plant in the garden, when its tiny lilac flowers are in bloom, and I smell its balmy fragrance, I recall those jovial times when people had the time to eat and a meal was a solemn event, a ceremony; and when the stuffed cabbage à la Bathory was prepared in an earthenware casserole lined with thin slices of bacon. And I also reminisce about the pig-slaughtering feasts, for savory—called by various pet names: garden cress, Viennese rosemary, pepper grass, balm mint, sausage grass—is a must in preparing pork liver or blood sausages as well as other kinds of sausages.

Dill—dried or fresh—is a frequent collaborator with savory, and there are certain delicate or sublime assignments that they can accomplish only in unison. For example, they are bound together in sauerkraut and "slushy" cabbage, and even in fresh spring cabbage; and they act unselfishly, adding their best to the undertaking, lending an inimitable flavor to the ever-popular cabbage dishes. Dill can also have an effect on its own. Excellent dill sauce can be prepared to garnish boiled beef or chicken, and it is prerequisite with fish, crayfish, and snail dishes. Stuffed squash or meatball soup simply cannot be made without it. However, it comes as a big surprise in a pancake, when it excels in the dilled cottage cheese filling. If you taste it once, you will never forget that flavor.

If the Transylvanian onion were lifted out from the pyramid of our dietary culture, the structure would collapse. It is one of our most ancient and most faithful condiments, and is of Central Asian origin. During the passage of time it was dominant as the "prince of spices," and moved with ease in royal courts and played a devilish solo in the orchestra of spices. Whatever noble place it attained, it never abandoned the barefoot wandering poor, in whose satchel one or two onions always rolled around next to the dry piece of bread or fraternally joined the meatless goulash cooked in the open air in a worn pot. Its faithfulness and omnipresent role made our ancestors fond of the onion; its piquant, hot scent when raw, and sweet taste when cooked, are unrivaled in the world. Today, hardly any recipe starts without it; it comes directly after the fat and is cooked briefly before being sprinkled with paprika.

Of course, onions are also grown at Makó (on the Hungarian Great Plain) and elsewhere, but tarragon is a plant truly of Transylvanian origin. Its thin, long leaves, resembling fresh lawn grass, are picked from their stem, packed in a jar, and soaked in salty vinegar. This is how the most refined tarragon vinegar is prepared. Otherwise the leaves can be chopped up and added to potato soup, soup of field greens, or white bean soup, which, of course, can also be cooked only with tarragon vinegar. The most delicious meal—where it is in complete harmony with other flavors and fully complements them—is the Transylvanian tarragon lamb soup.

Finally, the irreplaceable, though modest, caraway seed should also be mentioned: it's a domestic condiment that also grows wild. A proper goulash soup, roast leg of lamb, stuffed savoy cabbage, or savory crisp pastry fingers have a refreshing, pleasant taste from the caraway seed. Although it is grown in our environment, a seed bitten between our teeth can take us to faraway lands, perhaps to the Mediterranean, where aniseed comes from. We Transylvanians first became acquainted with it in our early childhood, when it was combined with onion leaves and brewed into a tea; it was a soothing remedy for teething. Then later it remained with us, on intimate Sunday mornings, when we heated the *krampampuli,* a punch with caramelized sugar and caraway seeds, boiled on the stove to burn off its roughness.

EPILOGUE

by Győző Hajdú

Paul Kovi, co-owner of The Four Seasons—perhaps the world's best-known restaurant, certainly North America's most innovative one—dreamed up and created this gastronomic volume, which can accurately be described as a Transylvanian feast. It is published here in a Krúdy-like nostalgic style. The birth of this work—in the genuine sense of the word—began in the editorial office of the literary magazine *Igaz Szó (True Word)* in Marosvásárhely with the Hungarian writers in Rumania, suggesting ideas during one of the workshops of Transylvanian Hungarian belles lettres. That informal meeting started with a friendly handshake, and from this handshake—a chain of handshakes, in fact—this book emerged. It is particularly interesting to note that in this volume many of the most outstanding writers of Transylvanian, Hungarian, Saxon, Armenian, and Rumanian literature are represented, having joined forces with an internationally renowned American connoisseur of wine and gastronomy. They intended to attract the interest of the world to the richness of Transylvanian cuisine, and the heavenly aromas and flavors of our dishes. And there is indeed plenty to whet the appetite and fulfill the healthy palate!

Several years ago, when touring the United States with my wife, Erzsébet Ádám, we met Paul Kovi for the first time at The Four Seasons. He honored us with a true feast in his elegant and grand restaurant. For us the dinner was an example of a happy marriage between art and gastronomy: a sparkling parade of light and palatable food, including a meat dish more than just a course for consumption—it was more similar to an aquarelle created by a master painter's fantasy. I dare to admit now, in retrospect, that during the first hours of our acquaintance, the ambience somewhat distracted my attention from the elevated dissertation—improvised by our host—about the past and possibilities of Transylvanian gastronomy. Nevertheless, our congenial host refused to be sidetracked. Paul Kovi, almost entranced, acclaimed with fire and passion: "It is a world sensation! Transylvania is the land of gastronomic wonders! Only the French and Chinese cuisine can be compared to the ancient, original Translyvanian food!" He sounded as if he were reciting Whitman's free verse. With his deliberate and purposefully "pro-grammed" plan—a long-fostered dream of many decades—my destiny was sealed by the time we had finished the Lucullan repast, long after midnight. Unknowingly, I had become inoculated with the serum of Transylvanian gastronomy, The Four Sea-sons' version à la Paul Kovi. And from that time on, events seemed to roll on without a break . . .

Mr. Kovi wrote letters, sent cables, and phoned, and at the precisely indicated time arrived in Marosvásárhely. It took many days and hours to accomplish our pioneering work: the reconnoitering of the Transylvanian gastronomic jungle. Then Paul Kovi left, and returned a year later, laden with recipes, the result of his worldwide collecting activity. And this routine was repeated year after year. In the breathless tempo of New York he had long learned that one's most precious asset is time, so he assumed a nonstop pace in the collection of recipes and organization of writings from all the contributors. This volume—this immense, generous Transylvanian feast—could not have been accomplished without his admirable expertise, his collecting of material over several decades, and his almost visionary, tireless, and self-sacrificing work and enthusiasm.

At the very beginning, when he arrived in a small village in Nyárád and was perusing recipes, handwritten on parchment and excavated from the depths of centuries long past, he remarked, "In collecting our work, we should follow the example of Bartók and Kodály. We will find native culinary treasures and unparalleled cultural discoveries in the Transylvanian gastronomy, just as these composers uncovered folk music. This find must be thoroughly explored; we have to descend into its depths, and the deeper we penetrate it the higher we ascend into the realm of knowledge and intellect."

A character in one of Gyula Krúdy's books remarked: "Ten million people in the world speak Persian. But can ten million people eat in the way that nature demands? People have to learn what to eat. According to the world calendar, this should be what is healthiest in every season and every month of the year. Everybody would immedi-ately feel better!"

This is Paul Kovi's *ars poetica*. Most probably he is guided by a somewhat similar motive. Perhaps this is why his New York restaurant is called The Four Seasons. It signifies that in every season of the year people should eat what is most appropriate and most healthy, because it gives the greatest pleasure and satisfaction and may help to better themselves. Dear reader, let us prove together, you over there, beyond the ocean on the other side of the globe, and we here, in our tiny, pine-embraced "fairy garden" of Transylvania, that by appreciating the spiritual and artistic values of eating, we can, in a small way, enhance the great civilizing force of the whole world.

SELECTED
BIBLIOGRAPHY

Acsády, Ignác. *The History of How Hungary Was Divided Into Three Parts*. Budapest, 1897.

Adventures in Gastronomy Throughout Europe. Budapest: Gondolat Publishing House, 1974.

Ágoston, Péter. *Our Ways*. Nagyvárad, 1916.

Alszeghy, Zsolt. *School Plays from Csiksomlyó*. Budapest, 1913.

Antalfy, Gyula. *Travels as "Once Upon a Time."* Budapest: Corvina Publishing House, 1980.

Apafi, Mihály. *Cookbook*. Edited by Imre Gundel and Iván Horváth. Budapest: Corvina Publishing House, 1982.

Apor, László. *Seklers in Bácska*. Budapest, 1942.

Apor, Péter. *Metamorphosis Transylvaniae* (facsimile). *Remarks by Mihály Cserey*. Budapest, 1927.

Arany, János. *Ouevre*. 14 vols. Budapest, 1913.

Asturias, Miguel Angel, and Pablo Neruda. *A Taste of Hungary*. Budapest: Corvina Publishing House, 1966.

Asztalos, Miklós. *Historical Transylvania*. Budapest, 1936.

The Austro-Hungarian Monarchy in Pictures and in Writing. 17 vols. Bucovina, 1899.

The Austro-Hungarian Monarchy in Pictures and in Writing. Gyergyószentmiklós: The Hargita Calendar, 1977.

Avraham, Y. *Le-korot ha-Yehudim bi-Transylvanyah*. 1951.

Babe, A., and E. Mach. *Handbook of Wine Handling and the Hospitality Industry*. Berlin, 1927.

Balásházy, J. *On Working Wine Cellars*. Pest, 1856.

Balla, Lajos, and István Tóth. *Supplementary Facts on the Pannonean-Datian Connection*. Debrecen: Yearbook of Debrecen Museum, 1966–67.

Ballai, K. *Album of Nagyenyed*. Nagyenyed, College Library.

———. *A Book on Hungarian-French Cuisine*. Budapest: Kultúra, 1938.

———. *History of the Hungarian Catering Industry*. Budapest: Kultúra, 1943.

———. *Pubs and Inns in Hungary in the 13th to 18th Centuries*. Budapest: Robert Lampel Publishers, 1927.

Ballai, Károly, and Kornél Tábori. *Forty Years of the History of the Hungarian Restaurant and Hotel Industry*. Budapest: The Museum of Innkeeping, 1938.

Balmez, Didi. *Carte de Bucate*. Bucharest: Technica Publishing Company, 1978.

Bányai, Elemér. *Armenian Anecdotes*. Vol. 2. Szamosujvár, 1902.

Bányai, János. *Natural Treasures and Rarities of the Seklers Land*. Budapest: Library of the Hungarian National Museum, 1935.

Barcsay, Domokos. *The Life and Stories of Domokos Barcsay.* Compiled by Vilmos Hegyesy. Kolozsvár, 1915.

Barczay, Oszkar. *Of An Old Hungarian Kitchen.* Budapest: Századok, 1893.

Baross, Károly. *Innovation of Our Vineyards.* Budapest, 1890.

————. *Operational Policy in Vineyards.* Budapest, 1900.

Basta, György. *His Correspondence and Papers, 1597–1607.* 2 vols. Budapest, 1909–13.

Báthy, Gábor. *A Special Grape Treatment.* Budget of the Transylvanian Economic Association. Kolozsvár, 1861.

Bátky, Zsigmond. *Did First Hungarian Settlers Eat Raw Meat?* 1903.

————. *History of the Hungarian Kitchen.* Budapest, 1937.

————. *Nutrition. Ethnography of the Hungarians,* Vol. 1, 1939. Published by The Hungarian Museum of Ethnography, University Press: Budapest.

Bátory, Stefan. *King of Poland, 1533–1586. His Correspondence with the Transylvanian Government, 1581–1585.* Budapest: The Archives of the Széchenyi Museum, 1948.

Bel, Mathias. *Ad Paratus Historiam Hungariae.* Poson, 1735–46.

Benkő, Josephus. *Historia de Rebus Transsylvanicis.* 6 vols. Szeben: Martini Press, 1793.

Benkő, József. *Seklers and Seklerland.* Kolozsvár: Helikon Publishing, 1944.

Bethlen, Farkas Gróf. *Findings in Grape Growing and Wine Handling.* Pest, 1868.

Bethlen, Gábor, Prince of Transylvania. *Unpublished Political Writings.* Budapest: National Museum Library, 1979.

Bethlen, Gábor, Emlékszám. Commemorative Issue in Honor of Gábor Bethlen published in *True Word,* monthly periodical issued by the Transylvanian Hungarian Association of Writers, Vol. 28, No. 9 (September 1980).

Bethlen, Zsuzsa. *Her Cookbook from 1692.* Marosvásárhely: Teleky Museum.

Bevilaqua-Borsody, Béla. *Cafés in Pest-Buda: The History of Coffee and Coffee Making, 1535–1935. A Study in Culture.* Budapest: Atheneum, 1935.

————. *Papers from the Pest and Buda Butchers, 1250–1872.* Budapest: Franklin Társulat Publishing, 1932.

Blond, Georges. *At the Table of the Centuries.* Budapest: Helikon Publishing, 1971.

Böldényi, J. *La Hongrie Ancienne et Moderne.* Paris, 1853.

Bonfini, Antonio. *King Matthias.* Compiled by László Gereb. Budapest: Atheneum, 1943.

Boros, György. *Unitarianism in the Age of Ferencz Dávid, and Later.* Kolozsvár, 1910.

Borza, Al. *Ethnobotanical Dictionary.* Bucharest: Academy Press, Rumanian Academy of Sciences, 1968.

Borza, Tibor, ed. *Yearbook of the Museum of Hungarian Commerce and Catering Industry.* Budapest: Museum of Commerce and Catering, 1976.

Bözödi, György. *The Seklers' Grief.* Budapest: Atheneum, 1943.

————. *Sekler People, Jewish Gods.* Cluj-Kolozsvár, 1935.

Brenner, D. *Histoire des Revolutions de Hongrie.* Le Haye, 1739.

Bright, Richard. *Travels from Vienna Through Lower Hungary.* Edinburgh, 1818.

Brulik, Eduard, and Jurajo Romanuk. *Let's Cook This Way.* Bratislava: Educational Publishing House of Slovakia, 1972.

Bruto, G. M. *His Hungarian History, 1490–1552.* 3 vols. Budapest, 1863–76.

Bunyitay, Vincze. *Religious Relics from the Age of Reformation in Hungary.* Budapest,

1902–1904.

Camilly-Weinberger, J., ed. *Memorial Volume for the Jews of Cluj-Kolozsvár.* English, Hebrew, and Hungarian. Tel-Aviv: 1970.

Capesius, Roswith. *Das Siebenburgisch-sachsisches Bauernhaus Wohnkultur.* Bucharest: Kriterion Publishing, 1977.

Champin, Aime. *Der Weinstock seine Kultur und Veredelung.* Leipzig, 1882.

A Complete Cookbook of High- and Low-Class Kitchens. Published in Pest and Poson, sponsored by Mihály Füstkúti-Landerer in 1801. Facsimile.

The Cookbook of Aunt Biri. Brassó. Book Division of the Brasso Papers. 1924.

Cookbook of the New Times Magazine. Budapest: New Times Publishing, 1931.

Counties and Cities of Hungary—Bihar County and Nagyvárad. Budapest, 1896–1914.

Csávossy, György, Ödön Horváth, Sándor Mezei, and József Szász. *Wine Growing.* Bucharest: Agricultural Publishing House, 1957.

Csekonics, Erzsébet. *Cultural Status Report in Transylvania.* Budapest, 1929.

Cselebi, Evlia. *Hungarian Travels of a Turkish Globe-Trotter.* On Request by the Historical Committee of the Hungarian Academy of Sciences, translated and interpreted by Dr. Karácson Imre. Budapest, 1904.

Cserey, Adolf. *Atlas of Botanics.* Selmecbánya, 1906.

Cserey-Rozsnyai-Bethlen. *Dying Transylvania, 1662–1703.* Biography of Miklós Bethlen. Marosvásárhely: Teleky Museum, 1935.

Cs. Pócs, Éva. *Superstitions about Christmas Dinner.* Akadémia Publishing, 1965.

Csutak, Vilmos. *Memorial Book in Honor of the 50th Anniversary of the Sekler National Museum.* Sepsiszentgyörgy, 1929.

Czelnai, Eszter. *Pastry Baking and Cold Buffet.* Cluj-Kolozsvár, 1930.

Czifrai, Istvan. *Hungarian National Cookbook.* 1st ed., 1826; 3rd ed., 1840; 7th ed., Pest, 1845.

Daniel, Gábor. *The Origin of the Daniel Family in Vargyas.* Budapest, 1896.

Décsi, János. *Hungarian History, 1592–1598.* Pest, 1866.

Derecskey, Susan. *The Hungarian Cookbook.* New York: Harper & Row, 1972.

Diószegi, Samuel. *Doctors' Book of Herbs.* Debrecen, 1813.

Dobos, J. *Curiola der Kuche.* Budapest, 1909.

Dobos, József. *Hungarian-French Cookbook. Indispensable Guide in Every Household.* Vols. 1 and 2. Budapest: Franklin Association, 1881.

Dömötör, Tekla. *Calendar Holidays.* Budapest: Magvető Publishing, 1964.

Drucker, Jenő. *Grape Economy in Hungary.* Budapest, 1905.

———. *Our National Beverage.* Budapest, 1907.

———. *Progress in Hungarian Grape Growing.* Memorial Volume, Budapest, 1909.

———. *Viticulture and Wine Production in Hungary.* Budapest, 1922.

Egy székely asszony (Anonymous). *By a Sekler Woman: Transylvanian Cooking. Cookbook from Cluj-Kolozsvár.* Kolozsvár: Lajos Lapage Publishing, Library of the Gundels, 1906.

Eisler, M. *From the Past of the Transylvanian Jews.* Kolozsvár, 1901.

Encyclopedia of the Hungarian Jews. 1929.

Ens, Gáspár. *Rerum Hungaricum Historia, Novem Libris Comprehensa.* Coldinae Agrippinae, 1604.

Entz, Ferenc, and Ignácz Málnay. *Viticulture and Wine Production in Transylvania.* Report by the Department of Agriculture. Vácz, 1870.

———— and Imre Tóth. *Wine Production in Hungary.* Report by the Department of Agriculture. Budapest, 1869.

Erdei, Ferenc. *Ethnographic Gastronomy.* Budapest: Minerva Publishing, 1971.

Erdélyi, Béla. *Turkish Habits of Gourmet Eating and Drinking.* Budapest: Tábori Kornél Library, 1889.

Erdélyi, János. *My Father's Wedding.* Folksongs and Ballads. Székelyudvarhely, about 1840.

Erdélyi, László. *History of the Árpád Age.* Budapest: Pallas Publishing House, 1922.

Erdész, Sándor. *About Food.* Manuscript. Sárospatak, 1753.

————. *Nyirség—Northeastern Corner of Hungary.* Sárospatak, 1755.

Fábián, Gyula. *Ginger-Honey Cake (or Bread).* Folklore Report Book. Budapest: Néprajzi Értesitő, 1913.

Fabríciusné, Bónyi Elsa. *Transylvanian Cookbook.* Secueni-Székelyhíd, 1926.

Fehér, Géza. *The Role and the Culture of Bulgarian Turks.* Budapest, 1940.

Fejérpataky, László. *Old Account Books of Hungarian Cities.* Budapest, 1885.

Ferdinándy, Gyula. *Reform in the Federal Structure.* Kassa, 1910.

Fine Arts Observer. Transylvania. About 1860.

Forgách, Ferenc. *History of Hungary between 1540 and 1572.* Pest, 1866.

Fornády, Elemér. *Craftsmanship in Wine Handling.* Budapest: Association of Budapest Hotel and Restaurant Owners, 1948.

Fraknói, Vilmos. *Clerical Personalities in the Middle Ages in Hungary.* Budapest, 1916.

Fuhrmann, K. *Count József Teleki and the Hungarian-French Intellectual Connections.* Budapest, 1929.

Gál, Kelemen. *The History of the Unitarian College in Kolozsvár.* Vol. 1. Budapest: Kultúra, 1935.

Galambos, Kálmán. *The Book of Mushroom Collectors.* Budapest: Agricultural Publishing House, 1970.

Galeotto, Marzio. *The Life of Matthias Rex.*

Gamauf, Vilmos. *The Grapes that Proved to Be Highly Productive in Transylvania.* Kolozsvár, 1879.

Gerando, A. de. *The Political Spirit in Hunland.* Pest, 1848.

————. *La Transylvanie et les Habitants.* Paris, 1850.

Gesta Hungarorum. Budapest: Corvina Publishing House, 1969.

Glück, F., and K. Stáder. *The Book of Gastronomy.* Budapest, 1889.

Göckel, Alfred. *Hungarian Wine History.* Article from *Borgazdaság* magazine, 1956.

Göllner, K. *Geschichte der Deutschen auf dem Gebiete Rumaniens.* Vol. 1. Bucharest: Kriterion Publishing, 1972.

Gombócz, Zoltán. "The Origin of Old Hungarian Food Names." *Magazine of the Hungarian Language,* 1905.

Gombos, I. A. *The History of the Peasant Rising in the Year of 1437.* Kolozsvár, 1898.

Govrik, G., and K. Szongott. *Armenia.* Szamosujvár, 1887.

Greenwald, Leopold. *Liflagoth Yisrael Behungariah.* Kolozsvár, 1929.

————. *Mekoroth Lekoroth Yisrael.* Kolozsvár, 1934.

Greger, M. *Ungarns Weinfrage.* London, 1873.

Greguss, Ágost. *The Esthetics of Eating.* Budapest, 1899.

Grünwald, J. and S. Scheiber. *New Findings to the History of Jewish Settlers in the First Half of the 18th Century.* Budapest: Corvina Publishing House, 1963.

Gundel, Imre, and Judit Harmath. *The Hospitality of Our Past.* Budapest: Közgazdasági és Jogi Publishing, 1979.

Gundel, Károly. *The Art of Hospitality.* Budapest: Atheneum, 1934. Magyar Szakácsok

Köre.

———. *Developments in Cooking and the Hungarian Literature of Cookbooks until the End of the 18th Century.* Budapest: Athenaeum, 1943.

Gunther, A. *Der Wein.* Leipzig, 1918.

Guttman, Mihály. *Simon Péchi's Sabbatarian Book of Prayers.* Budapest, 1927.

Gyürki, Antal. *The Grape: A Mine of Treasures.* A Study. Budapest, 1888.

———. *The Reforms in our Viticulture.* Vác, 1879.

Halász, Zoltán. *The Book of Hungarian Wines.* Budapest: Corvina Publishing House, 1981.

———. *Hungarian Wines Through the Ages.* Budapest: Corvina Publishing House, 1958.

Halmay, István. *The Transylvanian Princedom of Mihály Apafi the First. 1661–1690.* Szeged: University Publishing, 1934.

Hamm, W. *Das Weinbuch.* Leipzig, 1874.

Hangay, Octáv. *About the Paprika.* Budapest, 1887.

Harsányi, Adolf. *Coffee Traders, Waiters, Coffee Makers.* Budapest, 1909.

Hatsy, Pál. *The Genuine Hungary.* Budapest, 1920.

Hazai, H. *Treatment About the Sabbatarians.* Kolozsvár, 1903.

Hegyaljai, Kiss Géza. *Kata Árva Bethlen, Widow of József Teleki, Count of Szék, 1700–1750.* 2nd ed. Budapest, 1923.

Hegyesi, József. *Appetizers.* Budapest, 1895.

———. *The Latest Handbook of Home Pastry Baking.* Budapest, 1893.

Herczegh, Mihály. *The History of Viticulture and Wine Production in Hungary.* In *Viticulture* magazine. Budapest, 1896.

Herman, Ottó. *The Book of Hungarian Fishing.* Vol. 1. Budapest, 1887.

Hertelendy, Ferenc. *The Viticulture in Lekence, Tomaj, Csaliti.* Sárospatak, 1902.

The History of the Hungarian Hospitality Industry. Budapest, 1957.

Hódos, Zotti. *Masa leftina.* Sibiu-Szeben, 1914.

Hofer, Tamás, and Edit Fel. *Hungarian Folklore.* Budapest: Corvina Publishing House, 1975.

The Hoffgreff Songbook. Printed by György Hoffgreff in 1554–55. Facsimile. Budapest: Helikon Publishing, 1966.

Hollós, Józsefné. *The Latest Homemade Pastry.* Cluj-Kolozsvár: Helikon Publishing, 1931.

Hóman, Gyula, and Gyula Szekfű. *Hungarian History.* Budapest: Atheneum, 1936–39.

Horn, J. *Kitchen Use of Domestic Wild Plants.* 1916.

Horváth, Ilona. *A Collection of Folklore: Poems, Descriptions, Stories.* Budapest: Kossúth Publishing House, 1968.

———. *Cookbook.* Published by the State Council of Hungarian Women. Budapest: Kossúth Publishing House, 1970.

How the Tartars Returned to Their Homeland. The Calendar. Háromszék 1975.

Húnfalvy, János. *Hungary and Transylvania.* Darmstadt, 1860.

Hungarian Review of Economic History. Excerpts. 1894, 1895, 1897.

Hungary. Sovereigns. Articuli Leopold Dominorum Praelatorum. Poson, 1791.

Hunyadi, Erzsébet. *Cold Cuts from Bánfihunyad. Pates. Pig Slaughter.* Budapest, 1924.

Hutás, Magdolna R. *Cooking Instruments and How They Get Expressed in Our Language.* Budapest: Hungarian Linguistic Society Publishing, 1951.

———. *Cooks. Old Dishes.* Budapest: Magvető, Association of Chefs, 1953.

Illésházy, István. *Notes between 1592 and 1603* and *History between 1594 and 1603.* Pest, 1863.

Illyés, Gyula. *On the Boat of Kharon.* Budapest, 1969.

Incefy, Lajos. *Scents and Tastes.* Kolozsvár: Dacia Publishers, 1975.

Istvánffy, Gy. *Report of the Hungarian Royal Institute of Experimental Viticulture.* Budapest, 1907.

Iványi, Béla. *The Gyömrő Archives of the Teleki Family, Count of Szék.* Szeged: University Publishing, 1931.

Jakab, Elek. *The History of Kolozsvár.* 3 vols. Budapest, 1870.

Jakabfy, Elemér. *Transylvania. A Statistical Book.* Lugos, 1923.

Jankó, János. *The Hungarian-Sekler Population of Torda, Aranyosszék and Torockó.* Kolozsvár, 1893.

Jávorka, Sándor, Zoltán Árokszállásy, and József Bánhegyi. *Book of Botanics.* Budapest: Educational Publishing House, 1952.

Jewish Encyclopedia.

Jewish Family Journal. N.P. 1924–25.

Jósika, Miklós. *Sketches.* Kolozsvár, 1835.

Kádár, Gyula, et al. *Viticulture.* Budapest: Agricultural Publishing House, 1973.

Kaiter, Joseph. *Die alte und neue ungarische Welt.* Vienna, 1796.

Kallós, Zoltán. *A Book of Ballads.* Budapest: Hungarian Helikon, 1973.

Kányádi, Sándor. *A Little Bird Had Been Sitting . . .* Transylvanian Saxonian Poetry. Bucharest: Kriterion Publishing, 1977.

Karácsonyi, János. *The First Lónyais.* Nagyvárad, 1904.

———. *The Historical Rights of the Hungarian Nation.* Nagyvárad, 1916.

———. *The History of the Clergy in Hungary.* Nagyvárad, 1915.

———. *Hungarian Minorities in the 16th Century.* Budapest, 1900.

Kazinczy, Gábor. *The Works of Baron Péter Altorjai-Apor.* Pest-Buda: Library of the Gundel Family, 1863.

Kecskeméti, Ármin. *Universal History of the Jews.* Vol. 1. Budapest, 1927.

Keglevich, István. *Transformation of Our Vineyards.* Budapest, 1883.

Kelemen, Lajos. *A Guidebook to Kolozsvár.* Kolozsvár, 1902.

Kemény, Zsigmond. *The Enthusiasts.* Vols. 1 and 2. Budapest, 1904.

Kempelen, Béla. *Hungarian Noble Families.* Budapest, 1911–15.

Kerényi, András. *Datian Names.* Dissertations, Series I. Budapest, 1941.

Kertész, André. *Hungarian Memories.* New York: Little, Brown, 1982.

Kertész, Manó. *Proverbs.* Budapest, 1922.

Keszei, János. *About a New Way of Cooking.* Commissioned by Mihály Apafi. Erdély, Transylvania, 1680.

Kéza, de Simon. *Chronicon Hungaricum.* Buda, 1782.

Kisfaludy, Sándor. *Stories from the Hungarian Pre-Ages.* Pest, 1818.

Kiss, István. *How Ferenc Rákóczi II Was Elected the Emperor of Transylvania.* Budapest, 1906.

K. Mátyus, István. *Old and New Dietetics.* Presented to the Count József Teleki at Marosvásárhely. Poson, 1787.

Kocab, Frigyes. *Our Economy in the Second Half of the 16th Century.* Budapest, 1913.

Kofbauer, Anna. *Cookbook.* Translated from the German. Kassa, 1826.

Kóhn, Samuel. *The Sabbatarians.* Budapest, 1889.

Kohút, Adolf. *Aus dem Reiche der Karpan.* Stuttgart, 1887.

Kolozsvári, Nagy Naptár. *Kolozsvár Calendar.* 1867, 1869.

Konsza, Samu. *Hungarian Folklore in Haromszék.* Bucharest: State Publishing of Literature and Arts, 1953.

Kós, Károly. *Folklore and Heritage.* Bucharest: Kriterion Publishing House, 1972.

———. *Studies in Ethnography.* Kriterion Publishing House, 1976.

———. *Transylvania.* Kolozsvár: Dacia Publishers, 1934.

Kosutány, Ignácz. *The Clergy Law Book.* 2nd ed. Kolozsvár, 1903.

Kosutány, T. *Grapes and Wine.* Magyaróvár, 1896.

Kovachich, M. G. *Rare Hungarian Scripts.* 2 vols. Buda, 1798.

Kovachóczy. *Árpádia.* Nagyvárad, about 1825.

Kovács, János. *The Short Summary of the Hungarian Chronicle.* 3 vols. Poson, 1742–49.

Kővágó, Antal. *Of Forty-one Native Hungarian Grape Varieties. A Study.* Budapest: Mezőgazdasági Publishing, 1951.

Kőváry, László. *The History of Transylvania.* Vol. 1. Pest, 1859.

———. *How the Promenade of Kolozsvár Was Founded and Improved.* 1812–86. Kolozsvár, 1886.

———. *Regional Dresses and Regional Habits.* Kolozsvár, 1810.

Kramszky, László. *Facts on the Composition of Hungarian Wines.* Budapest, 1892.

Kreekné, Liben Etelka. *Homemade Pastries.* Brassó, 1886.

Kremnitzkyne, Frőhlich Ilona. *Homemade Honey Cookies.* Kolozsvár, 1917.

Krenedits, Ferenc. *Historical Facts of Hungarian Viticulture.* Budapest: Borászati Lapok, 1902.

Kriza, János. *Wild Roses.* Bucharest: Kriterion Publishing, 1975.

Krúdy, Gyula. *Poets' and Writers' Hangouts of Yesterday.* Budapest, 1927.

———. *Pest in 1915.* Budapest: Published by the Bookstore of Manó Dick, 1924.

Kubinyi, Ferenc. *Hungary and Transylvania in Pictures.* Pest, 1854.

Lakos, Imréné, and Ilona Pécskay. *Household Advisory.* Nagybánya, 1903.

Lang, George. *The Cuisine of Hungary.* New York: Crown Publishers, 1967.

László, Gyula. *The Life of the Settlers.* Budapest: Atheneum, 1944.

Letenyey, Lajos. *Regions of Wine Growing.* Pest, 1859.

Lőbl, Margit. *The Art of Cooking.* Tel-Aviv: Neografika, 1957.

Lőrincze, Lajos. *About the Food of Old-Time Shepherds.* Szentgál, Veszprém megye, n.d.

Lucullus. *The Cookbook of Old Hungary.* Budapest: Atheneum, 1937.

Lukanics, Imre. *Album from Nagyenyed.* Of the Collection of the College. Nagyenyed, 1926.

Magazine of the Hungarian Hotel and Restaurant Owners. 1896–1943.

Magazine of the Hungarian Jews. 1929–41.

Magazine of the Hungarian Wine Producers. 1895.

Málnássy, László. *A Short Book of Mushrooms.* Kolozsvár: Kriterion Publishing, 1972.

Malonyay, Dezső. *The Hungarian Folklore.* 5 vols. Budapest: Franklin Association, 1907.

Máramarosi Gottlieb, Antal nyomdája. *Obligations of the Best Men.* Printed in his workshop. Vácz, 1793.

Marencsics, Ottó. *Aphorisms.* Budapest, 1941.

———. *A Four-Language Dictionary of Food.* Budapest, 1957.

Mariechen's *Saxon Cook Book.* Edited by Elva J. Crooks. Cleveland, Ohio, n.d.

Márki, Sándor. *The Age of Matthias Rex.* Pest, 1866.

Márton, Katalin. *Wedding Habits at Magyardecse.* Manuscript.

Matthias I. Corvinus, King of Hungary. *Epistolae ad Ponifices, Imperatores . . . Viros Illustres. Datae.* Crassovie, 1744.

Mauthner, Klára. *Game, Fish and Other Fine Bites.* Bucharest: Editura Technica, 1978.

Mayer, Theodor. *Verwaltunsreform in Ungarn nach der Türkenzeit.* Vienna, 1911.

Mikó, Imre. *A Collection of Dances and Dance Tales About 1860.* Kolozsvár: Helikon Publishing, 1942.

———. *The Politics and the Rights of Minorities.* Kolozsvár: Helikon Publishing, 1944.

Miskolczy, István. *Hungary Under the Anjous.* Budapest, 1923.

Miskolczy, Mihály. *A Book of the Hungarian Grapes.* Pest, 1867.

Molnár, István. *Basics of Wine Handling.* Budapest, 1885.

———. *A Handbook on Viticulture and Wine Handling.* Budapest, 1883.

———. "The Wine Market." In *Viticultural* magazine. Budapest, 1877.

Móricz, Zsigmond. *Transylvania.* Vol. 1. *Fairy Land.* Budapest: Kultúra Publishing, 1960.

Nagy, Miklós. *Past and Present in Marosszög.* Budapest: New Helikon Publishing, 1947.

Nánási, István. *Cookbook.* Kolozsvár, 1771.

Németh, A., and A. Osztrovszky. *New Trends in Processing Grapes and New Wine.* Budapest, 1928.

———. *The Wine in Human Life.* Budapest: Mezőgazdasági Publishing, 1932.

Newham, Davis N. *The Gourmet's Guide to Europe.* New York, 1908.

Nyáry, Ferenc. *Wine and Cellar.* Selmecbánya, 1876.

"Official Statues of Hungary and Transylvania." In *Hungarian Quarterly,* Vol. 6, No. 4. Budapest, 1940–41.

Orbán, Balázs. *Description of Seklerland.* Marosvásárhely, 1870.

———. *Ten Hungarian Villages in Barcaság.* Marosvásárhely, 1873.

———. *The Town of Torda and Its Region.* Marosvásárhely, 1889.

Pach, Zsigmond Pál. *The History of Hungarian Economy.* Part 1, until 1848. Budapest: The Ministry of Economy of Hungary, 1963.

——— et al. *The History of Hungarian Economy.* Part 2, 1848–1944. Budapest: The Ministry of Economy of Hungary, 1963.

Paget, John. *Hungary and Transylvania.* London: John Murray, 1839.

Pálffy, János. *Noblemen in Hungary and in Transylvania.* Kolozsvár, Helikon Publishing, 1942.

Pálmay, Sz. J. *The Personal Archive of the Family of Writer Szobahói-Pálmay. 1526–1849.* Marosvásárhely, 1911.

Panek, Zoltán. *Pilat in the Kitchen.* Kolozsvár-Napoca: Dacia Publishing, 1980.

Panovin, Olga. *The House, the Furniture and the Meals at Székelykeve.* Kolozsvár: Dacia Publishing, 1979.

Passuth, László. *The Dragon's Tooth.* 2 vols. Budapest, 1963.

———. *Four Winds in Transylvania.* Budapest, 1971.

Past and Future. 1929–41.

Pasteur, L. *Études sur le vin.* Paris, 1866.

Pásztor, Lajos. *The Religious Life of the Hungarians in the Age of the Jagellos, 15th Century.* Budapest, 1940.

Pátay, Árpád. *The History of Grape Growing in Hungary from Ancient Times until the End of the 9th Century.* Budapest: Unpublished dissertation, 1965.

Perlaky, Mihály. *The Basics in Wine Growing.* Budapest, 1899.

Petrarca Codex. Basilica San Marco. Venice, 13th century.

Pettenkoffer, S. *The Good Cellarman.* Budapest, 1930.

———. *Guide to the Correct Handling of New Wine and Old Wine.* Budapest: Pallas Publishing, 1910.

———. *Wine: How It Is Made and Handled.* Budapest: Atheneum, 1936.

———. *Wine Production.* Budapest: Pátria Publishing, 1941.

Pray, György. *Epistolae Procerum Regni Hungariae.* Poson, 1806.

Radnóti, Dezső. *Guide to Transylvania.* Kolozsvár, 1901.

Radvánszky, Béla báró. *Hungarian Family Life and Household in the 16th to 18th Centuries.* Budapest, 1897.

———. *Old Hungarian Cookbooks.* Budapest, 1893.

Rákóczi, János. *Cookbook.* Budapest: Magvető Publishing, 1964.

The Rákóczi Archives. Budapest, 1871–77.

Rapaich, Raymund. *The Story of Bread.* Budapest: The Society of Natural Sciences, 1934.

Reső, Ensel Sándor. *Folklore Habits in Hungary.* Pest, 1867.

Révai. *Révai's Encyclopedia.* Budapest, 1916.

Ritoók, János. *The Double Mirror.* Bucharest: Kriterion Publishing, 1979.

Romváry, Vilmos. *A Book of Spices.* Budapest: Natúra Publishing, 1972.

Rosenmann, S. *Staatsrecht des Konig-Reichs Ungarn.* Vienna, 1792.

Rozsnyay, Dávid. *Historical Memories.* 8 vols. Pest, 1867–1971.

Schams, Ferenc. *Findings in Grape Growing in Hungary.* Pest, 1831.

———. *Ungarns Weinbau.* Vol. 1. Pest, 1832. Vol. 2, Pest, 1833. (Hartleben) Pest.

Scheiber, Sándor. *Folklore and History.* Vols. 1 and 2. Budapest, Corvina, 1977.

Schoen, D. *God-Seekers in the Kárpát-Valleys.* Kolozsvár: Kriterion, 1964.

Schőnherr, Gyula. *János Hunyadi-Corvin: 1473–1504.* Budapest, 1894.

Schram, Ferenc. *Similarities between High-Class and Low-Class Kitchens.* Budapest, about 1890.

Schuller, Gusztáv. *Saxon Peasant Household in Transylvania.* Translated from German by Dr. István Székely Nagyszeben, 1896.

Schuller, Victor. "Trauriger Herbst in Siebenburgen." Article in *Stern* magazine. March 1978.

Schullerus, Adolf dr. *Siebenburgisch-sacksische Volkskunde im Umriss.* Leipzig, 1916.

Schuster, Christine. *Kuche und Haushalt.* 2nd ed. Kolozsvár: Kronstadt, 1925.

Schwicker, J. H. *Die Deutschen in Ungarn und Siebenburgen.* Inaug. dissertation. Vienna, 1881.

The Second Cookbook of the New Times Magazine. Budapest: Uj Idők Publishing, 1943.

Sestini, Domenico. *Viaggio Curioso-Scientifico-Antiquario per la Valachia, Transilvania e Ungheria fino a Vienna.* Florence, 1815.

Sigerius, Emil. *Vom alten Hermannstadt.* Hermannstadt, 1922.

Sigray, Ferenc. *How to Prepare Some Dishes. A Notebook.* Facsimile. Budapest: University Press, 1972.

Siklósy, László. *Through Transylvania by Carriage. Of Wine- and Coffee-Drinking Customs in Transylvania.* Kolozsvár, 1927.

Sonklar, Karl. *Sketches of a Journey in the Alps and the Carpathians.* Vienna, 1857.

Spielmann, Mihály. *Jews and Sabbatarians in Transylvania.* Unpublished manuscript.

Steinbach, Béláne, and Anna Réczey. *Cookbook.* Szatmárnémeti, 1914.

Steiser, Anna. *Cookbook.* From the Collection of the Hungarian Museum of the Hospitality Industry. Budapest, n.d.

Studies in Ethnography, 1976.

Szabó, Dezső. *The History of the Hungarian Parliament.* Budapest, 1909.

Szabó, T. Attila, ed. *Etymological Listing of the Hungarian Language in Transylvania.* Bucharest: Kriterion Publishing, 1976.

Szadeczky, Lajos. *Gáspár Komjáti-Békés.* Budapest, 1887.

Szalay, József. *The History of Hungary.* N.p., 1897.

Szamosközy, István. *Historical Memories, 1566–1603.* 4 vols. Budapest, 1876–80.

———. *The History of Transylvania between 1598 and 1603.* Budapest: Magyar Helikon, 1977.

Szamota, István. *Old-Time Journeys Throughout Hungary.* Budapest: Franklin Association, 1891.

Szászné, Bene Ilonka. *Transylvania Hungarian Cookbook.* Nagyvárad, 1929.

Szathmáry, Louis. *The Chef's Secret Cookbook.*

Chicago: Quadrangle Books, 1971.

Szegedi, Joannes. *Tripartitum Juris Hungarici Tyrolinium.* Tyrnaviae, 1751.

Szekfű, Gyula. *Gábor Bethlen.* Budapest, 1929.

Szendrey, Zsigmond és Ákos. *A Study of the Ethnography of the Hungarians.* n.d.

Szeremi, György. *Memoirs of the Decline of Hungary, 1484–1543.* Vol. 1. Pest, 1857.

Szigeti, József. *Decameron from Kolozsvár.* Kolozsvár, 1936.

Szilády, Áron. *State Archives of the Turkish Times in Hungary.* Budapest, 1874.

Szilágyi, Sándor. *Documents of the Sessions of the Transylvanian Parliament.* Vol. 4. Budapest, 1878.

———. *Supplementary Facts to the History of the Bethlen-Alliance.* Budapest, 1873.

Szongott, Kristóf. *Armenia.* Szamosujvár, 1889, 1891, 1892, 1895.

———. *An Ethnographical Study in the History of Armenians in Hungary.* Szamosujvár, 1903.

———. *Genealogy of the Armenians in Hungar.* Szamosujvár, 1898.

———. *Hungarian-Armenian Metropolis.* Szamosujvár, 1901.

———. *Monograph of Szamosujvár, Independent Royal City of the Imperieum.* Vol. 2. Szamosujvár, 1901.

Tábéry, Géza. *Author Mór Jókai in Transylvania.* Oradea-Mare, 1925.

Tábori, Kornél. *The Bibliography of the Hospitality Industry.* Budapest, 1924.

Tarisznyás, Györgyi. *The Armenians' Christmas.* Budapest: Péter Pázmány Academy of Sciences, 1943.

Tarisznyás, Márton. *The History of Armenians in Transylvania.* Unpublished manuscript. Marosvásárhely, 1978.

Teleki, M. *Writings and Correspondence.* 8 vols. Marosvásárhely, 1905–16.

Teleki, M. and Dominik von Szék. *A Journey Through Hungary and Some Neighboring Countries.* Pest, 1805.

Thouvenel, Edouard. *La Hongrie et la Valachie.* Paris, 1840

Tököly, Imre. *Correspondence.* Budapest, 1882.

———. *Journal.* Budapest, 1896.

Tótfalusi-Kis, Miklós. *The Menu of the Household of Count Szaniszló Thurzó.* Galgócz, 1603.

———. *The Book of Cooking.* Kolozsvár, 1698. The Archives of the Rákóczi Family. *Hungarian Book Review, 1881.*

——— and L. Thaly. *The Transylvanian Royal Family's Cookbook at the end of the 15th Century.* Koloszvár, 1692.

Tóth, Béla. *Hungarian Rarities.* Budapest, 1899.

Tóth, György. *In Honor of . . . Ferencz Dávid.* Budapest, 1929.

Townson, Robert. *Travels in Hungary.* London, 1797.

Transylvania. Parliament. Monumenta Comitalia Regni Transylvaniae. Budapest, 1875–98.

Transylvanus. *The Ethnical Minorities in Transylvania.* Budapest: Akadémia, 1934.

Trócsányi. Zoltán. *A Trip to the Hungarian Past.* Budapest: Pesti Hirlap Publishing, 1939.

Túrós, Emil, and Lukács Túrós. *The Way We Cook.* Budapest: Magvető, 1961.

Ujfalvy, Sándor. *On Hunting in Transylvania.* Cluj-Kolozsvár, 1927.

Universal Jewish Encyclopedia.

Vágó, B. in R. L. Braham, ed. *Hungarian Jewish Studies.* Vol. 1. N.p., 1966.

Varjú, János. *The Poetry of the Sabbatarians.* Budapest, 1937.

Végh, Antal. *Hundred Peasant Dishes from Szatmár.* Budapest: Minerva Publishing, 1978.

Venesz, József. *The Hungarian Kitchen.* Budapest: Minerva, 1965.

———. *Technology of Cooking.* Budapest, 1964.

———— and Imre Gundel. *Old Dishes—New Tastes.* Budapest: Minerva Publishing, 1970.

Venesz, József, and Emil Túrós. *The Chef's Handbook.* Budapest: Publishing House of Economy and Law, 1976.

Venetianer, Lajos. *The History of Jews in Hungary.* Budapest, 1937.

Verancsics, Antal. *Oeuvre.* Vol. 2. Pest, 1857.

Vida, Zsigmond. *Preparation of Hungarian Mustard.* Bucharest: Kriterion Publishing, 1976.

Viski, Károly. *Hungarian Peasant Customs.* Budapest, 1932.

Weiss, Edward, and Ruth Buchanan. *The Paprikás Weiss Hungarian Cookbook.* New York: William Morrow, 1979.

Wenzel, Gustav. *Hungary and Transylvania in Pictures.* Vienna, 1878.

Wine Production and Viticulture. Weekly magazine. Pest, 1866.

Yearbooks and Journals of Hungarian History in the 16th to 18th Centuries. 3 vols. Budapest, 1881–1906.

Zilahy, Ágnes. *Transylvanian Kitchen.* Budapest: Singer and Wolfner, 1901.

Zilahy, Lajos. *The Dukays.* New York, 1949.

Zolnay, László. *Hungarian Chefs of the Middle Ages.* Budapest: Yearbook of the Museum of the Hungarian Hospitality Industry, 1970.

Zoványú, J. *Protestantism in Hungary Until 1565.* Budapest, 1921.

Zsemlyei, Oszkár. *History of Baking, Pastry, and Cookie Making in Hungary.* Budapest: Singer and Wolfner, 1940.

INDEX